LOVE AGAINST HATE

Karl Menninger, chairman of the board of trustees and chief of staff of the Menninger Foundation, was born in Topeka, Kansas, in 1893. He received his A.B. and M.S. from the University of Wisconsin, and his M.D. *cum laude* from Harvard. He is clinical professor of psychiatry at the University of Kansas Medical School; neuropsychiatrist at Stormont-Vail Hospital in Topeka; chairman of the dean's committee and senior consultant at Winter Veterans Administration Hospital, Topeka; senior consultant at Topeka State Hospital; consultant in neuropsychiatry for the Central Office of the Veterans Administration; consultant to the Department of Social Welfare of the State of Kansas; and chief consultant to the Office of Vocational Rehabilitation of the Department of Health, Education and Welfare. He is a former president of the American Psychoanalytic Association, and a member of various organizations. Among his books are *The Human Mind* (1930), *Man Against Himself* (1938), and *Love Against Hate* (1942). He is editor-in-chief of the *Bulletin of the Menninger Clinic,* and is connected in an editorial capacity with several medical journals.

Love

against

Hate

KARL MENNINGER, M. D.

with the collaboration of

JEANETTA LYLE MENNINGER

A Harvest Book

Harcourt, Brace & World, Inc.
New York

To the memory of Sigmund Freud

© *Copyright 1942 by Karl Menninger and Jeanetta Lyle Menninger*

152.4   Q.6.69

Printed in the United States of America

Acknowledgments

SOME of the material in this book is an elaboration or restatement of accepted psychiatric knowledge; some of it is new and, so far as I know, original. In presenting the entire thesis, I had to make the choice of employing a highly technical form available only to specialists within my field of the profession of medicine or a form which was understandable to any intelligent person, professional or non-professional. I have chosen the latter even at the risk of having it depreciated as mere "popular science." The substance of the book, however, I have been teaching to my students and discussing with my colleagues for many years. Parts of it have been formally presented at staff seminars of the Menninger Clinic and to the Topeka Psychoanalytic Society, the Washington-Baltimore Psychoanalytic Society, the New York Psychoanalytic Society, the American Psychoanalytic Association, and the American Psychiatric Association. Parts of Chapters 5 and 6 were published in the *Bulletin of the Menninger Clinic;* parts of Chapters 2 and 3 were published in *The Atlantic Monthly;* and parts of Chapters 4 and 6 in *The Virginia Quarterly Review.*

The original manuscript was read by a number of friends who sent in most helpful suggestions and criticisms, leading ultimately to a very considerable reorganization and recasting of the material. Among these I would mention particularly: Drs. Franklin and Helen McLean of Chicago; Frances Adams Gumberg, Dr. Gobind Behari Lal, Robert and Betty Lamont, Maurice Finkelstein, Dr. Iago Galdston, Margaret Blanton, Mary Reinhardt Lasker, Rabbi Louis Finkelstein, Ben Sonnenberg, and Seward Hiltner, all of New York; Bernice Engle of Omaha; and Dr. Robert Knight, Dr. Mary O'Neil Hawkins, and Nelson Antrim Crawford of

Topeka. Valuable suggestions were also received from other sources, including the late Dr. Irene Haenel of Los Angeles, Dr. Leo Bartemeier of Detroit, Dr. Ruth Mack Brunswick of New York, Lucy Stearns McLaughlin of Santa Fe, Dr. David Rapaport of Topeka, and the Research Service of the Encyclopaedia Britannica.

For help with many technical details, my secretary, Alice Dangerfield, deserves unlimited credit and appreciation. For assistance with bibliographic references, Clara Louise Meckel, Librarian of the Menninger Clinic, was most helpful. My daughter Martha retyped one entire draft of the manuscript, and my son Robert photographed the manuscript in microfilm. My brother Will has been a source of unfailing encouragement and sympathetic appreciation. Finally, I want to acknowledge in particular the great debt I owe to the collaborating author, who was the inspiration of the book in the first place, and supplied many ideas, rewrote passages, and read with constructively critical attention every word of the half-dozen drafts.

A search for a title of the book proved to be remarkably difficult, and we enlisted the aid of numerous friends and consultants. A great many titles were suggested, including: "Man for Himself," "The Will to Live," "The Life Instinct," "The Conquest of Hate," "Living and Loving," "The Education of the Emotions," "The Cultivation of Love," "The War of the Instincts," "The Conflict Within," "This Medicine, Love," "The Power of Love," and "Stronger Than Death." All of these were rejected, however, for one reason or another, after repeated conferences with our publishers and colleagues. It became more and more evident, in the course of trying out various titles, that the average person has a curious aversion to words that treat of love as a constructive scientific force. There was a general tendency to shrink from the use of the word "love" as being sentimental, romantic or weak. Titles using the words "hate," "war," "conflict" and the like were, on the other hand, considered more acceptable to many people because they sound strong, scientific, and dignified—but at the same

time somewhat deterrent. This experience seemed to epitomize the
commentary made by the book on our civilization, indeed, its
chief message. Someone suggested that we might have called the
book "The Truth that Nobody Believes." But because we feel that
it sets forth simply and specifically the basic conflict of human life
and of our civilization, the primary issue at stake in the present
World War, we chose the title that the book now bears.

K. A. M

Karlyle Woods
Topeka
Oct. 1, 1942

Contents

Contents

LOVE AGAINST HATE

Chapter 1. This Medicine, Love

SCIENCE is a slave. It is commandeered by war to kill men and by medicine to save them. It fires guns and it allays fevers. It builds bridges and it blows them up. In science man found a slave to minister to his comfort and safety, but one which could take away both. The slave may even destroy his master, a possibility some now feel to be imminent. But the slave can also save his master, if the master will give the command.

With the world set on fire, it is time we reordered our slave. War is a disease, a world sickness, for which we know no ready cure. We cannot even agree upon the diagnosis. But no one will maintain today that "all's right with the world." It is full of hate and murder and bitterness and hunger and waste and pessimism and fear and sorrow. And we command our slave to further them.

But why? We are all human—we human beings. We all want the same thing in life, and there is enough for all. We have a world full of resources. We have emerged from the ignorance and lawlessness of savagery. We have captured a slave that works for us all, and with it we have become civilized. But—we still have war.

Perhaps civilization is to blame. Perhaps it is a disease, too. A strange and ironic paradox that would be—that the magic which made savages into men now makes men into savages! Could it be that our social structure, our cultural ideals—built by such painful increments to enable us to live in community and peace—may become a threat to the individual and to the world?

What's the matter with civilization? Is it sick? Is it fundamentally defective? Is it a juggernaut which is crushing man? Or is it too weak for the nature of man?

3

The nature of man! Does it perhaps all come back to that—this world sickness? Is it possible that human phenomena can all be related to human beings? Science has said so, but science is only a slave. The psychologist, speaking for science, is like a voice crying in the wilderness. "The disease of the world is the disease of the individual personality," he says. No one listens. "The World War of today is a reflection of multiple miniature wars in the hearts of individuals," he persists. He is met with silence. "The war of nations is a magnification of the war of human instincts, human motives," he cries. "What of it?" someone asks.

The world is made up of people, but the people of the world forget this. It is hard to believe that, like ourselves, other people are born of women, reared by parents, teased by brothers, adored and importuned by sisters, solicited and threatened by playmates, exhorted and reproved by teachers, courted by lovers, consoled by wives, worried by children, flattered by grandchildren, and buried by parsons and priests with the blessings of the church and the tears of those left behind. It is hard to believe that there are not some supermen and some archfiends who manipulate the rest of us and guide our destinies. It is easier to speak of fate, and destiny, and waves of the future than to consider the ways we determine our own fate, right now and in the immediate past and future.

What if science, the slave, were right? What if he were listened to, and put to work, according to his lights? What if science were to be applied to making—not a more deadly machine gun, not a more convenient refrigerator, but a more peaceful world community?

"Write us another book, please," said a thoughtful friend, "a book that tells us what to do. You've told us in *Man Against Himself* what science has discovered about man's innate destructiveness. But now you must tell us what science has learned about controlling it. Write us a book called *Man for Himself.*"

"My son is in the Army," wrote another reader. "He may never come back. He has a little girl . . . and I'm wondering if she and her generation will be different. Or must the same old cycle go on—hating—arming—killing? Is there no science of peace?"

Yes, there is a science of peace, a science of man *for* himself, and, by the same token, there *is* a remedy for war. "Two contrary laws seem to be wrestling with one another nowadays," said Louis Pasteur; "the one a law of blood and death ever imagining new means of destruction . . . the other, a law of peace, work, and health ever evolving new means of delivering man from the scourges which beset him." It was Freud who related these two contrary laws to the innate nature of human beings; it was he who recognized that the destructiveness of human beings is not the result of some passing fever, some incidentally occasioned accident in the normal course of life, but the expression of a deep persistent instinct. And it was also Freud who showed us that the impulse to live and love is likewise an instinctual endowment of human beings and a source of strength in opposition to the self-destructiveness. Die we must, ultimately, but in the meantime we can live, if we can love.

"This medicine, love, which cures all sorrow" was prescribed by Jesus long before Donne and by Gautama Buddha long before Jesus. What Freud did was to analyze the ways in which hate becomes fused with love and threatens to overcome it. No one realized better than Freud that he had given no final answer; not long before his death he wrote: "This point of view is still too new; no one has so far attempted to make practical use of it." [1] *

This is, however, precisely what I have attempted in this book. The practical problem may be stated thus: What resources do we have at our command with which to favor the life instinct and oppose the death instinct? How can we encourage love and diminish hate? How can we promote their fruitful fusion? Is it possible to dispose of our aggressions more expediently than by killing our-

* Explanatory footnotes have been placed at the bottom of the page and technical references and source notes at the end of the book.

selves and one another, and to foster and cultivate that tremendous power which draws men and men, and men and women together, that sovereign remedy which stills the hate that forces men apart?

It would seem logical to believe that we *can* do this. The clinical experience of the psychiatrist encourages him to believe it, for he sees it happen every day, in particular instances. The question is how to give this a general application. To do so involves risks of presumption, omission, incompleteness, unconscious personal bias. But I must run those risks and beg the reader's forbearance.

Such a presentation likewise involves the necessity of a systematic progression from the earliest expressions of emotion in the child to their final pattern of display. I hope the reader will bear this program in mind; otherwise he may find the next few chapters somewhat gloomy. But until we courageously examine the underlying groundwork of hate which breaks through to such disastrous expression, we cannot deal intelligently with it. To know ourselves means to become aware of our destructiveness as well as of our constructiveness. There is no need to shut our eyes to the former, to pretend that it is not there, or to say that we find it unpleasant to see either in ourselves or in others and prefer, therefore, to avert our eyes in pious fatuity. The logical inference of Freud's theory is that hate means death and that love is stronger than hate, and, therefore, stronger than death. Water is stronger than fire, too, and yet fires continue to destroy; water can win its victory only when the fire is sought for, discovered, and scientifically combated. The *laissez faire* people have had their day and what has the world come to? Is it not logical to assume that, given an opportunity, scientists could do no worse and might conceivably do better?

Chapter 2. The Frustrations of the Child

IT IS an ancient and still moot question what it is that the new-born child brings into the world with him. There have been religious wars over the question, philosophical arguments which have lasted for centuries, and scientific disputes which are still unsettled. The various theories about it can all be classified into those which assume that everything has been decided at the time of the child's birth—whether by heredity, destiny, predestination or whatever; and those which assume that the child is something of a *tabula rasa* on which his environment immediately begins to write its signature.

Lay people quite generally reflect in their own attitudes the scientific and theological and philosophical theories which best fit in with their own prejudices and fears, even when the favored theories are basically contradictory. Take, for example, the ups and downs of the theory of heredity. The foundation of the American democracy was in essence a repudiation of the principle that abilities and authority are transmitted by heredity. No sooner does our country get established, however, than we ourselves begin to exalt the principle that "blood tells" and develop our own lineal aristocracy and theories of blood superiority. In agriculture, in horticulture, in racing stables, dog kennels, poultry yards—in short, wherever science is applied to biological phenomena—the theory of hereditary dominance is taken for granted. But in the case of human beings, it is and it isn't. We develop aristocracies, to be sure, but we consider careful inbreeding to be immoral; we exalt the potentialities of the individual and turn a deaf ear to the eugenist.

But it is possible for scientists also to be blinded to essential facts by their prejudices and fears. These may be of a general character; some people believe that scientists are influenced by popular notions as much as popular notions are influenced by scientific discoveries. Or there may be prejudice of a type that distinguishes scientists—the fear of subjectivity. There was a time when physicians and psychologists were determined in their attitude toward human beings by experiments with guinea pigs and starfish, or, perhaps I should say, by what laboratory scientists had been able to see in their experiments with guinea pigs and starfish. I make this amendment because I have no way of knowing that even a starfish may not have some feelings which escape the observation of the laboratory man. It was long assumed that the newborn baby has no emotions and very few sensations; now we have fairly good evidence that he has both emotion and sensation even before he is born. Scientists in general and medical men in particular have been slow to modify their ultramaterialistic physiochemical view of the newborn child because of the long and painful route they have traveled. Religion and theology fought doggedly against the biological concept of the human being, and it took several centuries, stained by the blood of many martyrs, for scientists to be able to think without prejudice about the biological nature of man. But in thinking without prejudice, as they believe they are doing, such scientists are actually thinking with a very strong prejudice. They are prejudiced by the fear that religious philosophy, mysticism, doctrines of the divinity of man, and the pervading influence of theories about the soul will again invade their objective thinking about "facts." They are so much afraid of this—some of them—that they cannot acknowledge the evidence of their own senses, nor can they accept the theories of fellow-scientists who submit that psychology, though it deals to some extent with intangibles, nevertheless deals with facts. We might even call them the facts of the soul, if that word did not so regularly throw scientists into a panic.

Not all scientists are like that; some scientists have much of the priest in them. For them, human suffering consists not of broken bones and ulcers alone but also of frustration, despair, anxiety, and depression. Disgusted with the refusal of fellow-scientists to concede the importance of these realities, some scientists begin to deny entirely the hereditary and biological influences upon the human personality. They turn to sociologists and the general public with the frank appeal: "Biology is less important than sociology. Listen, now, to us." When one stops to reflect that there are several hundred thousand teachers and almost an equal number of social workers in this country whose lifework is predicated upon the truth of such a theory, it can be seen how influential such a theory is. But if we concede that what people do and how people feel are facts no less than the movements of the heart or the chemical constituents of bile, we can avoid the fallacies of the sterile, hardboiled biologists on the one hand and of the opportunistic, softboiled environmentalists on the other.

Let us observe a newborn baby with a willingness to consider everything about it as a scientific fact. Our sentimental and proprietary feelings about babies make this difficult to do. But it has been done and we have accumulated a certain body of knowledge about the physical and chemical structure of the newborn. In addition, we have some (although less) definite knowledge about the psychological structure of the newborn.

Such evidence as we have indicates that, however sweetly we may interpret the fact, the human child usually begins his life in anger.* The painstaking observations by Margaret Blanton [1] and

---

* It would perhaps be more accurate to say that fear is probably the first emotion experienced, fear incident to the process of birth. But apparently this fear is quickly superseded, so far as we can judge, by anger. Throughout this book some readers may think I have overstressed hate to the exclusion of fear. Fear, they will say, is surely a more obvious, more universal and more crippling emotion than hate. In answer, I would say that fear and hate are emotions so inextricably fused and regularly associated that it is difficult to make useful distinctions. This we can say however: conscious rational fear serves a useful function; it warns us from real dangers and has impelled mankind to build up defenses against danger, hunger, disease and other external threats. The irrational fear that cripples and inhibits us is, as we shall see, not fear of real danger but rather

others of the first minutes and hours of infant behavior justify
Kant's statement that the cry of the child just born has the tone
not of lamentation but of wrath.

One is easily led into apologetic explanations for the baby's
earliest rage. Rebecca West, for example, in a magnificent chapter, concedes (in agreement with Freud) that "hatred necessarily
precedes love in human experience." But she assumes that this is
"an early error of the mind, which becomes a confirmed habit before reason can disperse it."

After the tideless peace of prenatal existence the child is born into a
world of uncomfortable physical experiences and terrifying uncompre-
hended controls. It must feel that in order to preserve itself it must lay
about it; it must beat with its hands and plot evil against the aggressors.
Thus a habit is initiated; thus a fantasy is engendered. It is imagined
that it is right to inflict pain, which is given the most intricate and
noxious ramifications by early experience. When one inflicts pain on
the surrounding world one is punished, one suffers a greater pain than
the one inflicted, one is treated as guilty. This does not rob pain of its
majesty, for punishment is pain, and punishment is acclaimed as good
and holy. Is it not a way of salvation to be punished? (Rebecca West,
Living Philosophies, Series II, Simon & Schuster, Inc., 1939.)

Scientists cannot accept the assumption that the child's anger or
any other consistently observed natural phenomenon is "an error."
It would be a rather serious error if the child did *not* learn to hate
certain things. The real fact seems to be that he does not *learn* to
hate; he comes into the world equipped with it, for better or for
worse, and then he learns to use it, wisely or unwisely according
to his experiences. Under proper tutelage and with what we may
call normal experience he gradually becomes more and more able
to distinguish between those objects which are properly to be
feared, hated, and fought against, and those which may be more
promptly accepted, utilized, and loved. So long as this discrimi-

a fear of ourselves, a fear of our own hatreds or of the hatreds engendered by
us in others or projected upon them. Fear is often the only external manifestation
of hate.

nation is an accurate one, the aggressive or destructive tendencies can be advantageously expressed in the services of self-preservation; that is, in support of the expanding of constructive tendencies.

However, early in his life even the child of most fortunate environment does make mistakes in his differentiations. He mistakes friends for foes, and vice versa. The hot fire looks pretty and attractive, but it burns him. The cat looks soft and safe, but scratches. The fierce, noisy person, who later turns out to be an older brother, is not nearly so dangerous as he at first appears, but is actually a protector. The new baby sister does not deplete the mother of all her capacity for love as at first seemed to threaten. All sorts of such misunderstandings and wrong estimates must later be corrected by a continuous testing of reality which requires many years for the achieving of even a fair degree of accuracy. In the meantime the expression of hate is mobilized and dispersed in unpropitious directions, while the outflow of love is either scanty or overexpended in inexpedient and unprofitable relationships.

In their observations on children being cared for at the Hampstead Nurseries in London during the present war, Anna Freud and Dorothy T. Burlingham write: [2]

It is a common misunderstanding of the child's nature which leads people to suppose that children will be saddened by the sight of destruction and aggression. Children between the ages of 1 and 2, when put together in a play pen, will bite each other, pull each other's hair and rob each other's toys, without regard for the other child's unhappiness. They are passing through a stage of development where destruction and aggression play one of the leading parts. If we observe young children at play we notice that they will destroy their toys, pull off the arms and legs of their dolls or soldiers, puncture their balls, smash whatever is breakable, and will only mind the result because complete destruction of the toy blocks further play. The more their independence and strength are growing, the more they will have to be watched so as not to create too much damage, not to hurt each other or those weaker than themselves. We often say, half jokingly, that there is continual war raging in a nursery. We mean by that, that at this time of life, destructive and aggressive impulses are still at work in children in a manner in which they only occur in grown-up life when they are let loose for the purposes of war.

It is one of the recognized aims of education to deal with the aggressiveness of the child's nature, i.e., in the course of the first four or five years to change the child's own attitude towards these impulses in himself. The wish to hurt people, and later the wish to destroy objects, undergoes all sorts of changes. It is usually first restricted, then suppressed by commands and prohibitions; a little later it is repressed, which means that it disappears from the child's consciousness. The child does not dare any more to have knowledge of these wishes. There is always the danger that they might return from the unconscious; therefore all sorts of protection are built up against them: the cruel child develops pity, the destructive child will become hesitant and over-careful. If education is handled intelligently, the main part of these aggressive impulses will be directed away from their primitive aim of doing harm to somebody or something, and will be used to fight the difficulties of the outer world: to accomplish tasks of all kinds, to measure one's strength in competition and use it generally to "do good" instead of "being bad," as the original impulses demanded.*

* Speaking of the effect of actual war conditions on children, the authors continue:

"In the light of these considerations it is easier to determine what the present war conditions, with their incidents of wholesale destruction, may do to a child. Instead of turning away from them in instinctive horror, as people seem to expect, the child may turn towards them with primitive excitement. The real danger is not that the child, caught up all innocently in the whirlpool of the war, will be shocked into illness. The danger lies in the fact that the destruction raging in the outer world may meet the very real aggressiveness which rages in the inside of the child. At the age when education should start to deal with these impulses, confirmation should not be given from the outside world that the same impulses are uppermost in other people. Children will play joyfully on bombed sites, around bomb craters, will play with blasted bits of furniture, and throw bricks from crumbled walls at each other. But it becomes impossible to educate them towards a repression of, or a reaction against, destruction while they do so. In their first years of life they fight against their own wishes to do away with people of whom they are jealous, who disturb or disappoint them, or who offend their childish feelings in some other way. It must be very difficult for them to accomplish this task of fighting their own death wishes, when at the same time people are killed and hurt every day around them. Children have to be safeguarded against the primitive horrors of the war, not because horrors and atrocities are so strange to them, but because we want them, at this decisive stage of their development, to overcome and estrange themselves from the primitive and atrocious wishes of their infantile nature."

Thus what might be called "error" or ignorance or inexperience in the child plays a part in forming the early patterns of hate. For the present, I am neglecting the contribution made to these early reaction patterns by parental ignorance and inexperience; we shall come back to this in a moment. For there is yet to mention the effect of certain great "natural" disasters, those unpredictable, unpreventable blows from the hands of Fate or Nature which all too early fall upon the heads of some children. Against these he has no defense but resentment. His mother dies, his home burns, his favorite sister sickens, he is subjected to a surgical operation, his father and mother separate, the country is visited by a famine or a war. No adult can be quite objective in the face of such disasters, let alone an immature, inexperienced personality whose pattern of loving and hating is still in the process of formation.

It is not surprising, therefore, that no one grows up entirely logical and sagacious in his program of loving and hating. At times everyone to some degree hates unwisely and loves unwisely. Perhaps it would be more accurate to say that we sometimes hate the wrong persons and love the wrong persons, or that, since love and hate are always fused, there is often too much hate in our relationships with some whom we ought to love, and too much love for some whom—in our own self-interest—we would do better to hate.

These confusions begin in childhood, as I have already said, through misapprehensions, misinterpretations, and inevitable conflicts in purpose. Dr. Smith Ely Jelliffe used to say that the child's first major decision was whether "to holler or to swaller," when he discovers that the two cannot be done simultaneously. Yet simultaneous emotions exist in the heart of the child which he finds it as difficult to reconcile as he does crying and swallowing. How shall he resolve the problem if the same person who brings him his bottle also takes it away? No matter how ideal the mother is therefore, the child is bound to have both positive and negative feelings toward her.

In discussing how these confusions arise, I have perhaps over-emphasized their logical, rational aspects. Logic and reason imply some ability to see beyond the immediate present, and this, of course, the child cannot do. His earliest reactions are not rational; they are entirely emotional, based upon the feelings induced by the immediate stimulus and the way it is followed up.

For, just as certain deprivals evoke the hostile capacities of the child, so certain gratifications allay them. If we can imagine a parent sufficiently skilful to replace each satisfaction of which the child is deprived by another satisfaction which the child could ac-cept as approximately equivalent, without disloyalty to the re-quirements of reality, we should expect to see in the progeny of such a parent an ideal person, not one without aggression but one without a sense of being thwarted in the adventures and misad-ventures of life, and without hate for anything except those things which should be hated and fought against in defense of his own ideals and best interests.

2

But parents are only human beings; they, too, had childhoods and they, too, had parents who made mistakes; and they, too, un-derwent accidents of fate which always upset the otherwise ideal milieu. Consequently what it comes to is that we should seek to determine precisely what sort of thwarting gives rise to serious childhood dissatisfactions.

So much has been said in recent years about the responsibility of parents for the early habit formations of the child, good and bad, that many parents have become very self-conscious about it and some of them a little hysterical. Some psychiatrists, in turn, have raised their voices to assure parents that such anxiety is worse than no concern about the problem at all. The state of confusion which exists among parents is, therefore, not surprising; it is a

question whether anxiety or smug indifference is the more pathological and harmful.

In what is to follow I shall make no attempt to offer specific
suggestions (until the end of the chapter) in regard to parents'
behavior with respect to their children, because our first concern
is with the fundamental psychological principles underlying the
attitude of parents and their treatment of the children, and particularly those general trends which, as I believe, tend to increase
frustrations and thus determine certain hate patterns.

We shall begin with the psychological and physiological interactions of the earliest period.

When the baby is born, his lungs and kidneys take over the
responsibility of purifying his own blood stream. This means that
he begins to absorb oxygen, exhale carbon dioxide, drink water
and a watery solution of sugar, fat, and protein, and excrete by-
products of tissue disintegration diluted in water. In short, the
baby begins to breathe, suckle, urinate, and defecate. For the most
part these processes develop automatically, but parents and nurses
take a hand in regulating them. The child is always allowed to
breathe as he pleases, and for a time he is allowed to urinate and
defecate as he pleases; but almost from the beginning certain
regulations are placed about his eating. He can't eat all the time,
and his elders have themselves become so much the slaves of time
and schedules that it seems to be a simple and natural expedient
to feed the child at certain regular intervals, which correspond
only approximately as far as we can discover to the child's needs.
The feeding intervals are gradually lengthened, and after some
months the child is induced to accept other methods of feeding
than that of suckling and is introduced to other foods than milk.

All of this is very revolutionary as far as the child is concerned,
and we could assume hypothetically that the process is accompanied by considerable psychological disturbance even if we did
not know it, on the one hand from pediatric observations and on
the other from psychoanalytic explorations. In fact the far-reach-

ing influence of these early experiences has certainly been under-estimated in the past; some scientists today go so far as to believe that "the infant who has had generous breast feeding and a be-nevolent weaning will face life with a benign, generous, and opti-mistic attitude or disposition, while the infant who has been denied adequate nursing and mothering, and has been abruptly weaned, will feel deprived, suspicious, and fearful, and bear resentment that may be crystallized into active hostility and aggression." [3]

But there is more to the emotional experience of the infant than the question of feeding regulation; sooner or later the parents de-cide that the functions of excretion must likewise come under the influence of social control. For reasons that to the child must seem inadequate, if not totally lacking, he is "taught" (forced) to regu-larize his urination and his defecation. And again we know em-pirically, both from the observation of children and from the recollections of psychoanalytic patients, that these processes are accompanied by turbulent emotional reactions and that vestiges of the conflict between the child (as a representative of nature) and the parent (as a representative of society) persist throughout life. That these reactions are inculcated into the character structure as stubbornness, retentiveness, extravagance, exhibitionism, and other traits is now no longer a matter of theory.

Some readers will perhaps feel that this interpretation puts too much emphasis on nursing, weaning, and toilet training to the neglect of many subsequent frustrations. Others will conclude that it applies to a minority of persons, and explains very little of the present worldwide epidemic of hatred. Surely, think such readers, not all those who clamor for war or gloat over the oppression of the weak are to be regarded as the children of parents exceptionally unskilful in the inauguration of weaning and toilet training.

The fact emerges, however, from the observation of young chil-dren and the personality study of a large number of adults whose life adjustments have failed, that there are certain striking and undeniable correlations of the adult behavior with the early childhood traumata. It is quite a uniform finding that the inability of adults to endure frustration in the degree in which we are subjected to it in the ordinary experiences of daily life is regularly connected with the childhood experience of having been frustrated too considerably, or too rapidly, or too inconsistently (as in the case of the "spoiled" child), and thus having had aggressive patterns overstrongly developed. Such children are weaned (not only from the breast but also from subsequent satisfactions) in such a way as to make them feel that they have been robbed or cheated.

Here again, I repeat, I am speaking of attitudes and not of techniques. It is possible that a child could be weaned at six months with less thwarting than another child would experience after nursing for a year. Many modern infants are prematurely weaned, literally, but the premature thwarting of other infantile gratifications, or an insufficiently skilful and adequate substitution of other gratifications produces the same psychological result. A child discovers that it is pleasant to pour water (or urine) on the floor; the tendency of many parents is to forbid such a gratification and to substitute no other. It is the same with other "bad habits"— toilet play, thumbsucking, manual manipulation of the genitals. Parents often look upon these things with undisguised horror and do everything within their power to take such pleasures from the child without making any attempt to replace them with something acceptable and more approved socially. We must admit that parents are often encouraged in these frustration patterns by physicians, especially in the matters of feeding and fondling. Both pediatricians and psychiatrists have been influenced adversely by false conclusions drawn from the schools of behaviorism and dietetics.

The interaction between an infant's psychology and his physiology has been well stated by a pediatrician, Dr. G. F. Weinfeld: [4]

The instinctive need for food is physiologically expressed through the medium of hunger contractions. Pain occurs and tension accumulates as a direct result of these contractions. Gesell in his intensive studies on feeding behavior has shown that there is a great variability in the chronological rhythm with which these contractions occur. This rhythm differs from infant to infant and in the same infant at different times, but as growth proceeds hunger occurs with progressive regularity. It is obvious, then, that any feeding schedule which provides for the presentation of food to the young infant at regular intervals is physiologically unsound. Such a schedule would not anticipate the natural rhythms of hunger and therefore food would be offered when it was not required and withheld when it was demanded. . . .

The emotional aspects of hunger are also concerned with the irregularity with which hunger contractions occur. . . . When the feeding program is adjusted to the individual rhythm of the infant, his hunger is always followed by gratification. When there is gratification the sensory apparatus is released for ultimate recognition of an intermediary between hunger and gratification—the mother. When the feeding experience is satisfying and not frustrating, the infant comes to have confidence in the mother and his environment. He can depend upon the certain satisfaction of his instinctual needs and has learned to wait. He has made his first adaptation to reality. Equipped with a new attribute—confidence, all of his senses are expanded so that the rooting at the breast, the handling of the breasts, the odor and taste of the milk, the sight of the mother and the sound of her voice, in fact all his perceptual senses, are constantly enlarged for the purpose of exploring reality. . . .

There can be no doubt that the ideal feeding program should be based on the physiologic and emotional needs of the infant. Such a program would involve no fixed feeding schedule whatsoever and the parent would be instructed to offer food to the baby whenever it is hungry. Because the older ideas of regularity and discipline are so firmly entrenched in our culture, many parents find it difficult to carry thru a program based on indulgence and gratification. In most instances it is necessary to spend a great deal of time and much patience in re-educating the parent to the physiological and emotional reasons upon which this program is based.

In those primitive societies where adults leave their children alone and do not thwart them, the child can find for himself substitute gratifications which may subsequently appear to him better than the original ones. He comes to like guavas or bananas as well as—ultimately better than—mother's milk. He learns to "come in out of the rain," to step on grass rather than thistles, to avoid dangerous animals and insects, because it is more pleasant and not because he is ordered to do so. Thwarting, when it occurs, is ascribable to nature, not to his parents. The resentment he feels can be charged against those malignant forces of nature which it is the duty of mankind to combat.

In contemporary society, on the other hand, when substitute gratifications are made, their choice is largely determined by adult tastes. And not only does society demand that the child restrain his natural healthy impulses and give up some of his greatest satisfactions, but it also demands that he express no untoward resentment at this frustration. Not only must he sacrifice much of his freedom, but he must do so politely and willingly. He cannot even have the satisfaction of screaming, kicking, and fighting. "Children should be seen and not heard" is an old-fashioned slogan, but the motive behind it—the idea that children must be kept in their place and not allowed to rebel—is still very important to many parents, as witness the letters they write to child-guidance experts asking how to "make" the child obey, how to "break" the child of bad temper, and so on.

How the child feels about even the most reasonable requirements of civilization could be attested by child psychiatrists and child psychologists in thousands of instances; but in all the clinical literature I know of nothing so eloquent as the story brought to national attention a few years ago in a most unexpected place, the columns of the *New Yorker* (July 1, 1939). I quote it without change and without comment:

A young mother we know has sent us a song, or a chant, or a poem, or something that her four-year-old son made up and sings every evening in his bathtub. It goes on practically forever, like the Old Testament, and she was able to copy down only part of it, but even this fragment seems to us one of the handsomest literary efforts of the year, as well as another proof that children are the really pure artists, with complete access to their thoughts and no foolish reticence. It is sung, she says, entirely on one note except that the voice drops on the last word in every line. We reprint it here because seldom, we think, has the vision of any heart's desire been put down so explicitly:

"He will just do nothing at all,
  He will just sit there in the noonday sun.
  And when they speak to him, he will not answer them,
  Because he does not care to.
  He will stick them with spears and put them in the garbage.
  When they tell him to eat his dinner, he will just laugh at them,
  And he will not take his nap, because he does not care to.
  He will not talk to them, he will not say nothing,
  He will just sit there in the noonday sun.
  He will go away and play with the Panda.
  He will not speak to nobody because he doesn't have to.
  And when they come to look for him they will not find him,
  Because he will not be there.
  He will put spikes in their eyes and put them in the garbage,
  And put the cover on.
  He will not go out in the fresh air or eat his vegetables
  Or make wee-wee for them, and he will get thin as a marble.
  He will not do nothing at all.
  He will just sit there in the noonday sun."

Most people do not remember having had such feelings in childhood, or remember them only dimly. For when emotions are stimulated which it is dangerous to express outwardly, their suppression is gradually replaced by repression—that is, by denying the experience and then by excluding it from consciousness and from conscious memory. But a repression is successful only if the child has attained sufficient maturity to accept it temporarily and to find other outlets later. If the experiences are not too severe, the child forgives and "forgets." But if repression is forced upon him prematurely or excessively, it is almost certain to break down, sooner or later, releasing unmanaged impulses in the form of neurosis, behavior disorder, or other forms of "abnormality." In discussing her daughter's childhood eating and drinking habits, a mother once told me this: "We were advised by the best pediatricians in New York that she should be given spinach. And spinach she got. But it was necessary for my husband and the nurse to hold her down with a sheet draped over her body, screaming and sobbing, while I forced spoonfuls of spinach between her clenched teeth." This mother was not a heartless woman; she was cultivated and socially prominent in a great city.

I recall an otherwise intelligent father telling with pride of slapping his three-year-old child's face every time the child said, "I can't eat this oatmeal." Since the child was almost as determined as the father, the slapping continued at intervals of a few seconds for ten or fifteen minutes at each meal. Finally the child would eat the oatmeal, and then vomit it up!

How many parents have placed a child upon the toilet with instructions to remain there until he has moved his bowels, how many have shown their senseless anxiety over the child's constipation by an onslaught of soapsticks, enemas, cathartics, and purges —these can only be conjectured.

I mention these illustrations as extreme instances only to remind the reader of the contrast between the way many primitive children grow up and the way many of our so-called civilized children are obliged to grow up. A significant comment on this difference is contained in a letter from Dr. Nancy D. Campbell, executive medical officer of the United Pueblos Agency of Albuquerque, New Mexico:

One fact in the rearing of the Indian child has interested me greatly. Babies and small children are treated with great kindness and indulgence. If a child cries, it is suckled or provided with whatever it appears to desire, whether by our standards this would be good or bad. No disciplinary measures are offered unless restraint by use of a cradle board is considered in this light. During childhood they do very much as they please. I have often seen the parents defer to a six-year-old's whims as to whether he would or would not be hospitalized, regardless of the child's degree of illness. Yet at adolescence that same child becomes a thoroughly law-abiding citizen who conforms in every respect to the tribal customs, takes part in the ritual ceremonies and dances, and defers in every matter of great or little importance to his elders.

Homburger Erikson [5] has reported similar observations among the Sioux Indians, and George Devereux [6] among the Mohaves. The latter writes:

The Mohaves never strike their children or punish them in any way. One who did so would be regarded as "crazy." When asked why he did not respond to the blows administered to him by a child, one of the Mohaves said, "Why should I strike him? I am big, he is small. He cannot hurt me. If I did so I should be like the white people who beat their children."

In recent years the influence of the government schools at which the children are * sometimes whipped has extended to the Indians, so that mild corporal punishment is occasionally administered, but this is attributed by the Indians entirely to white influence. As for juvenile delinquency and rebellion among the children, Erikson's and Devereux's impressions were that they are far less in evidence than among civilized peoples, indicating that failure to punish children cannot be said to be followed by adult disrespect of authority; more likely the reverse is true.

It may be objected that civilization requires more restrictions than life on a desert island or under the primitive conditions of savage life. We feel it necessary, for example, that our children learn to control their excretions in accordance with adult prejudices. It helps them if they begin early to learn the intricate social code to which they must conform all their lives if they are not to be conspicuous. It would be unkind indeed for parents, in the light of their own painfully gained knowledge, to withhold such training from their children.

Some neurotic parents, however, do precisely this thing. They overreact, as it were, to the dilemma that our culture forces upon

* I mean "were"—because I feel sure this has been changed during the progressive administration of John Collier.

the child. I have in mind those parents who try to introduce the non-regulatory, *laissez faire* methods of primitive society into the twentieth-century urban home. They take pride in letting the child do whatever he chooses, within very wide limits, on the theory that they may hurt his development by restraints. Some acquaintances of mine, for example, were accustomed to allow their six-year-old boy to appear naked in the living-room if he so desired. Another couple alienated many of their friends through their refusal to restrain their twins from destructively handling other people's possessions. I am sure the experience of every reader will supply additional examples. Such privileged children do not escape the penalties which civilization imposes on primitive behavior. They soon learn that their parents' attitude is not truly representative of life in their community, and therefore cannot be trusted. But how is one to introduce a child into a civilized world and educate him in its complicated restraints and customs without injury to his mind and emotions?

Civilization demands more thwarting of immediate gratifications than does most savage life; and although, in theory, it offers more compensations, these are surely not apparent to the child in the first years of his life. Thus one might say that the difficulty in bringing up children in our modern life is that immediate tangible goals must be denied and distant abstract goals ubstituted which are beyond the child's understanding. The problem is to provide stop-gap substitutions which will give the child legitimate pleasure in the present.

But this statement of the problem is not quite the whole truth. It overlooks the most important factor in learning: the immediate pleasure that the child obtains in the form of love whenever he gives up a socially disapproved habit or attitude. The encouraging smile of the mother when the baby remembers her prohibitions, his parents' beaming pride in observing his efforts to use a spoon instead of his fingers—these are tangible rewards for which the child barters his naive ideas of comfort and selfish ease. This is why parents are more important to the child in civilized communities than in primitive communities. The tremendous task of the child's first four or five years of education devolves almost exclusively upon the parents, the persons who can, theoretically, best give this love and attention in repayment for renunciations he is asked to make. Never again in his entire life will the child learn so much with such rapidity as he does in these first years. From then on, no matter how brilliant he may appear to be, he is a dull and stodgy person in comparison with the triumphant flowering of his babyhood.

But without love to sweeten each step in this prodigious uphill climb, the boundless energy and curiosity of the child are diverted into easier paths. The great frustration which the modern child in civilized society suffers is not entirely due to the rigid curbing of his natural pleasures and unsocial habits; it results also from the fact that he is deprived of the extra supply of love which his sacrifices require. A restriction imposed upon him may be demanded by society, but when it is accompanied by expressions of the parents' hostility toward him and re-enforced by their resentment of his intrusion upon their comfort, it is small wonder that the child reacts with bitterness and confusion. Under these discouragements, some children give up altogether the idea of attaining adulthood and become irresponsible weaklings.

Thus far we have been considering the frustrations of the infancy period rather than the frustrations of the older child, although to some extent these two are inseparable. During the first two years the problems of feeding and toilet training are the most important, but by the end of the second year there are dawning evidences of the child's sexual life, and in our civilization this involves additional frustration. Parents are prone to assume, in spite of vast quantities of scientific evidence to the contrary, that the child has no sexual life and no sexual feeling. The child quickly learns that he must act in accordance with this myth so far as external evidences are concerned. One of the most frequent memories uncovered by psychoanalytic patients is their profound disappointment and bitterness when they came to recognize (often before the age of seven) that their parents indulged in sexual activity forbidden to themselves and represented to them as "bad." Coupled with this are the experiences of masturbation, sexual curiosity regarding the opposite sex, anxieties regarding the possible loss of the penis in boys and a corresponding assumption on the part of little girls that they have been injured or slighted in some way, and, finally, emotions of jealousy directed toward the parents in the form of the well-known "Oedipus complex." This last is likely to be interpreted popularly as a child's guilty incestuous feeling toward the parent of the opposite sex; but it should rather be thought of as hostility toward the parent of the same sex—a phenomenon more easily recognized and also more significant in its consequences. In addition, the child tends to regard the parent as a seducer or a seductress, encouraging or inviting an affection whose complete realization would be fatal.

We shall have more to say about the psychosexual development of the child in another chapter; all that needs to be said at this point is that parents are obliged to enforce an authority regarding sexuality which is in turn dictated to them by social attitudes; the technique with which they enforce this authority will depend largely upon their degree of freedom from ambivalence toward the child.

Parents often treat their child as they themselves were treated by their own parents, many years previously, thus achieving a long-deferred and displaced revenge for the indignities and suffering they endured. But, queerly enough, such parents rarely recognize the hate implied in their behavior. They defend their position with the most respectable rationalizations. "They knew how to bring up children in those days." "The old folks were pretty hard on me, but it didn't hurt me any." "What was good enough for me is good enough for my child." "One thing I can say for my parents, they didn't spoil me." So they say; and while they claim to be teaching their child to obey, to control himself, to endure hardship and criticism without flinching, they are actually teaching him that might makes right. The child learns quickly enough that his parents do what *he* is forbidden to do, and that such hypocrisy is possible because of their superior size and strength. It is therefore likely to become his object in life to attain adulthood in order to aggrandize himself and to punish and restrict those who are weaker than he; thus the revenge of parent upon child is perpetuated for another generation.

We must emphasize again that not all the unwise restrictions and mistakes of the parents in rearing their children are to be ascribed to hostility, conscious or unconscious. Some of these mistakes are certainly due to ignorance and still others to a faithful adherence to the advice of false prophets. Much harm, in my opinion, has been done to the children of the present generation by the dogmatic, opinionated instructions delivered to young mothers by faddists of one kind and another, sometimes in very respectable garb. The fad of beating the child into submission was succeeded by the fad of ignoring the child's emotional needs completely. The fad of purging the child gave way to the fad of enema and dietary rituals. Vitamin worship replaced spinach fanaticism. The authority for these various regimens was sometimes that of a psychologist, sometimes of a physician, and sometimes of a psychiatrist. Often, perhaps, it was a grandparent or a neighbor, though —having mentioned grandparents unfavorably—I must add that I have also seen instances in which it was they who exerted the most normal and favorable influence.

I am constantly impressed by the fear of parents lest they be too kind or too loving to their children. Although for a time they may heed the advice of a psychiatrist to be considerate and patient with a child who shows evidence of being under severe tension, they will often turn with alacrity to sterner measures as soon as the child shows signs of improvement. A little boy who had developed strong hostilities toward his parents and younger sister was brought to a psychiatrist, who recommended that he be placed in a psychiatric boarding school where, in contrast to his treatment at home, he was given a great deal of encouragement and approbation. In this congenial atmosphere, no longer in competition with his favored younger sister, he showed an immediate improvement in his school work and in his social relations with adults and children. In fact he was so unusually adaptable, co-operative, and affectionate that he soon became one of the leaders in the group. He spontaneously wrote glowing accounts of the school to his parents, who began to fear that he was having too good a time and was not being disciplined severely enough. After several months of growing dissatisfaction with his improvement, they abruptly transferred him to a military academy for small boys, in spite of his tearful entreaties to be allowed to stay in the school he liked. His father declared he did not believe in "mollycoddling" children, and his mother said that while they appreciated the fact that he had been made happy and had seemed to take a new interest in school work, they wanted most of all to see him taught to be "responsible."

But there is another extenuation for mothers who seem to offer less than the necessary amount of love to their children. Consider the fact that a third of the families in the United States live on incomes of under $780 a year, two-thirds on incomes of under $30 a week.* This means that during the child's pre-school years, which are so formative, the average mother has a very large reality problem in getting enough for her family to eat and keeping her home in some kind of working order. In most homes the mothers cannot avail themselves of labor-saving devices such as washing machines, refrigerators, furnaces, and bathrooms. Many of them are definitely overworked. Their hours are long, their labors hard, their anxieties great. As a very intelligent reader, Mrs. Marion E. Lewis, put it in a personal communication:

* The figures are for 1935.

The young mother's day is too long, and if she has a little baby besides two other pre-school children, as is certainly very common, there are too many tensions. Just consider how she spends her day! She awakens at six o'clock, tidies herself and her baby, and gives the baby her breast. At half-past six she dresses herself. If the baby seems sleepy she leaves it in the chamber; if not, she takes it with her and places it where it can watch her get breakfast. Meanwhile, the other members of the family awake. She dresses the three-year-old child and perhaps helps the five-year-old a little.

After breakfast she changes the baby, and reminds the three-year-old to go to the bathroom. She washes the dishes and sweeps the kitchen; she makes the beds and tidies the bathroom, taking care of soiled clothing and misplaced articles. At half-past eight, if it is a fair day, she puts some washing through her washing machine, then hangs it out. At half-past nine she bathes and nurses the baby, meanwhile keeping eye and ear alert to the activities of the other two. Between ten-thirty and eleven-thirty she probably sweeps and dusts. She makes sure the baby is comfortable, persuades the other children to wash their faces and hands, and serves a simple lunch for herself and them at twelve. After that she washes the dishes. At one she lies down with the children for a rest. At two she gets up softly and nurses the baby. When the three-year-old wakes, she takes him to the toilet, dresses him, and then sits down with him on her lap for a little while. She also tries to give the five-year-old some of her attention.

About three o'clock she brings in her washing and irons or mends for an hour. She makes sure the baby is comfortable. Between four and six she cooks. At six she nurses the baby. At six-thirty she serves supper, then washes the dishes. At seven-thirty she bathes one of the older children—they get their baths by turn—and puts them both to bed. It is eight o'clock before she can join her husband in the living-room, and she has already put in considerably more than a twelve-hour day. Actually her day is not finished yet, for she must feed the baby again at ten o'clock, and it will be wise to wake up the three-year-old and put him on the toilet for a moment. Of course, I do not mean that this schedule is a fixed one. It varies some, as you know.

What this all comes down to is that the machinery of civilization requires so much of the mother (as well as of the child) that she has insufficient time to express love for her child in the ways

which he can most appreciate. She is too busy seeing that he excretes in the prescribed way, gets dirt washed off him in the prescribed way, eats food prepared in a prescribed way. The baby
must eat out of clean dishes, and while she is washing his dishes
she can't be petting him.

I realize that these practical difficulties exist and that nothing
either the reader or I can do will change them immediately. Whatever the causes, the child often gets an insufficient amount of love
and too great an amount of hate; and not only that, but in the
lack of love, the neglect, the restrictions, sometimes even the attempts to be loving, there is an implicit element of hate which
the child feels and reacts to.

3

Whenever we speak about the hostility or hate of parents toward
their children we are met by vigorous defenses, often from the
very persons who are the most guilty. "Why, I love my children
devotedly!" exclaims the mother who is obviously behaving in a
way most likely to harm them or in a way which has already
ruined them beyond redemption. President Neilson of Smith College brought showers of abuse upon his head by making the very
intelligent observation that much that passes for mother love is
really self-love. Some remarks of my own in a lecture to the effect
that we should study "mother hate" as well as "mother love"
were picked up by newspapers all over the country and used as
the text for sentimental editorials about the great sacrifices that
mothers make and the callousness of modern scientific opinion. It
is natural for us to recoil from observing our own aggressions. To
admit them is often to bring our guilt feelings into such an acute
stage of awareness as to provoke severe anxiety. It is pitiful to see
the self-reproach of some parents (usually on the wrong scores)
for their earlier treatment of a child who has become maladjusted
or mentally ill.

Let me be more specific about some of the crimes unwittingly committed against the child by the mother. I mean such things as inconsistency, threatening, objecting to his activities because they are disturbing and because they arouse her neurotic fears, refusing his reasonable requests, ignoring his efforts to be pleasing or interesting, breaking promises, quarreling with him over trivial matters, impressing her own anxieties or worries upon him, discussing him in the presence of other people, embarrassing him, neglecting him, bribing him, lying to him, shielding him from the consequences of his own acts, comparing him unfavorably with others. The greatest crime of all, perhaps, is the inculcation of a dishonest, hypocritical philosophy of life.

Swamping a child with "advantages" is often a substitute for giving him time, interest, companionship, and love. Frequently the material gifts to him are given because the parent feels guilty of an unconscious hostility, and hence, as is always the case, they actually accomplish in the long run the hostile purpose which was their original incentive. The same is true of the mother who "lives only for her child," who is uncomfortable when she is away from him if only for a few minutes, who threatens to leave the house if her husband dares lay a finger on the child, who accompanies him to school, helps him with his studies, allows him no friends lest they contaminate him.

As a dramatic instance of the outburst of long-smoldering, unrecognized hate, consider this example from the Kansas City *Star* of April 30, 1939:

SNAPS AFTER 30 YEARS

Minneapolis, April 29.—A.B.C., respected 47-year-old Federal Reserve bank clerk who was to have been married today, was held tonight in jail accused of beating his crippled 82-year-old mother to death with a chair.

After he killed her last night, he tried to commit suicide by slashing his wrists, by turning on the gas, and by setting fire to a pile of rags to burn the house.

"I don't know why I did it," C. sobbed. "She was a perfect old lady. Something just came over me."

For nearly thirty years C. had been the sole support of his widowed mother. They lived together in his mother's home. C. was regarded by his acquaintances as a "model man." He neither smoked nor drank and was known for his untiring devotion to his feeble mother.

"I can't understand it," said Miss B. She and C. had been engaged for eleven years. Only recently he completed construction of their "dream home" in South Minneapolis. He had purchased their marriage license. This, with the intended wedding ring, was found in his mother's dresser. He had given them to her for safekeeping.

I once talked with a white-haired mother whose terrific but unrecognized hatred of her son had driven him into hopeless mental illness; he had been confined in a hospital for a dozen years. She told me proudly that she visited him regularly every month, in spite of the disapproval of the hospital physicians. "I know he is glad to see me," she said, "and I think it does him good. Of course he never speaks, but I know he loves me." Such a tragedy wrings one's heart. Perhaps it is just as well for her that she cannot now realize the part she played in her son's retreat from life; but there are other mothers and sons for whom it is not too late to understand.

What I have said thus far will perhaps seem self-evident to many, or so well recognized and accepted scientifically that my careful restatement seems trite. But what I shall say next is not mere restatement; it has been pointed out occasionally, but it is by no means generally accepted or even recognized.

We know that most children are reared by women. The child's early frustrations that we have been discussing, as well as his earliest gratifications, come to him most often from a woman. Not only this, but his subsequent training throughout the formative years, and sometimes even in adolescence, is in the hands of women. It is, therefore, a presumptive conclusion that the patterns of emotional behavior, both of loving and of hating, are to a far larger extent than any of us realize determined not by "the parents" but by *the mother*. The child is born of her, and his first interpersonal experiences are with her; she is his first and greatest source of pleasure and love and food; but since every mother transfers her child from the comfort of her own womb and her own breast to the relative discomfort of a realistic world, one could postulate that she is also the one who first stirs up bitterness and revenge wishes in him.

For this reason I feel that a careful study of the particular effects of civilization upon women and the way in which it deprives them of instinctual gratifications is important in understanding why we grow up so much more prone to hate than to love. In the next chapter I shall discuss some of the ways in which women are, in their adult life, increasingly frustrated and cheated by the prevalent cultural patterns. They have good and abundant reason, I believe, for the resentments they feel consciously and unconsciously. But there is a vicious circle here: The women who must rear the children are themselves so thwarted and resentful that they tend to impose the same restrictions upon their children; and the children grow up and re-enact the same error. Males frustrate females, and females divide their aggressions between their male partners and their dependent children.

This may sound to some as if I were placing the responsibility for the present sorry state of world affairs chiefly upon women; I would not be the first to do so. In the very connection we have been discussing, Havelock Ellis [7] quotes a few comments from thoughtful writers of all periods which are rather startling to see collected in such an array: "Give me other mothers and I will give you another world" (St. Augustine). "Of ten blows which a child receives, nine are from its mother" (T. Hippel). "Maternal love easily becomes pernicious, an animal affection, overlooking, forgiving, and sparing all the child's faults, immensely injuring the child itself, and imparting at the outset the germ of future illusions in life" (Forel). "Many women wish to abolish war; but these very same women, in the sphere of education, cannot give up those methods of force which call out rough passions and un-worthy ideas of right, and are the counterpart of war" (Ellen Key). "Poor child! Your father is tied to his office, your mother is vexed today; tomorrow she has a visitor, the day after, her moods" (Pestalozzi). "The family, the hell of the child, the home of all social vices!" (Strindberg). "If the punishment of the crimi-nal is justified, we must first ask: How did he become a criminal? What was his mother like?" (Brockhaus).

These sentiments, of course, are utterly contrary to those usually cited; and—though one may feel that the positive virtues of mothers are sometimes overstressed in order to conceal resent-ment—the following *also* are true: "Mother is the name for God in the lips and hearts of little children" (Thackeray). "Mothers are fonder of their children than fathers, for they remember the pain of bringing them forth" (Aristotle). "God could not be everywhere, so he made mothers" (Yiddish proverb). "Her chil-dren rise up, and call her blessed" (Proverbs).

Certainly these things are true; scarcely anyone can think of his mother without emotions of gratitude, tenderness, and poignant yearning. I have not stressed the positive elements of the mother-child relationship simply because these are so powerful, so uni-versal, and so well known that they need no recital. No deprivation is so great and so irreparable to the child as the loss of a mother.

But it is just because of the solemn and frightening power that mothers exert that it is important to consider their role anew. It is customary to pay them homage and to exalt their sacrifices, and in doing so to ignore their status as human beings. Women have long recognized that the tendency of men to put them on pedestals and to idealize them has great disadvantages and penalties, and some of them have properly rebelled against it, preferring under-standing and recognition of their individual needs. It is the need of the child to receive help, food, care, kindness, and love, with·

out making adequate return, that leads him to see the mother as omnipotent and superhuman. The mother can tolerate this dependent attitude in her babies, but she cannot support it in all her relations in life.

It is therefore an obligation of the psychiatrist, whose experience brings him into sympathetic touch with the continual struggles of mothers to carry on their difficult tasks and with the unhappy consequences of their failures, to point out the inherent dangers in the mother-child relationship. In doing so, he must refrain, even at the risk of being misunderstood and accused of misogyny, from laudatory sentimentalism and easy compliments.

Most certainly it is not my intention to represent mothers to be the "precipitating cause" of all the present woes of the world. It is philosophically naive to talk about personal causes, as distinguished from impersonal causes, because of course everything is related to, and in that same sense *causes*, everything else; hence, we get nowhere by the antiquated sophistry of inquiring "who is to blame." Blame is a legal and religious concept, not a scientific one. Science conceives of causation in the sense of regularity of natural phenomena, and the scientist does not attempt to ascribe blame but rather tries to describe as accurately as possible just what is happening and in what order.

Nor would I give the impression that fathers have no responsibility in the injuring of children. Men's preoccupation with their business and with each other is a source of widespread disappointment to women, acting to fan the flames of their discontent. In this and many other ways, men are certainly accountable for some of the unnecessary embitterments which are stimulated in children. I shall have more to say about these things in the next chapter. In the way in which the average person would think of it, however, men are less closely related to the parent problem because they are less important to the child.

Critical readers will remind me of innumerable examples of the harsh father—the father who beats his children, the father who scorns or ignores them, the father who deserts them, the father who forces them into celibacy, hard work, martyrdom, or flight. Surely such fathers excite hatred, and in such instances it may seem unfair to incriminate the mother.

The answer to this will probably tax the credulity of the reader, but I must state it as an empirical fact: even in such instances as those I have just mentioned, where the father gives plenty of occasion for the child's conscious hatred, it is often the mother who is accorded the deeper resentment. Logically or illogically, correctly or incorrectly, the child of a severe father is likely to feel in the secret places of his heart that his mother should have protected him from such harshness, or that it was through her neglect that he was exposed to the father's mistreatment. Of course, *consciously*, the resentment is entirely displaced, as we say, onto its more conspicuous provocateur, the father. His harshness makes such a displacement the easier; the child can justify his feelings to himself more convincingly. But if we penetrate the many layers of hatred we come eventually to the deepest hurt of all—"Mother failed me."

I remember a conscientious schoolteacher who had led a very hard life. She had never permitted herself any pleasure except intellectual application and devotion to her work. She had been reared by pioneer parents—a kind, hard-working mother and a stern, harsh father. "I remember many times," she said, "being struck in the face by his fist and knocked to the ground for such an offense as dropping a teacup." And yet, as it developed, it was not her father—much though she consciously hated him—against whom this woman harbored her *inmost* feelings of injury; it was against her mother. Her rationalization was that her mother should have protected her and her sisters from such cruelty. I say "rationalization" because under it were hidden more infantile grievances, not the least of which was that she had been the eldest child and had been forced, while still almost a baby herself, to make way for younger children, to care for them, and to share her mother with them.

Another instance that typifies this frustration was the weaker son of a very strong, self-made Danish-American father. The father was proud of his elder son but extremely disappointed in this younger one and punished him severely for his poor school work. The boy was sent to a succession of boarding and military schools where he was lonely and frequently mistreated. When he begged to be allowed to come home, his father refused, calling him a "nitwit" and a "mollycoddle" and comparing him unfavorably with his elder brother. In spite of this the boy's misery at school was so great that he eventually ran away and refused to return. At home the father continually showed his contempt and dislike for the boy; his mother, on the other hand, was a quiet, tender-hearted woman who indulged and comforted the poor boy in every way she could, although remaining loyal to her husband. Yet, curiously enough, it was not the father against whom this boy's bitterest hostility was felt, nor yet against the elder brother. He thought that his mother should—in some mysterious way that he could not express—have "explained things" to him, helped him to get along, and prevented his friction with his father.

In both these cases the mother was (as always) the first and most important link with the world. She was the first antagonist in the child's battle to get his own way. These apparently unreasonable and unfair accusations, therefore, had a peculiar validity in that they related to a conflict more important to the child than the later battles.

If the early conflict between mother and child is not too severe and the child is not too bitterly thwarted, we may expect him to reorient himself with respect to women as he grows older—no longer to consider them exclusively as agents of nourishment or disciplinarians who curb his pleasures. But the opportunity to do so is considerably lessened by the fact that the child's care and education are entrusted almost exclusively to women, who quite often reinforce and strengthen his idea that women exist to frustrate him. When the child is turned over to a substitute mother at an early age, it often increases his burden of hate without expanding his capacity for love.

The tendency toward the use of substitute mothers is quite understandable in the light of the widespread change in women's vocational interests in late years. Formerly only the very rich could entrust entirely to nurses and governesses the duties ordinarily performed by the mother. But, since the turn of the century, woman's entrance into the economic world has extended this custom to families of even moderate means, although the percentage of families having servants is still a relatively small one. Ostensibly such help is for the purpose of relieving the mother of the menial tasks associated with the care of the children, but in reality such maids or "nurses" or governesses are frequently assigned all the major responsibilities of the child's care. Not the least important of these, from the psychological standpoint, are the toilet training and eating habits discussed at the beginning of this chapter.

Of course it is conceivable, and no doubt frequently true, that these hired women may be more objective, stable, and affectionate than the mothers themselves. But they certainly do not have the same incentives to give the child love or to exert their utmost skill in managing the hard transition stage from uncontrolled instinctual life to life according to difficult social standards. Sometimes they are neurotic; not infrequently they are actually feebleminded. When the subject is discussed in a group of young mothers, the aspect that seems paramount is wages—the apparent objective being to get a sufficiently docile girl at the lowest possible wage. If mothers who are disinclined to care for their own children were as seriously concerned over the problem of getting the best possible substitute parents as they are over getting the best beauty-parlor operator, or the best dressmaker, or the most competent dentist, they might really do their children a favor by putting them in more skilful hands. But this isn't what happens. Here and there, where a little nursery school has been organized by a few intelligent and energetic members of the community, with trained personnel employed to operate it, it struggles against almost insuperable difficulties arising largely from the reluctance of parents to pay what it costs to get really competent persons with whom to place the responsibility to which they themselves feel unequal.*

At any rate, for better or for worse, substitute mothers are almost always women, and the necessity of thwarting and controlling (the slightest mismanagement of which the child resents) is again relegated to a woman. Any way one looks at it, the earliest struggles and, hence, the patterns of subsequent hostilities are developed by the child's experiences with women, and are therefore with the greatest facility displaced in later life to other women.†

* Early in my experience as a psychiatrist I was struck by the fact that parents would willingly spend ten times as much for the psychiatric treatment of a twenty-five-year-old child as for the much more effective treatment of a five-year-old child. The only financially successful—or, I might say, solvent—institutions for the psychological help of children in the United States today are those limited to feeble-minded children—that is, children who must, for practical reasons, be moved from the home. Time after time psychiatrists have attempted to provide schools, clinics, and foster homes for the psychiatric treatment of children who could be cured, the "problem children" who suffer chiefly from the mistakes of their parents. But these institutions have regularly failed, not scientifically but financially.

† At various times it has been proposed that children would be better off generally if they could be raised scientifically in boarding homes away from the influence of the parents for the first few years of life. Sometimes, in the case of orphans and neglected children, this is actually necessary, and the consequences on the personality of the child are incredibly disastrous. Dr. Lawson G. Lowrey ("Personality Distortion and Earliest Institutional Care," read at the American Orthopsychiatric Assn. Meeting, February 23, 1940, Boston, Mass.) has studied a series of children so reared, both in the orphanages and in their subsequent development, and he concludes that these children follow a strikingly similar pattern of personality development: all of them show isolation trends and behavior typical of accentuated feelings of rejection, which includes certain typical sadistic oral aggressive patterns. It is interesting that children placed in such homes after the age of two do not develop these patterns of behavior to anything like the same extent as do those placed there before that age, emphasizing our contention that the very earliest months and years of the child's life are the most important.

4

Although I intend to go further and examine the psychology of women and the special frustrations which they endure, I would not end this chapter without drawing certain obvious practical conclusions of a constructive nature. Everything I have said points to the desirability of improving the early management of infancy in such a way as to decrease the unnecessary frustration of the child which creates in him patterns of hate and distortions of his basic behavior patterns. Clinical experience shows us some definite ways in which this can be done, and many readers have asked for them.

Every child should be guaranteed seven things:

1. He should have the opportunity for frequent sucking periods not limited in time, not artificially interrupted, and preferably at the mother's breast.

2. There should be no attempt to train the functions of excretion in accordance with adult standards until the child can sit alone securely, until he has acquired a primitive sign language by means of which he can make known his bodily need, and until he shows some autonomous inclination to learn. In both excretion and feeding there is an innate rhythm for each individual child which must be observed and respected, since these rhythms are fundamental in the evolution of his feelings of satisfaction, body control, and personal adjustment.

3. There must be a long and uninterrupted period of consistent and skilful "psychological mothering" by one individual. This brings about a biological and psychological symbiosis in which two organisms with essentially different needs profit mutually, the mother getting the satisfaction of completing the creation of her child and the infant receiving both food and the primary experiences of need-consciousness and gratification which assist in bringing his sensory nervous system into a regulated functional activity.*

* These first three recommendations, wholly in line with the thought of this entire chapter, are paraphrased and elaborated from Margarethe A. Ribble ("Dis-

4. He should have a father and mother in harmonious relationship with one another to set a consistent pattern for his love development.

5. He should be spared reproaches, intimidations, threats, warnings, and punishments regarding physical manifestations of his sexuality. The example of the parents and the quickly perceived attitude of society are sufficient deterrents from unsocial behavior.

6. He should be accorded the dignity of a separate individual possessed of his own needs, rights, and feelings, which means that he should be given reasons and explanations within the reach of his understanding for the compliance required of him by parental authority.

7. In all communications with the child, truthfulness, honesty, and sincerity on the part of the parents are unequivocally essential.[8]

organizing Factors of Infant Personality," *Am. J. Psychiat.* 98 :459-463, Nov. 1941).

Chapter 3. The Frustrations of Women

TO PLACE the major responsibility for the formation of the child's personality upon the mother is to put woman in the center of the universe, psychologically. This is not in contradiction to biological concepts; in many of the lower forms of life, there are no males but only females. Recently it has been demonstrated that even in mammals fertilization of the female ova may be accomplished artificially without either the mechanical or the chemical assistance of the male; he could, so to speak, just as well not exist.

Our social order, on the other hand, our economic order, our religious concepts, our legal codes, all make a quite different assumption, a historic assumption. Man is the more important figure; woman is born to serve him, love him, be protected by him, and assist in reproducing him. In the English language the word "man" is used synonymously with "human being."

It is important to emphasize this contradiction between the psychobiological and the prevalent social concept, because it makes for certain difficulties in grasping what is to follow, difficulties of a sort that psychoanalysts call resistances. The average woman reader, for example, may be somewhat pleased to think of herself as more important than the world seems to consider her; she will like this, but she will not like its logical consequences—namely, that she has a greater immediate responsibility for the troubles of the world. Men, on the other hand, are glad enough to hear women blamed for anything and everything, but male narcissism rejects the thesis that woman is biologically and psychologically more important than man.

The reader, therefore, whether man or woman, must remember that the empirical facts are as we have stated them: women bear the children; women suckle and feed the children; women largely rear the children; women (in the United States, at least) educate children; and women, far more than men, determine the personality patterns of the children. Some of these children are little females who grow up to be women and form the next generation of mothers; others are little males and grow up to govern, pursue, support, flatter, and frustrate these women, meantime thinking themselves (and often being thought by their mothers) to be the center of creation. But, as we too well know, friction begins to develop between men and men and between men and women, and the fact that there is too much of it we have blamed on certain frustrations inflicted upon the child by the mother. But the mother inflicts these frustrations because she herself is frustrated. Our problem, then, is to examine carefully how, where, when, and by whom she is frustrated.

Perhaps the most obvious frustration that women experience depends upon the point just mentioned; namely, that this appears to be a man's world. Men are physically stronger than women and, as a carry-over from childhood feelings of helplessness, the expression of physical power assumes an undue importance in their minds. To be sure, the power of the purse strings has long since superseded the power of muscles, but men continue to use their advantage through politics, economics, and legal codes to keep women in abeyance under the guise of protecting them. Society is to some extent still organized as if only men were human beings and as if such rights as women have were "conceded" to them by the generosity of their male governors. This situation is frustrating to women, not so much because of what it actually denies them as because of what it implies.

But since women think of themselves as a part of the social order, even though a subordinate part, they think of themselves as part-authors of this state of affairs, and it is therefore very difficult for them to express their resentment against it. In fact, as a general thing women are more conservative than men on questions of change in the economic order and in the regulations of civilized life. They tend to want to preserve the *status quo* even though they suffer unduly from it.

Nothing is more illustrative of this than the attitude of women toward war. War probably injures women even more than it does men, everything considered; yet, except in such male fantasies as the play *Lysistrata,* women have rarely used their power—personal, political, or economic—to put a stop to war. They are often reminded of their responsibility for doing so; especially in times of peace we hear, over and over, that women could stop war if they wanted to.

In 1938 C. E. M. Joad of England wrote—as quoted by Virginia Woolf in *Three Guineas:* [1]

I doubt whether at any time during the last fifty years young women have been more politically apathetic, more socially indifferent than at the present time. . . . Before the war, i.e., the First World War, money poured into the coffers of the W.S.P.U. in order that women might win the vote which, it was hoped, would enable them to make war a thing of the past. . . . Is it unreasonable to ask that contemporary women should be prepared to give as much energy and money, to suffer as much obloquy and insult in the cause of peace, as their mothers gave and suffered in the cause of equality?

Mrs. Woolf waxes ironic over this accusation. Addressing women, she writes:

According to Mr. Joad, you are not only extremely rich; you are also extremely idle; and so given over to the eating of peanuts and ice cream that you have not learnt to cook him a dinner before he destroys himself, let alone how to prevent that fatal act.

She goes on to insist that women are in reality poor, and so dependent upon men for their livelihood that they feel helpless to oppose men's self-destructive impulses even when these are turned directly upon women.

But these are not the real reasons. The difficulties go much deeper than Mrs. Woolf's explanations. Our civilization is based to too large an extent upon the principle that might makes right, and women are a part of that civilization and they believe in this principle and practise it just as do the men. Their instincts and their intuition ought to tell them otherwise, and in many instances do so tell them.* But women are susceptible to frustration, disappointment, and fear, just as men are, and they, too, have the urge to fight. We can be absolutely certain that the German women today, for all the suffering and humiliation that have been inflicted upon them by their government, share with their husbands the feeling that German men were heroes to invade and devastate France, and that Germany should extend the blessings of Nazi idealism to others as it has to the Austrians, the Czechs, the Slovaks, the Poles, the Greeks, the Norwegians, and the Dutch. They cannot see how aggressive, how senseless, how suicidal this looks to the rest of the world. They are caught in the same delusions and illusions that possess their men, hypnotized by the same empty words and the same ignoble dreams of national power. But their reaction to these delusions does differ from men's: they fight in a different way.† To some extent they fight

---

* I should certainly not want anyone to misconstrue these remarks about war's being an evil consequence of some defect in our civilization which women might repair—to mistake me as opposing the present war against Germany and Japan. We cannot reconstruct civilizations in a day, and for the present situation war is in my opinion our only salvation. Appeasement, isolation, and other such maneuvers in the name of peace in the present conflict seem to me to be either suicidal self-deception or calculated treason.

In mentioning political power, I do not mean to accord it much importance. I doubt if this is the best technique for women to use, as the world is now organized. It will be recalled that in the First World War an International Congress of Women met in 1915 under the leadership of Jane Addams and attempted to use the influence of women to bring about peace. An armistice was sought by representatives sent to the powers involved in the conflict. Some refused to see the women, and others were little more than courteous.

† Readers will recall Maupassant's story "Bed Number Twenty-nine" in which a woman, the beloved mistress of an army officer, suddenly disappears and is found by him, later, in a hospital bed, dying of syphilis. She had been captured by the enemy and infected with syphilis; when she could have escaped or been cured, she had done neither but had seduced and infected as many of the enemy soldiers as she could. "I took no thought of myself . . . I wished to kill them and I have killed them!" she screams to her stupefied lover. "I have killed more Prussians than you . . . more than all your regiment together!"

by proxy. Lillian Smith and Paula Snelling [2] have pointed out other feminine differences:

Women do not have the age-old undertow of group loyalty to combat which would impel them to stand together right or wrong, and to rationalize their acts; nor have they as much thirst to merge themselves with the group in sensuous enjoyment of its pervasive erotic attraction (both of which male characteristics may have their origin in those banished-brother days). And if it be true that women hate no less than men, are impelled no less than they to destroy, are no more inclined to turn their destructive impulses inward, still they would be less likely to choose war as a solution; for they are less given to symbolism, less likely to be satisfied with killing the wrong person.

The conception of women organized as a civilizing force to oppose the barbarous depredations of men is untenable, because it requires of women that they betray their deepest loyalties and interests. Woman will continue as in the past to throw in her lot with her mate and to share his fate even to her own sorrow. Any organization that aimed to promote peace by aligning woman against man would fail in its purpose. Only when men and women work together in understanding and sympathy for the same causes, turning their aggressiveness outward toward a joint threat, can useful ideals be realized.

Mrs. Poyser's observation (in *Adam Bede*) on the fallibility of women—"The Lord made 'em to match the men"—is applicable to aggressiveness, which waxes in women as it increases in men, so that neutralization of hostility by one sex becomes impossible. The expedient described in *Lysistrata*—by which a war was stopped and fighting men were brought to their senses when the women suddenly realized the latent power implicit in the function of love —has never been put into practice. Women have been too busy (and usefully so) cheering their soldiers as they marched off to war, urging them to stand fast in defense of their homes and children, nursing their wounds, growing food, mending clothing, manufacturing ammunition, and encouraging their men in what both sexes believe to be the preservation of their common security, to try to stem the torrent of hate in which they with the rest of the world are engulfed.[3]

From the psychological standpoint, however, *Lysistrata* * set forth a profound truth, but a truth that burns with a feeble flame compared with the incandescence of modern invention, and one that is likely to pass unnoticed in the confusion of so-called civilization, if indeed it is not extinguished. Fundamentally, woman *is* more predominantly than man the embodiment of the erotic power which is arrayed against self-destruction. While she shares his hostilities and his illusions, her role, even in war, is healing and sustaining. The erotic instinct, properly conceived of, does not refer solely to impulses toward physical contact, but to the drives in the direction of social and biological life, with the ultimate object of race preservation. A better term for it is simply love.

All the privations and oppressions which man inflicts upon women, including war, they would probably accept without a murmur if they were not frustrated in a more fundamental respect, the one just hinted at. Women are frustrated not so much by the infliction of tyranny, in one form or another, as by the

* With regard to the *Lysistrata* motif, it may be relevant to quote some ethnological remarks made to the author in a personal communication from Dr. Weston LaBarre. Among the Plains Indians, as is well known, nearly all the mechanisms of male prestige revolved around war exploits and war prowess. But in some groups it was the women who had the final say whether or not there would be a war-raid. An old woman—a mother, for example—could forbid her grown son to go to war, often by the touching symbolism of exposing her breast and reminding him of his childhood dependence upon her. Among some of the Iroquoian-speaking tribes, an old woman in the council could veto a proposed aggressive war.

On the other hand, it was the women who, ceremonially at least, stood to profit from a successful war. Among the Kiowa (and typically in the southern Plains) sisters and mothers and daughters of warriors (never the warriors themselves) took the bloody scalps of enemies, placed them on willow hoops, and danced publicly with a peculiarly blood-curdling ululation.

Here, the culture certainly afforded the women a means for opening and closing the channels of prestige to men, when the price to the women became too great. (Polygamy was common in the Plains; men killed in war left an excess of women.) But it also opened the way to expressing their hostilities as well—passively in what effectively amounted to *permission* to go to war; actively, in the triumphal scalp dance, etc.

denial of love. Love is expressed in material ways such as protection and support, and in psychological-physiological ways such as tenderness and caresses. Custom, convention, and law have long since insured for women a relative degree of security in the material expressions of love; they do not, however, guarantee her a continuation of the psychological representations of love, although these are just as necessary to her as the material aspects. There are some who oppose the legal institution of marriage because, they maintain, it tends to insure the latter at the expense of the former.

Husbands and wives want to love one another; they are encouraged in it by society, sanctioned in it by the church and the law, and confirmed in it by the observation of nature.* We think of the love of a man for a woman and her love for him as being the most intense expression of the life instinct. Theoretically, to love and to be loved should exclude the possibility of frustrating, hating, destroying, and permitting oneself to be destroyed. Yet with all this impetus in the direction of mutual affection, we know that too many husbands and wives are unhappy together. Separation and divorce are too frequent—though from another standpoint they are perhaps not frequent enough. A silent war between the sexes seems to be waged continuously so that, instead of working toward a better personal integration and mutual helpfulness, marriage seems to stimulate mutual aggressiveness; men and women aid and abet one another in self-destructiveness rather than in greater creativeness. In the eagerness of winning a wife or the elation of obtaining a husband, the hatchet is buried, but only for the time being. The event of marriage represents a temporary victory, but it is also for both parties a contract of mutual obligation which begins to draw heavily upon the erotic reserves. Unless these are replenished they become depleted, and as time goes on the old aggressive feelings of hostility toward the opposite sex

* Some animals observe strict monogamy and give evidences of sentimental attachment; others do neither.

which the heightened emotion held in check are reawakened within the marital union.

In the light of modern psychoanalytic theory, living and loving are almost synonymous; one may say that eating one's food and kissing one's bride are merely differently directed expressions of the same drive. And in marriage we must recognize that economic, legal, and religious factors have all taken advantage of the vital need of men and women for a mutual expression of love for one another. Marriage is a compromise, molded legally, economically, and religiously, for providing a dependable opportunity for the expression of the erotic life. Such a basis for marriage is intrinsically important enough to justify tremendous sacrifices, but the unfortunate thing is that in conventional thinking the sexual life *per se* is accorded only a low degree of respect. It continues to be regarded by many if not most people as something of a necessary evil, *permitted* only under certain carefully supervised conditions.

For, conditioned as they are by their childhood experiences, men and women in contemporary civilization grow up ill prepared to reap the full benefits of the erotic opportunity provided in marriage. As the result of the patterns of hate inflicted upon children, as described in the previous chapter, the tendency is for men to fail to attain that degree of masculinity, and for women to attain that degree of femininity, which can find in the constant associations of marriage an unfailing source of spiritual helpfulness. In clinical terms, too many women tend to be frigid, too many men tend to be impotent. For many couples it is simpler to discontinue any attempts at a union which provides so little satisfaction to one or both. For others it continues with episodes of promiscuity, with what Freud once described as the empty, superficial flirtations of American social life, which clearly indicate how deeply dissatisfied such persons are, and how incapable of correcting that dissatisfaction. I do not imply that marriage has been— or was—any more successful in Europe, or that I have a better alternative to suggest. I can only say that, dissatisfied though many are with marriage as an institution, any suggestion for improving it provokes outbursts of rage on the part of the very ones most dissatisfied—the women.

When I say that women complain of sexual dissatisfaction, I do not mean that most of them put it in those words. In fact, only a small minority are even conscious of feeling this reproach against men, let alone being articulate about it. Their complaints are more likely to be expressed in symptoms, symptoms observed to be related to their daily dissatisfactions. The neurotic part of their dissatisfaction lies in the fact that they cannot always accept or encourage the love from their husbands which they want and need; the normal and objective part is that they actually are frustrated not only in their immediate sexual life but in the ultimate purpose of the erotic instinct, the bearing and rearing of children.

There is a popular fantasy that men are the ones who desire sexual gratification and seek it selfishly from passively compliant, more or less victimized women. This myth of the male as a sexual beast and the female as a frigid madonna is a vicious, hypocritical residuum from Pauline and Victorian ethics which simply has no basis in fact. Indeed, its very persistence in the face of the evidence proves the extent to which sexual frustration is present among women. Numerous scientific investigations,[4] statistical and otherwise, indicate very clearly that most American women are sexually frustrated. Most American wives fail to achieve complete sexual satisfaction. This fact was once accepted by all these women as inevitable, but today many of them are at least partly conscious of their sexual needs and their sexual disappointments, although an attitude of pessimism prevails with regard to the possibility of bettering matters.* Some women blame their own physi-

---

* The question whether in the sexual sphere men frustrate women more, or women frustrate men more, reminds one of the legend about the quarrel of Zeus and Hera as to which received the more pleasure from physical love. Tiresias, it will be remembered, was called in to act as umpire, and when he declared that woman has nine times as much pleasure as man, Hera became furious and blinded him.

ology—which is absurd, since physiologically (not psychologically) the woman's sexual capacity is unlimited. Some blame the physiological limitation of their husbands, which, though it *is* limited, is rarely so much at fault as the husband's psychology. Some women simply accept sexual frustration as an inexplicable fact without blaming anyone.

As I write this I have a feeling that to many readers it will seem overstressed; but sexual frustration is so shrouded in secrecy and so likely to be obscured by secondary emotions that it can, and I believe does, exist to a far wider extent than a nonprofessional person can realize. By secondary emotions I mean the sense of shame, or the feeling of loyalty to one's partner, or the inhibition of good taste—all the things that deter both husbands and wives from discussing the matter with anyone else. It might be supposed that physicians would hear so much of it that it would become a well-known medical problem; but the fact is that both husbands and wives generally refrain from mentioning it even to their physicians, and physicians generally neglect to investigate it. Indeed, I would say that most physicians completely fail to realize its importance, in spite of all the work of Havelock Ellis, Ellen Key, Sigmund Freud, and many others. Sexuality is still a taboo subject in the medical schools of American universities. Psychiatrists, on the other hand, see such dramatic examples in their daily practice that they cannot forget. To them it is important, and this is why even those psychiatrists who do not use Freud's technical methods unite with the psychoanalysts in their gratitude to him for his clinical demonstrations.

I am thinking of an accomplished and sophisticated woman, a college graduate, a social leader, the mother of three children, the wife of a very masculine and successful husband. She had been married for fifteen years without ever having had any sexual pleasure of which she was aware, and without ever having suspected—according to herself—that this was other than normal. Her husband, on the other hand, had never guessed that she was rigid. I might add that her body cried out its protest against her enslavement through a dozen different symptoms, for the medical and surgical relief of which the husband had paid out thousands of dollars—all in vain, of course.

I think of another case of a woman who was conscious enough of her sexual desires but who had to content herself with sexual intercourse once a year only—which apparently was sufficient for her husband, and which she only vaguely suspected to be somewhat less than the average frequency. I mention these examples to indicate the persistence of a taboo on the recognition of sexual needs and sexual frustration as such.

But sexual frustration in the woman is not limited to being deprived of sufficient physical gratification, for her sexual needs include not only her husband's affectionate demonstrations and the enjoyment of sexual intercourse, but also the experiences of pregnancy and childbirth. For since the ultimate objective of the erotic drive is the preservation of the species, and since this includes the production of children, interference with its normal biological expression acts as a smothering blanket upon the fires of life. This interference is apparent in the diminished importance of childbearing. It is no secret that many couples now dread to have children. By far the majority of illegal abortions are performed upon married women, women who have a legal right to bear children, but who do not want to do so or feel they cannot. Whereas childbearing was once a woman's most important function and the mark of her success, it is now regarded sometimes as a sign of resignation, of carelessness, or of lack of ambition.

One often hears the blame for this shift put chiefly upon our politico-economic system, but in the last analysis it must be chalked up in part to something in the psychology of the individual. Instincts will always rise above economics, ultimately. When they do, as in the case of the poor families on relief who go on having more children whom they cannot support, we call it slovenliness—criminal improvidence. The very fact that these people do not have enough food or shelter or anything else to give them a sense of security increases their need for the psychological support which reproduction furnishes. They are less corrupted by modern education and have a greater appreciation of the satisfaction of progeny. It is much easier, of course, to explain this in terms of moralistic condemnation, as is often done; but it is not very philosophical, and it allows us to sidestep the psychological necessity of reproduction. Thus we fall again into the error of minimizing the importance of the erotic life, including childbearing.

Many intelligent people *think* they can substitute other gratifications; but that they are mistaken in this appears in the neurotic consequences that are so often observed—by psychiatrists, for example—to follow. There are many women who could well afford to have children but who, following in the tradition of the times, think themselves more comfortable without these responsibilities. Other women consciously desire children—so they think—but find themselves sterile. And finally, nothing in our civilization is more disgraceful and tragic than the fact that millions of women are childless simply because they are—against their wishes—unmarried.

Since the bearing and rearing of children is woman's greatest achievement and the climax of her erotic expression, one would expect it to be not only her greatest joy but the source of her greatest power. By means of it she acquires an inner determined sense of security and is thus in a position to counteract not only her own aggressive impulses but the occasional eruptions of aggression and self-destructiveness on the part of her husband. Hence to be thwarted in this objective, whether by the restrictions of economic reality or by lack of socially approved opportunity or by conflicting wishes engendered within her by her early childhood experiences, makes for a deep inner resentment. To put it another way, it deprives her of her primary safeguard against her own aggressive impulses.

2

We must now consider another aspect of the frustration of women. We know that frequently, in their fantasies and fears, women assign to men the role of powerful, brutish oppressors, tyrants, and assaulters. Here and there one sees an actual realization of this fantasy. There certainly is such a thing as a sadistic husband, and probably there are many fairly masterful husbands who exemplify the ideals of the patriarchal system. But the fact that a play portraying the head of the house being consistently defied and outwitted by every member of his family was the most popular play on Broadway in 1940 * suggests the rarity and obsolescence of the masterful father. For better or for worse, the dominance of the male is undoubtedly passing.

If I were to try to express in a single word the accusation brought by wives against husbands and by children against fathers, as I have learned in my clinical experience, I should say that the chief sin of men with reference to their wives and children is not harshness, not parsimony, not tyranny or injustice or eccentricity, but *passivity;* and under this I should include overdependence, inattentiveness, helplessness, overmeekness, indifference, neglect, and (in extreme instances) desertion. Many a wife tells a story something like this: "My husband is good, kind, loyal, but he just takes me for granted. He is really not personally interested in me except as a part of his surroundings. It seems to me I compete unsuccessfully with his business interests, his hobbies, and even with the children, although he takes little enough interest in them. I don't think he is unfaithful to me, although he may be; sometimes I almost wish he showed enough interest in women as women to be suspect. I would feel then that I was at least in the running; I could fight against the situation on my own terms. But when a man prefers his newspaper, his golf club, his poker game,

* See *Life With Father*, not as originally written by Clarence Day, but as dramatized by Howard Lindsay and Russel Crouse.

his political meetings, and everything else to any real satisfaction he gets out of me as a woman, I feel as if there were nothing for me to do but slump back into a combination of housekeeper and nursemaid. He probably has some justification for saying that i don't make myself as attractive or as interesting as I should, but what's the use?"

The daughter of such a man talks like this: "Oh, Dad loves us all right, but he doesn't pay much attention to us; he's got his business worries on his mind, and he'd rather smoke and read his magazines than talk with us about things. Naturally we turn to Mother and depend on her for what advice and encouragement we need. She is *really* interested."

Such men do not feel inadequate or unmasculine; they are too busy being very masculine, very manly, in the meaning of those terms current in a society which prizes success in everything except mature sexuality. But it is definitely felt by the woman as an aggression. There are two elements in it: the general passivity that makes the man seem to surrender to the woman the masculine prerogatives which she wishes he would retain, that makes him lean upon her in a dependent way as if to make her a mother rather than a wife; and the withdrawal of his erotic interest from his wife and the transference of it to male associates at the club, the store, the Legion meeting, the golf foursome, etc. These two things, not necessarily connected, are responsible for deep frustrations in women and they arise from disturbances in the psychosexual development of men.

We have spoken of the fact that mothers discourage the dawning sexuality of their sons; * we could have gone further and re-

* In spite of this fact, the mother frequently appears in the role of a seductress in the fantasies of the child, sometimes, with some justification. The fear of the mother as a seductress is a minor but important theme in individual and social psychology. Mrs. Bernice Engle believes from her researches concerning the Amazons that the Amazon myth represents a defense against this fear; woman as a warrior is less to be feared than woman as a seductress. One sees the same thing in the tendency of many neurotic men to deny sexuality in their concept of motherhood. This is related to many inevitable disappointments of the child in the mother, discussed by Brunswick.[5]

minded the reader that society itself puts a very strong taboo on any conscious sexual interest in his own mother on the part of the boy child. It is normal and universal for this to occur, and every little boy does love his mother secretly in a forbidden way. He surrenders his secret hopes in this, however, or postpones them for a time, turning his chief affections both consciously and unconsciously away from his mother, who seems to be a dangerous love object, and toward his father.

This turning to the father represents a stage in the child's emotional development which is highly approved in contemporary civilization and in most primitive cultures. It is approved for various reasons. In the first place, it seems to be nonsexual; parents do not like to believe that the love of the child for his parents has anything erotic in it, and especially so the son's affection for his father. In the second place, it pleases them because the child appears to be growing up when he is no longer such a "Mama's boy." In the third place, it flatters the father, if he is at all interested in his children, and makes up for the feeling which every father has that his wife and her son have formed a love coalition which to some extent excludes him. Parental counselors encourage fathers to take advantage of this inclination on the part of the child. "Be a pal to your son," they urge. There is nothing to be disapproved of in such exhortations, and yet every parent knows that sooner or later, just as the child has relinquished a part of his interest in his mother for his father, so he will, if he is normal, relinquish this interest in his father for an interest in other boys, and in turn for an interest in girls.

The main trouble is right at this last point. The American boy too often does not turn his interest to girls in any deep, enduring way,* but remains unconsciously and sometimes quite consciously attached in a passive way to his father or to his mother. Instead

* Conspicuous, feverish "dating" of one or many girls is no proof of normally developing heterosexuality. I mention this because I have heard mothers speak with pride of this symptom as a proof of their sons' manliness.

of identifying himself with his father, such a son identifies himself with his mother. He does so in an effort to escape what seems
to him to be the too great danger of masculine identification. It
is as if he said to himself, "I am afraid of my father's power, so
I will make peace with him by passive, friendly submission. I will
play the same role toward him that my mother does. I will become like a woman and a better woman than she is, because it is
less dangerous to compete with her for his love than to combat
him and all the other obstacles placed in the way of my being a
man. I will outplay her at her own game." Such a boy then becomes a man's man—passive, friendly, and popular with other
men, and often inwardly inhibited in his relations with women.

One can see from this how the mechanism of identification is
one that covers with ostensible love and admiration much unconscious hostility. It is true that we tend to imitate and resemble
those whom we like, and this may be considered a compliment;
but at the same time such an identification is always determined
in part by a wish to replace the person with whom we identify
ourselves. Many a politician begins by revering, adoring, and
serving his superior, and ends by dethroning him and taking over
his authority and power. Imitation is said to be the sincerest flattery, but it is still flattery; it contains a threat based on unconscious hate, in addition to the obvious love.

There is a still more incomplete development of masculinity,
which is popularly regarded as the classical outcropping of an
unsolved Oedipus complex. Nearly every individual of this type
who comes to a psychiatrist announces that he has "a mother fixation" or "a mother complex." Like the general public, he understands this to mean an unconscious sexual attraction to his mother
which is so great that all other females are unsatisfactory and
second-rate substitutes. What such a man never recognizes, and
what the general public never recognizes, is that this attraction to
the mother is not comparable to the adult sexual interest of a man
in a woman, but depends rather upon an infantile attachment

which is partly *dependence* and partly *hostility*, but very little "*love*." It is an even more immature stage of development than the "father fixation" described above. Such men have no sexual attraction, in the adult sense of the word, to their mothers or to any other woman; if they consort with women at all, it is with women who are much older or much younger than themselves, and these are treated either as protecting mothers or as inconsequential childish amusements. As the reader will infer, it is only a step from this pattern to the acceptance of overt homosexuality which we shall discuss later.

It is important to emphasize that fixations of any type are determined more by hating and fearing than by love, and that they only masquerade as love. One might say that persons who have "a mother fixation" fear their mothers more than their fathers; they fear to leave the mother either for a passive, submissive relation to the father which brings them into competition with the mother, or for active masculine interest in available women. The mother is safe as a love object because she is not accessible. By a pretense of attachment to her such a boy can conceal his hostility to her, eliminate the necessity of any fear of her, and avoid the consequences of attempting to express his masculinity in a normal way. (D. H. Lawrence described this classically in *Sons and Lovers*.) It is really more pathological to be thus passively attached to the mother than to be passively attached to the father, because it is a more infantile, parasitic relationship and therefore contains a larger element of hostility and a smaller component of real object love. But both represent essentially a repudiation of masculine aims and character.

In seeking to fix the responsibility for such inhibitions in development, I have said that various traumatic events occur which augment the natural influences opposed to the development of masculinity. By natural influences I mean the fact that the world of men does not welcome more competitors, and the boy has to fight his way into recognition as a man. He has to overcome certain unconscious attitudes on the part of adults which oppose the maturing of younger rivals. Among savage tribes this opposition is symbolized by painful initiation ceremonies known as puberty rites; the adolescent has to go through a ritualistic ordeal before he is accepted as a man in tribal affairs. In our civilization the ordeal is not so particularized or acknowledged; it extends over the entire adolescent period and even earlier, and is generally described as "adolescent rebellion" with little recognition of adult participation in the struggle.

In addition to this, there are the inevitable neurotic fears of the child due to false interpretations and assumptions; each step in his development is dependent upon the overcoming of fears—fears that he will be punished, castrated, rejected, or killed. These fears can be augmented by neurotic attitudes on the part of the parents or by especially traumatic events, as I have outlined. The net result is in the direction of inhibiting the evolution of psychosexual development. Normally, of course, these inhibitions are overcome, but too frequently they are not overcome, or are not sufficiently overcome and a relative sexual immaturity results. Whenever the development of masculinity is inhibited with a consequent feminine identification, the inhibition is accompanied by a negative attitude toward that femininity within the man himself as well as toward femininity in others. Not only does such a man feel competitive with women and justified in fighting them in all sorts of subtle ways, but also to some extent he projects his own femininity upon them and hates in them those traits which are actually present in himself, traits that are normal in women and which, if he were objective, he could accept with tolerance and delight.

Hence it is that men who fail to live up to their masculine responsibilities, and assume the role of leadership and dominance that the normal woman expects of them, seem to be afraid of women. Actually they are afraid of themselves. They are afraid of the hostility which is stirred up in them because of their neurotic retention of feminine traits which they do not recognize but hate and cannot relinquish. The practical result is that they constantly thwart, disappoint, and injure the women they try (and often pretend) to love.

General misogyny is not unfamiliar, although rarely in history has it been made a national program to the extent that has occurred in Germany. The German *Fuehrer* is notoriously uninterested in women, and exalts a masculine cult which glorifies homosexual satisfactions and relegates women to the role of serfs. How Hitler exhibits and at the same time hates his own femininity is quite transparent, and this is precisely in line with his treatment of German women (*and* German men).

Don Juanism is another familiar pattern in which the seducing, disappointing, and abandoning of women leaves no doubt of the hostility felt for them. Promiscuity is a symptom, whether in men or in women, of an essential inability to find deep satisfaction anywhere. Such persons do not love their sexual objects; they seek rather to conquer them or to destroy them. What is often described in such moralistic terms as selfishness or caddishness or faithlessness is from a psychological standpoint unexplained by such terms. It is rather a relative "malelessness." Such men are constantly trying to prove to themselves and sometimes to others that they are as masculine as their inner voices tell them they are not. This explains why such men so often "kiss and tell," bragging about their exploits to other men. Even if they do not do this, they are impelled to reassure themselves constantly that only a superman could be so potent, so casual, so irresistible. Sooner or later this device breaks down, and such men become alcoholic or ill in such a way as to give themselves an excuse for impotence on some face-saving grounds.

This raises the question of sexual impotence, which in one form or another is far more frequent than promiscuity (many promiscuous men suffer from various kinds of impotence). Sexual impotence represents a somewhat localized way in which fear of and resentment toward women are expressed by automatic devices within the body for which the conscious ego can exonerate itself of any responsibility. The importance of this subject is recognized by everyone, it would seem, except physicians. It is the subject of discussion on the stage, in novels, and in the daily conversations of private life; but the medical textbooks have not yet gotten around to regarding it as worthy of scientific consideration.*

To some extent the same is true of homosexuality. In spite of the fact that overt homosexuality is technically a crime (so is suicide in some states), surely no one doubts that it is also a disease. Yet—at my hand is a classical textbook on *The Principles and Practice of Medicine* which has for many years been considered almost a Bible for physicians. Not a word concerning homosexuality is to be found in its 1200 odd pages. Next to it is an equally large book, equally classic, on *Diseases of the Nervous System*. In it is a paragraph, one-fourth of a page in length, devoted to homosexuality, and a little later one page devoted to the treatment of all perversions. This is in strange contrast to the frequency with which the problem is encountered by physicians.

Within certain rather vague limits, the attraction between persons of the same sex is highly approved in our society, and properly so, for it is psychologically normal. When that interest becomes excessive, when it becomes exclusive, when it impels adult persons to establish physical contact and enjoy physical pleasure with one another, it is certainly abnormal. From our previous discussion, the reader will correctly infer that it represents a more extreme repudiation of one's own sex and a more complete identification with the opposite sex than do the previously mentioned forms of incomplete (male) development. The femininity of homosexual men is sometimes apparent from such secondary manifestations as effeminate carriage, gestures, speech, and physical appearance. These are often very misleading; many homosexual men lack these and some individuals have them who are

* For a fuller discussion of the psychology of impotence, see *Man Against Himself*, pages 337-350.

not overtly, or even fundamentally, homosexual. On the other hand, emergent unconscious homosexual feelings may arouse great anxiety, even panic, with the result that certain "defense reactions" are stimulated which appear as violent condemnation of homosexuality, ultra-masculine appearance and behavior, ostentatious heterosexuality, etc.

Homosexual behavior should certainly be distinguished from homosexual leanings, and conscious homosexual leanings should be distinguished from those which are unconscious. No normal person is entirely free from the latter. But the man with conscious or unconscious homosexual propensities which preponderate over the heterosexual ones is certain to be a man who frustrates women; he will betray his essential lack of interest in them by showing fear, contempt, jealousy, suspicion, alcoholic escape, or patronizing paternalism. These attitudes may not preclude his seeking a woman's company and even consummating a marriage, but they will and do preclude satisfying the emotional needs of the woman.*

The difference in the basic psychological configurations of misogyny, Don Juanism, sexual impotence, and homosexuality is not so great; the general pattern of all of them is as I have outlined above. The different pictures result from differences in the degree and kind of traumata experienced in infancy and the various stresses that are thus produced. In all of them, the essential fact is that there is a self-destructive repudiation of masculinity.

3

I should like to cite some categorical illustrations from clinical practice of this repudiation of masculinity in some persons who, in appearance and in their own opinion, were normal; they were all considered normal by their friends. They were certainly not

* Homosexuality in women, to which we shall refer briefly in a later chapter, represents a corresponding renunciation of one's own sex in favor of a pseudo-identification with the opposite sex.

homosexual or consciously misogynistic or impotent or "feminine."
They were all successful men; all married (although I might
well have included a typical bachelor). Here they will naturally
be given unreal names so as to insure anonymity. Nevertheless,
they so much resemble thousands of other men—if not millions—
that I shall not be surprised to receive many letters from wives
who feel sure that I have been describing their husbands. For,
after all, it is the effect on their wives that I am most concerned
with in this chapter. *These*, I might say, are the husbands that some
women get for themselves, and are then frustrated by, for a life
time.

Jeffrey Mason belonged to one of the "first families." Both his
father and his mother inherited fortunes. His father died when he
was quite young, and, as the only son in the family, Jeffrey was
expected to carry on the family business, a large insurance agency.
Of course most of the work was already in the hands of competent
experts, but Jeffrey's father, and then for a time his uncle, had
been very active in the general management and in the investment of the surplus funds.

Jeffrey went to an Eastern preparatory school, graduated from
Yale and then from the School of Business Administration at
Harvard, and was regarded as a highly promising candidate to
continue the work his father and uncle had developed. It had been
assumed all during his years at school that he would, upon gradua-
tion, step into the position of assistant to his uncle, who was
anxious to give Jeffrey what help he could in a practical way before retiring.

To everyone's surprise, however, Jeffrey suddenly decided that
the business was too much for him. He didn't think he wanted to
"worry about insurance." It made him "nervous" to be confined in
an office, anyway, and he didn't think he would be successful in
selling, in training and supervising salesmen, or in handling the
territory. Through the influence of his uncle and other friends
he obtained a position in a bank in his home city. After a few

years, however, during which he did not distinguish himself, he announced that there was no future in banking and that a great deal of money was to be made in the manufacture of airplanes. Of course, he knew nothing about manufacturing and rather little about airplanes, although he had one of his own. He persuaded his mother to invest a considerable sum of money in a company which he organized, and for the next few years he showed considerable enthusiasm in developing a factory and marketing its product. Unfortunately, the same idea similarly inspired a hundred other men about this time and plants were springing up all over the country, many of which collapsed, as did also that of Mr. Jeffrey Mason.

He expressed his regrets to his mother for having dissipated the money she had given him and persuaded her that he could recoup his (and her) losses by another venture in which his interest had been solicited by an acquaintance. This acquaintance proved to be a rascal, and Jeffrey's confidence in him and devotion to him was the means of extracting and wasting another quarter of a million dollars of his mother's money.

By this time the family-owned insurance business was seriously threatened, as the result of the financial depression of the thirties, and Jeffrey's uncle insisted upon retiring and throwing the responsibility for the business upon Jeffrey, whose reluctance to take over was equaled only by the misgivings of the other insurance executives. No better arrangement could be thought of, however, and so Jeffrey became general manager of the company. He insisted that it could only be saved from bankruptcy by the investment of more capital for the purpose of paying dividends to the policy holders so that they would not know the condition of the company's finances. In spite of this, however, the business continued to fail and a year later was declared insolvent.

Leaving this dismal account of economic disintegration, let us take a look at another aspect of Jeffrey Mason's life. In college, because he was good-looking, because his family was prominent socially, and because he was wealthy, he was exceedingly popular. From the standpoint of the marriage market, he was highly eligible and, in keeping with the mores of his group, vigorous efforts were made by numerous mothers to make a good "catch." His friends thought that this had something to do with causing his extreme wariness with regard to women, which, of course, was a very superficial interpretation. The fact is, however, that he was more sought after than seeking, so far as women were concerned. He participated in the various formal social activities of his city, was made chairman of the social committee of the country club, and tried to learn to play polo, but wasted a good deal of time in the studied effort to enjoy himself according to the prescribed pattern. In the course of all this, he was the escort of many attractive young women of his own set, but never went with one girl more than two or three times. No one of them seemed to interest him very much, although it was rumored that several of them had been intimate with him.

One of these women was the sister of a polo-playing friend, and to everyone's surprise he and this girl were married one morning by a Justice of the Peace, following a lively and very alcoholic all-night party. After the consternation and disappointment of the relatives on both sides had subsided, the couple settled down to housekeeping on a rather grandiose scale and for a short time their home was the center of a number of parties which drew the same feverish, distraught, artificial friends with whom Jeffrey had played for several years.

I must say a few words about the characteristics of this social set, not because similar groups are not to be found in other cities, but because what characterized them is typical of the psychosexual immaturity in which we are interested. There were perhaps fifty people involved; many of these were married couples. Although most of the latter had children, the care of these children was relegated entirely to servants, and "the gang" would manage to get together somewhere every evening. Quite often this would begin

in the afternoon with the women playing bridge and the men playing golf or polo. At five o'clock they would begin to have cock-
tails and by eight many of them were mildly intoxicated. They
would go somewhere and have dinner, following which they
would either dance or play poker or journey from house to house.
But the external form of these social activities is less important than
the interpersonal relationships among members of the group.
There was always a highly charged consciousness of sexual stimulation. No wife ever sat, danced, or rode in the car with her own
husband. Occasionally one mixed couple of this sort would stop
off at the home of one of them for a few hours and rejoin the
others later, to be greeted with great teasing and much hinting
at the possibility of what was a probability. This polite and tolerated adultery was not universal; in fact, it was condemned by
many members of the group who regarded themselves as the saving remnant. It occurred infrequently, but when it did it was not
considered important. Violent scenes of jealousy and quarreling
between husbands and wives often developed, to grow more
maudlin after the party had reached the usual stage of intoxica-
tion. A common topic of conversation was how Jim ever got home
last night, what Gwen said when Bob carried Grover in, and
what they did after Helen "passed out." If the poker and bridge
games did not occupy everyone's attention, there was a certain
amount of retiring to automobiles for "necking parties" or even
semipublic exhibitions of the same thing.

Now from personal observation or from moving pictures, everyone is familiar with this monotonous, immature routine. It is apt
to be looked upon as typical of the debauchery of the idle rich,
although the same thing occurs in a somewhat different form
among groups of people who have very little money, who eat
cheaper food, drink cheaper liquor, go to cheaper dance halls,
and play for smaller stakes at poker. I am describing it not to
condemn it but rather to furnish an illustration of sexual maladjustment which bears on the present theme.

If one has an opportunity to study psychologically the individuals composing such a group, one has all his preliminary suspicions confirmed: that these persons, if married, cannot endure to remain at home alone; that when they get together the men gravitate quickly to the men and the women to the other women for their greatest pleasure; that this state of affairs can be effectively broken up only with the aid of alcohol; that under the influence of alcohol there are fervid, amateurish, adolescent gestures in the direction of heterosexuality which occasionally become flagrant and aggressive violations of loyalty; that there ensues bitter quarreling on the basis of intense jealousy; and that the responsibilities of the women to their children and of the men to their business life seem to be forgotten. What this adds up to is that neither the men nor the women involved can be said to be sexually mature or even sexually normal. None of them realizes this; they regard themselves as exceptionally sophisticated, oversexed persons who have found a way to obtain pleasure in an otherwise dull and stupid world.

One can partly understand the psychology of the members of such a group by concentrating on the psychology of one of them. Jeffrey Mason participated in all the activities described. He and his wife had quarrels following several private adventures of his, and even more violent quarrels following private adventures of hers. Then he began to be so jealous that if she so much as danced with another man in the crowd he would become sulky and drink himself into a stupor, or precipitate a fight, or jump in the car and go home. The rest of the group took this good-naturedly because it added to the general excitement, but he and his wife suffered a good deal. Sometimes he would refuse to go on one of the nightly parties, whereupon his wife would accuse him of wanting to deny her an opportunity for pleasure and of being pathologically jealous, and would threaten to divorce him. It would usually end in their going, but they would come home with fresh ammunition for another quarrel. He would protest that he hated the

round of drinking because it interfered with his business responsibilities, and would accuse his wife not only of wanting to be unfaithful to him, but of wanting to see him fail at his work. Nevertheless, if they stayed at home, he was sure to become restless
and bored. Their only pleasurable evenings seemed to be those
occasions when his wife would play bridge with a group of
women and he would play poker with several men. He would
have preferred to play at his club, but then he would not have
known where his wife was and would have been tortured with
suspicions. In wishing to be near her he was never dominated by
any sense of responsibility for her or any feeling that it was in
his power to satisfy her so completely that he need not be jealous. The truth is he liked to be with men better than he liked to
be with her or with any other woman, and his occasional gestures
in the direction of flirting with women were chiefly for the purposes of reassuring himself of his own potency and of hurting his
wife's feelings. Even these casual gallantries, however, he could
rise to only with the aid of large doses of whisky.

As one might suppose, these homosexual predilections and
these compulsions toward demonstrating masculinity made his
sexual life with his wife very unsatisfactory. For weeks they
would have no relations with each other. Sometimes she would
actually importune him to pay some attention to her physically
and he would dutifully but resentfully comply. At other times
he would suddenly feel great sexual need and would approach
her with a violence to which she could scarcely respond. Even
upon these occasions his physical capacity was not always in
keeping with his psychological inclinations, whereupon he would
blame her lack of attractiveness or receptiveness for his failure.
Her frustration and resentment can be imagined.

Jeffrey's mother had been an exceedingly sharp and envious
woman. She treated her two daughters in an entirely different
manner from the way in which she treated Jeffrey, her only son.
It would not be accurate to say that she preferred them, because

in many ways she seemed to prefer him, but she seemed to want all three of her children to become perfect ladies. Jeffrey was constantly compared unfavorably with his sisters in respect to behavior, manners, school accomplishments, and appearance. He grew up with the feeling that in order to win the approval of his mother (his father's frequent absences left her in virtual control of the home) he must be like her or his approved sisters. To accomplish this it was necessary for him to repress the expression of his instinctual urges in the direction of masculinity. The sacrifice of the most important part of his personality—his masculinity—in order to live and to be loved inflicted a terrific injury upon his ego, an injury which produced great resentment. As he grew older he found some compensation for his initial humiliation in the fact that he was flattered and sought after as a man, and this led him to adopt the outward gestures of masculinity, though without any inner confidence in his ability to maintain the role or to secure and hold love through it.

It might have been possible for him as a child to *pretend* to be feminine, to act outwardly as if he were accepting the maternal program, while defeating it as a result of his own more intense inner strivings. That he had not been able to do so indicates how deep the injury really was, how early in his life his hope to achieve some independence from women which would permit him to be tender toward and considerate of them was crushed. All his life women continued to seem to him to be powerful creatures from whom he could get pleasure only by being dependent upon them and thereby injuring his own self-respect, or by flouting and ignoring them in a kind of small-boy defiance.

On this basis it was fully understandable why he should have successively failed to accomplish a man's job in business and a husband's job in the home. He was incapable of being a husband, incapable of being a father, incapable of acting as other than an adolescent socially. For he was still an adolescent when he was forty years old, whose chief erotic pleasure not inhibited by fears and hatred was derived from association with men in such circumstances that he could keep from consciousness the fact that his interest in them had a sexual element. Had anyone told him that he was latently homosexual, that he hated women and that he was not really a man, he would have charged at the accuser with his tongue and probably with his fists. Yet no one can survey his behavior as a whole and not recognize that this was the case, and one may be sure that his wife felt the full impact of it.

The second illustration I have in mind is in many ways the exact antithesis of the one related above. Mr. Morgan Lafour was anything but a playboy. In fact, it might almost be said that he never played a moment in his life. He never drank a drop of liquor. He did not smoke. He prided himself on paying strict attention to business.

He had begun as a poor boy and worked up, like the hero of a Horatio Alger story, to become the head of a large business. He was in every sense of the word a self-made man. He commanded the respect of his business associates because of his prodigious capacity for work.

Everybody knew Mr. Lafour; he was in every organization; he was on every committee, in every charity drive; he was on the board of directors of a score of hospitals, settlement houses, schools, etc. He was a Rotarian and a member of the Elks, Masons, three country clubs, two town clubs, and sixteen business organizations This does not include the religious and charitable organizations in which he took various active roles. People came to ask his advice upon every conceivable subject. He generally managed to see them and helped them if he could, but in the meantime he did not neglect his own business; in fact, he used his social and charitable contacts advantageously. His office was a model of efficiency; he had the latest business machinery, the most approved technique of office management. Business men from other cities were frequently taken by their friends to see his extraordinary equipment and methods.

Mrs. Lafour was a woman of modest attainments and rather more than average feminine charm, but all of this charm was completely wasted on her husband. He told her early in their married life that he did not want children and that he was not much interested in the ordinary satisfactions of married life. His wife understood this to mean that he did not enjoy social gatherings and did not want her to expect him to join her in evening parties and such engagements. She soon learned to her amazement and chagrin that he literally meant that he was not interested in her as a woman, had no sexual inclinations toward her, or, for that matter, toward any woman. His emotions were completely absorbed in his business and he regarded it as strange that his wife should be disappointed in this. He was completely loyal to her, gave her plenty of money, showed her respect at all times, but confined himself constantly to his office in the daytime and to his own room at night. His wife saw him at breakfast, sometimes at dinner, and occasionally on Sunday. It disturbed him very much to have her go out of town because he did not like to come home and find her gone; he wanted to feel that she was managing this branch of his business just as his various employees managed other branches of it. In fact, it might be said that he treated his wife like a highly respected employee.

I shall say more about Mr. Lafour, but this is enough to picture a type that in less extreme degree is surely not unfamiliar to many readers. What might be unfamiliar to them is the complete renunciation of the sexual life which is common to many such persons—far more common than most people suppose. There is a legend about the hard-boiled business man whose wife fails to show him sufficient affection and whose virility is perversely deflected to more receptive love objects; he is supposed to have a girl in every port, a mistress in every suburb, a sweetheart in every night club. Of course, such business men exist, but this is such a typical potency-fantasy that I regard it as relatively rare. I do know several men who have this *reputation;* one of them took his so-called mistress to Europe, gave her a mink coat, an automobile, and a great deal of jewelry, but never slept with or made any sexual overtures to her whatsoever. I know another one who had dinner with a woman every night regularly for several years, bade her goodnight at ten o'clock, went home to his wife (until she left him), and was never sexually intimate with either his wife or his regular dinner companion.

Of the Lafour phenomenon, some will doubt whether there was actually a repudiation of masculinity—perhaps Mrs. Lafour was not the type that appealed to him, it may be suggested, or perhaps he simply turned all his energies into his work. There was surely nothing effeminate about him; he was almost a superman.

On the contrary, there certainly was something effeminate about Lafour, extremely effeminate, though not on the surface. His prodigious application to work, his determination to make a success in his struggles, combined with his compulsion to keep everyone his friend by extravagant charity, and the like—these were activities substituted for genuine masculinity. They were, in Lafour, closely patterned on the life of his mother who had led the dreary, intensely arduous life of the mother of five children on a South Dakota farm. In her life there had been nothing but work, from early morning until late at night, with constant fears—of poverty, of drought, of hunger, of more pregnancies, of an incapacitated husband, and of the mortgage falling due. It was with this mother that Morgan Lafour identified himself instead of with his far less energetic, less provident, less intelligent father. His identification with her was so strong that it compelled him to make the renunciation of the masculinity that was represented by the biological activities of his father. His one goal in life was to succeed and to conquer difficulties, to put the anxiety-ridden mother-spirit within him at rest.

Dr. Blake was something like Mr. Lafour. I knew him very well. He had an enormous practice; he thought of nothing but the practice of medicine; everything else was sacrificed to it, including his family. At one time he had considerable money, but he could not even concern himself with investing it properly and lost most of it.

He was actually a very good doctor although he took no time off to read, to study, to take postgraduate work, or even to attend medical meetings. He simply devoted himself to his patients. He was rather more like an old grandmother than like a doctor; he spluttered, fumed, and stewed over every case. He spent an unnecessary amount of time hovering over the patient, walking back and forth with an air of great concern, looking into certain minutiae such as the temperature of the drinking water or the consistency of the bowel movements as if they were matters of the utmost importance. He would scold the relatives and scold the patient and caution everyone about innumerable dangers and possibilities. He would swamp the nurse with a score of very particular orders—most of which were scientifically baseless. He was exquisitely sensitive about his orders, his diagnoses, his opinions, his possessive relation to his patients. He regarded it as almost incomprehensible that any patient of his should consider going to any other physician. He treated them all as if they were his children. But the role that he played was not a paternal one; it was distinctly and transparently a feminine, maternal role. And in his home life he had little capacity for assuming the responsibilities of father and husband.

4

It is an axiom in psychiatry that a plurality of direct sexual outlets indicates the opposite of what it is popularly assumed to indicate. Dividing the sexual interest into several objectives diminishes the total sexual gratification, and men whose need for love drives them to the risks and efforts necessary to maintain sexual relationships with more than one woman show a deficiency rather than an excess in their masculine capacities.* This is why I include as another example of partly repudiated masculinity the phenomenon of the man with two (or more) women.

In one such case, which we shall call that of Ogden Smith, psychoanalytic study revealed that the man had had a very weak, neurotic mother and a strong, aggressive father of whom Smith as a child was in more or less constant terror. Intimidation by his father led him to cling to his mother as a protector long after he should have been able to stand on his own feet, and yet this clinging to his mother was one of the things that served as a basis for his fear of his father. In other words, his fear drove him to do something which only increased his fear. His anxiety and guilt over appropriating his mother and requiring her constant care and attention led him to try to conciliate his father. He regarded himself as his father's rival for his mother's love, but feared to appear in this light to his father. Yet he could not bear to give up his mother's solicitousness, upon which he was utterly dependent. He solved his problem temporarily by sacrificing his natural masculine aggressive development and remaining a dutiful and dependent child. This meant the repudiation of any sexual development since that would emphasize his rivalry with his father. Sexuality came to mean to him a dangerous and threatening temptation since it would bring down his father's displeasure. It was as if he said, "I have all of my mother—her love, her companionship, her kindness and care— everything except sexual union with her; that belongs to my father and is strictly taboo."

The adolescent normally solves the anxiety aroused by the changes of puberty, first by masturbation and later by experimental

* I ought to modify this by the phrase "in our culture," since this probably does not apply in communities where polygamy is an accepted social practice.

heterosexual relationships of a romantic nature. As he grows more mature he renounces both of these and begins to be capable of a consistent, stable, constructive, and realistic interest in a contemporary of the opposite sex, which indicates that he is ready for marriage.

But if his childhood experiences were such as to inflict upon him unduly great burdens of anxiety and guilt feelings with reference to all expressions of his masculinity, he cannot meet the increased pressure put upon him by physical changes in adolescence. He is likely to plunge immediately from his first adolescent attempts to solve his sexual problems into an irrevocable legal heterosexual relationship on a life-contract basis, which he thinks will absolve his guilt, afford him some outlet for his sexual desires, and give him undisputed possession of one woman who will take the place of his mother. This relieves his anxiety and gives him a temporary peace, but the relationship soon gives rise to a renewed feeling of need for sexual gratification on a more manly basis, uncomplicated by the guilt and narcissism implicit in a flight marriage.

Let me make this clear by returning again to the case of Ogden Smith. In high school he became interested in the woman who became his wife. During his freshman and sophomore years he was in a terrific stew much of the time over the problem of masturbation. In spite of the encouragement and example of some of his companions, he regarded himself as sinfully guilty whenever the urge mastered his resolution to refrain. He attended religious meetings in which its dangers were stressed by speakers who advised invoking the help of God to overcome this vicious and demoralizing habit. He got hold of some so-called "sex-books," and while some of them suggested that the habit was not "permanently" harmful, he was more inclined to credit those that said it ruined the body and mind. His unconscious self-destructive impulses were gratified by the notion that he was getting an appropriate punishment for his sin. During the height of his anxiety about himself, he was not interested in girls; but gradually they seemed to offer a solution to which he responded by becoming intensely attached to one of his classmates. This reduced his anxiety but gave rise to a new problem: he began to have increasing desire for sexual relations with the girl and, according to the conventional code, this meant marriage. Consequently, after an engagement of two or three years, the tension became unendurable and he quit school and married her.

Marriage reduced his sexual tension but not his sexual inhibitions. In marrying a woman who was to him a maternal figure he felt obliged once more to depreciate his masculinity in order to please her and to separate his sexual wishes from his love for her. This resulted in incomplete gratification and dissatisfaction for both of them. Many men baselessly accuse their wives of frigidity: the wife would like to respond but she is not permitted to; she is not given time to; her efforts are not acknowledged— sometimes they are even strongly disapproved. But a boy cannot conceive of his mother approving or co-operating in his sexual activities, and a man who marries a woman who represents his mother is in precisely this dilemma. It is also true, however, that an inhibited man may marry an equally inhibited woman who takes a deprecatory attitude toward sexuality in her husband and children and who does nothing to restore her husband's pride in his masculinity.

This man's tendency was to try to please women by giving them material gifts and kindness and attention, rather than by giving them a more mature form of love, chiefly for the reason that he *felt* that he could not give any woman sufficient love to hold her. This, in turn, was because his mother had accepted his devotion as a child, only on condition that he deny his true self and remain a charming but inhibited child. She was the active partner in their relationship, and he was constrained to be lovable, adaptable and passive.

Yet he needed to give and receive love in a more active, masculine relationship than his marriage afforded him. Having reproduced in his marriage the pattern of the relationship which had pleased his mother, he felt again the old dissatisfaction and rebellion and sought an outlet for his masculine strivings. Although his capacity to love was inhibited it was not blocked completely, so that he did not fall ill as the psychotic person does. Nor did he turn all his love toward himself as the hypochrondriacal invalid does, preoccupying himself with the organs of his own body. This man was more healthy in that he sought satisfaction in other women and found in them an incomplete and guilty outlet for his erotic needs. Thus we have the paradox of a man satisfying his conscience but sacrificing his manhood in one relationship, and asserting his mature masculinity at the expense of his conscience in another relationship. This conflict between two impulses—both of which he recognized as necessary and essentially good for him in his relation to society—was so confusing that he found it insoluble and came for psychoanalytic help in consolidating the two sides of his character which should not be opposed but were.

As I said at the beginning, this is an exceedingly common phenomenon in American life. There are many aspects of it that we could discuss, such as the psychology of the women involved who are willing to accept, or who even encourage men in giving them, half a loaf. It is important to recognize not only the dilemma and suffering of the man caught in this typically neurotic solution, but also the hostility it represents. The incompleteness of the man's love for both women is accompanied, as we would expect, by evidences of overt aggressiveness toward both. This aggressiveness is not incidental or accidental but is a fundamental part of the whole pattern of his relation to women. In the case of Ogden Smith it was implicit in his early relationship with his overprotective mother. The hate that he dared not express resulted in an unconscious fear not only of women in general, because of what they could do to him, but also fear of what he might do to them. It was particularly these fears of his own hostility that bound him so closely to his mother and drove him to extraordinary efforts later to insure himself against the possibility of losing the women he loved, feared, and hated.

The man who acquires two love objects, or occasionally three or four, is partly motivated by this fear of loss. Having acquired this plurality, he can always feel a little more safe, and furthermore he can then indulge his hostility for them with greater impunity— he can always align himself with one against the other. Some men habitually play one woman off against the other. They do not want a divorce, not so much because of sentimental attachment to the wife as because of dependence upon her, based upon this feeling of need for protection against the consequences of putting themselves completely in the power of one woman.

One sees this not only in married relationships but in many business relationships. A patient of mine is one of two secretaries to the administrative head of a large organization. It is proverbial among his employees that he is always at outs with one of the two; but if he is angry with one of them, he is careful to be very friendly with the other, to whom he confides the shortcomings and mistakes of the one with whom he is provoked. But a week later the arrangement may be just the reverse.

The superintendent of schools in a large city worked for years to obtain a social worker for the investigation of certain school problems and was finally successful; but he neglected to remove the clerical assistant who had formerly done some of the work which the newly acquired social worker was supposed to take over. In this overlapping they were constantly at swords' points, the one feeling that her position was threatened and the other feeling that her opportunities for doing a good job were being jeopardized. The superintendent would never take a definite stand, however; he would listen to the grievances of one and tell her what a difficult time he was having with the other one, and then repeat this formula, but he would never define precisely what each of them was to do. In this way he protected himself against the imaginary catastrophe which would result if one or the other of them decided to leave him. One is reminded of the story of the Rabbi who is said to have listened to one faction of his divided congregation state their position, and to have said, "You are absolutely right"; and then to have listened to the other faction with the same comment. When his wife reproached him for having told both factions that they were "absolutely right," he listened penitently to her strictures and then said, "My dear, you are absolutely right."

It is not that such individuals are either so spineless or so two-faced as they seem. It is rather that they have unconscious fear which impels them to placate and at the same time to antagonize two opposed women. Thus, they may release certain hostilities toward one woman, and turn for comfort to the other, or they may reverse the formula. Such a preoccupation with fear, aggression, defense, and atonement indicates an incomplete psychosexual evolution. In terms of popular attitudes, this appears as sin, sophistication, smartness, lustfulness, unscrupulousness, immorality, deceit, or adultery; in terms of the present thesis, it represents an incomplete or partially repudiated masculinity and, hence, a form of self-destruction.*

Self-destruction is always aggressive; one cannot injure himself without injuring others. The sacrifice of masculinity which the various forces that we have outlined lead men to offer is an indirect injury to women. It is a frustration, and frustration begets more aggression. The frustrated woman becomes the aggressive mother and the next generation pays the bill. It is no wonder that many a woman says to herself, "There is no ad-

---

* If I have seemed to discuss the psychology of the frustrating man more than that of the frustrated woman, let me justify it here by stating my endorsement of the comments of Havelock Ellis on this point: "It has always been common to discuss the psychology of women. The psychology of men has usually been passed over, whether because it is too simple or too complicated. But the marriage question today is much less the wife-problem than the husband-problem. Women in their personal and social activities have been slowly expanding along lines which are now generally accepted. But there has been no marked change of responsive character in the activities of men. Hence a defective adjustment of men and women, felt in all sorts of subtle as well as grosser ways, most felt when they are husband and wife and sometimes becoming acute." [6]

vantage in being a woman, only disadvantage. Would that I were a man!" For all she feels the impact of it, she does not realize that part of her dissatisfaction comes from a reciprocal but less conscious envy on the part of men. Men do not let themselves say, "Would that I were a woman! Would that I were spared the dangers and responsibilities of masculinity!" But they act it out unknowingly. In this women, because they less frequently fool themselves, are more realistic. It was two very wise and eloquent women [7] who made the following practical suggestions as to what the woman herself can "do about it":

. . . She must learn to live as a civilized, humane, informed world-citizen, refusing narrow provincialisms of thought and feeling, remembering that she has let her love through too many uncounted centuries carry her across the enemy's lines into his arms, for her now to deem insurmountable the historic and arbitrary boundaries of race, of nation, of class on a globe already shrunk so small by radio and aeroplane and interlocking needs as to make anachronistic and suicidal all artificial barriers to human relations.

. . . In her home she must use the knowledge which psychoanalysis offers her to level her own and her family's mounting frustrations, to gain understanding of human needs and ways of fulfilling them, to find outlets in creative directions for destructive instincts, using hate as manure, to make green fields for living children—not cemeteries for dead sons. She must, in addition, learn again the ancient ways of the female, the subtle strengths of her sex—birthrights she has sold for the pottage of a specious "equality" in man's world. Not that she must retire from his world (as Hitler and others suggest, perceiving, though crudely, some of man's basic trouble), but rather bring with her into it as substitutes for a competitor's tricks the old wisdom and versatility which if understood by her and used with scruple would enable her to play with brilliant virtuosity the complex, modern role of mother-companion-lover.

Chapter 4. The Depreciation of Femininity

WE HAVE considered the ways in which woman is frustrated by civilization in general and by men in particular. In this chapter we shall consider the ways in which she frustrates herself. Feeling herself oppressed and frustrated by males, woman identifies herself with the aggressor and depreciates her own femininity.

In my book *Man Against Himself*, I elaborated Freud's thesis that each of us has within him what Poe called "the imp of the perverse"—a tendency to do exactly the opposite of what would contribute to our own best interests. I pointed out how men defeat themselves in the attaining of their avowed objectives, how they handicap themselves, fight against themselves, ruin themselves, and even kill themselves, in spite of all we believe and feel about the instinct of self-preservation. I did not restrict this self-destructive tendency to males, but neither did I elaborate the ways in which it is peculiarly enacted or illustrated by females. These ways are not different in principle but only in form. The form of self-destructiveness peculiar to women is the repudiation of femininity itself.

"Femininity" denotes certain qualities characteristic of women. The fundamental basis of these qualities will be discussed later; for the present it is convenient to assume that everyone knows what they are—qualities that women have and men do not have. So strong is the taboo on the possession of feminine qualities by men that they conventionally renounce many pleasures and responsibilities which it would be in their interests to retain. The repudiation of femininity in themselves by men is taken for granted as a normal attitude.

It is much more difficult for a man to identify himself with women than for a woman to identify herself with men, not alone because women are adaptable but because masculinity has (erroneously) more prestige in contemporary civilization and because all men have from childhood a peculiar horror of being "reduced" to the anatomical status of women.

These same influences operate in an attenuated way on women. They too, paradoxical though it may seem, have an inclination to renounce femininity. In their minds, as well as in the minds of men, femininity comes under a certain taboo. Obviously, however, a woman's repudiation of her femininity is self-destructiveness, and to the extent that she accomplishes it she frustrates herself.

Naturally, I do not refer here to any intellectual decision on the woman's part that she will not be a housekeeper, that she will not get married, that she will not have children, that she wants a career, and so on. I refer to deep emotional trends and attitudes that are usually not known to the woman at all. "I would never do anything so unfeminine," said a certain woman referring to an act of one of her friends. Yet that same woman sued her husband for divorce because he insisted upon their having a child.

Look at this repudiation of femininity in the forms that it takes in a little girl at that period in life when these attitudes are crystallizing. One little girl, disappointed in her mother's love, might feel: "I want to grow up, but I don't want to be a woman— I want to be a man like father"; and she would proceed to identify herself with the more admired parent. Another girl, also hostile toward her mother but unwilling to forego feminine privileges, might say: "I want to be a woman, but not like mother. I'm going to have a good time and not slave for a man"; and thus she might prematurely decide to give up the joys of wifehood and motherhood, or at least to maintain her independence of men, in or out of marriage. A third child might resign herself to her fate with something like this: "I'm a girl and I have to be a woman. Everyone prefers boys. Boys have all the fun. I've nothing to look forward to but drudgery, boredom, and suffering. And it's all mother's fault for bringing me into such an unfair world." Still another girl might formulate her unconscious strivings in this way: "I'm a little girl and I want to stay one. I don't want to grow up and take on women's responsibilities. Women have a hard time. They suffer and even die having babies. I'd rather stay a child and be petted and protected."

Now look at some of these same little girls twenty or thirty years later:

Mrs. Jones had been a popular and extraordinarily capable young executive in a department store when she met her future husband. Many men had admired her, but she fell in love with a young lawyer because of his good looks and his tender, romantic devotion which her business associates did not accord her. They were engaged for eight years, during which time Mrs. Jones, absorbed in the excitement and competition of a growing department store, never found time to get married. Finally, however, she became aware, through a friend's remark, that her fiancé's patience was wearing thin and that he was turning to other women for reassurance. This roused all her fighting determination, and she bent to the reconquest of her lover all the vigor and energy hitherto spent on her business. They were married, and she made a clean sweep of all her business ambitions, determined to "live happily ever after." Although she hated housework she organized it with dispatch. But soon disillusionment set in. Her marital life was totally devoid of joy to her and, although she protested that she loved her husband, she soon came to feel secretly that he was a weakling, a romantic, impractical idealist. He wished to have children, but she refused. She despised what she called the weak and petty interests of women and was utterly bored by their social events. To escape from her home she took up golf and soon became so proficient that she began to play in tournaments in other cities. When this palled on her she entered politics where, with her usual competence and executive ability, she soon attracted national attention. Few of the thousands of people whom she met realized that she had a husband, and—as she confessed—she sometimes forgot it herself, although she always counted on his loyal support and sympathy in the background of her life.

A less obvious form of repudiation was illustrated by another woman, whom I shall call Mrs. Jackson. Unlike Mrs. Jones, she was very domestic and her housekeeping was exemplary. She was scrupulously conscientious in her devotion to her children and denied herself many pleasures for their sake. In fact, she had little pleasure of any kind, for her duties were performed with a heavy heart and a weary spirit. She managed to convey to her family the feeling that she was sacrificing her life for them; the cooking, the mending and the cleaning were all done to satisfy their heedless and insatiable demands. She was wont to refuse invitations to take part in social or community activities which required any responsibility on her part, by saying wistfully: "I'd like to do something clever and interesting like that. If I only had the time! But I'm afraid I'm just a homemaker." Needless to say, this attitude annoyed some other women, who felt that their own domesticity was impugned. Nevertheless, Mrs. Jackson was highly regarded for her modest unassumingness and patient devotion.

It was this gentle resignation that impressed the psychiatrist to whom Mrs. Jackson came one day—not for her own sake, because this type of woman never consciously does anything for her own sake, but in the interest of her daughter, Mary. Mary was a high-spirited, ambitious girl who, in a spirit of antagonism, had announced to her mother that she did not wish to marry and subject herself to the humiliations of being a good wife. Mrs. Jackson was alarmed at such "abnormality" and consulted her clergyman, who sent her to me.

Mrs. Jackson was firmly convinced that marriage was the career which every young woman should choose, and that to attain this end a girl ought to preserve her virtue and her dignity in order to attract the finest type of husband, who could take care of her and provide for her for the rest of her life. Sexual freedom was greatly to be feared because it reduced a woman's marriageable value. Mrs. Jackson was no prude; a moderate amount of drinking and smoking she condoned if it was essential to her daughter's competing with other girls in making herself "good company"; but any unconventionality that reduced the chances of a good match was anathema. "Men may be attracted to such women, but they don't marry them," she would say.

It was quite apparent, however, that Mrs. Jackson felt that her own life had been sad and disappointing, in spite of the fact that she had so sedulously followed the career she regarded as most ennobling for women. When this discrepancy was called to her attention, tears came into her eyes and she confessed that her own lot was really an unhappy and unrewarding one. She felt neglected and unappreciated by her husband and her children. All of them manifested in various ways a curious aversion to the home which she had devoted her life to making. The unkindest blow of all was dealt by her daughter who said that she dreaded to come home from school for the holidays because the house was so cheerless.

A talk with Mary after the conference with her mother was like a brisk breeze after the doldrums. "Of course I want to fall in love and to be married," she said seriously; "but not for security —not just to get my bills paid for the rest of my life. The women who talk sweetly of wanting to make a home for some man are often seeking a safe retreat for themselves. That's why ne'er-do-well men appeal to me, I suppose—because I don't want to be a parasite. Mother pities herself because she thinks we children aren't grateful to her for bearing us. She thinks she has sacrificed her life to being womanly, and I think that's hypocritical. If I ever have a child I'm going to be grateful to the man who makes it possible, and I'll try not to make motherhood an alibi."

To understand why Mrs. Jackson felt so cheated by life in spite of the fact that she had had an unusually good opportunity to fulfill the fundamental feminine urges, one must seek beneath the camouflage of womanly tastes and preoccupations to find her basic conception of femininity. Briefly it was that women are the injured sex. Since they come into the world under a heavy handicap and have no choice but to accept their fate, they should capitalize upon their helplessness. Like the man in the parable who buried his one talent because he assumed that *nothing* should be expected of him, such women exploit the privileges of their sex and resent the responsibilities of it. Since no one "rides free" in life, a woman who tries to wrest immunity from what seems to her a man's world actually suffers a surplus of hate and a lack of love. This confirms her original impression that life is hostile and unfair to women, and makes her cling all the harder to the prerogatives of femininity while rejecting its actual meaning.

Mrs. Brown represents a still different type. She was not an Amazon like Mrs. Jones, nor a martyr like Mrs. Jackson. She declared to everyone that she "loved" to be a woman and a wife and a mother, "loved" to keep house and to have children—or rather, *would* love to do so if it were not for her sinuses and her asthma. For these afflictions she had consulted all the doctors in her own town and specialists in the larger cities. She reported that they "couldn't do a thing" for her, but had recommended that she go away each summer. This seemed to help her, "even though it cost a great deal." She was reluctant to do it, too, because she loved her home and her children and her husband so much and "just hated" to be away from them.

The reader should not think that I am being satirical about Mrs. Brown. She was as totally unaware of the meaning of this illness as were most of her doctors. She had been encouraged in thinking that her illness was a blow of Fate, and that it alone stood in the way of her greatest happiness. It is very difficult to get such people as Mrs. Brown to see that illness is the price they pay for their unconscious resentments toward the very things they protest they love. It is much easier for doctors to agree with such a patient's theories about herself, and to give her a pill or perform an operation or recommend a trip, than to try to show her the truth. The attempt is likely to make her angry enough to march into another doctor's office with a tale of the former doctor's stupidity and heartlessness. Meanwhile the femininity of such women is sacrificed to their hypochrondriasis.

Nor should the reader assume that I have drawn conclusions about Mrs. Jones, Mrs. Jackson, and Mrs. Brown merely from the brief, circumstantial evidence which I have recited here. A great many hours were spent with each of them before it was possible to be definite, not so much about the fact that they felt aversion for their role as women as about the particular reasons for it and the details of its evolution. And while none of the three women came to the doctor's office announcing that they despised their feminine role or envied men or wanted to be masculine, these trends were specific in all of them and were more fundamental than the more obvious rejection of mature adult behavior.

Sometimes repudiation of femininity is definitely conscious and frankly avowed. Some women, like some little girls, freely declare their preference for things male; they look upon other women with contempt and despise their own femaleness; they often dress, talk, and behave as much like men as possible.* Others are, however, very feminine in appearance and behavior and only secretly, even unconsciously, hate their sex. I remember a rather prominent woman, the mother of several children, whose repudiation of femininity was particularly conspicuous because she was so pretty, so gracious, so apparently feminine. This is her story:

Her mother had been a very beautiful woman. She was also very skilful in adapting herself to the exacting demands of an exclusive social set, and it was in this atmosphere that the patient was reared. The father, on the other hand, was something of an *enfant terrible*. He was so lovable and accomplished that his gaucheries and his iconoclasm were overlooked by his wife and her

---

* Hypsipyle, leader of the Amazons, symbolically expressed her (and their) repudiation of femininity by attributing to the Lemnian women "a noisome smell." (Bernice Engle, unpublished manuscript.)

social group. But the contrast between the conformist mother and
the nonconformist father was very striking. Throughout her childhood the daughter was extremely self-conscious, insisting that she
was homely, whereas actually she was as beautiful as her mother,
if not more so. Her mother told me that many times she was em-
barrassed by the way in which acquaintances and strangers would
exclaim at the beauty of the little daughter. How shall we interpret the little girl's wish to deny her beauty, her apparent disbe-
lief in it? One could suppose that perhaps she felt guilty in being
her own mother's rival, or that she felt toward her mother as
many young sons do toward outstandingly successful fathers—
"The disparity is too great; I can never compete with that." But
I think the most important determinant was her rejection of
beauty as being a feminine characteristic.

The little girl very complacently followed in her mother's
footsteps up to the age of eighteen, in every way a dutiful, decorous
child and debutante. Then she suddenly exploded. She renounced
her mother's ways and wishes and adopted her father's views and
manners. She became rebellious, profligate, and indiscreet and soon
got herself into a great deal of trouble. She went on occasional
drunken bouts like a man; she was sexually promiscuous in a
casual way like certain men; she liked nothing better than to
wear men's clothes. She was physically very courageous; I could
give a long list of astonishing feats of strength and daring which
she undertook successfully. She married—but took no interest in
her children and very little in her husband. She was completely
frigid sexually.

Why should this girl have suddenly repudiated her femininity,
the identification with her mother which she had managed so well
until then? I have already mentioned the early feelings of competition with her mother toward whom she felt so inferior. When a
little girl feels overwhelmingly outdistanced by her mother as a
rival, one easy solution is to turn toward the father as an ideal for
identification. This girl's mother felt superior to her husband and

showed it; thus it was very easy for the daughter, discouraged in her attempts to emulate her mother, to turn toward an imitation of her father.

But there is another reason. A girl does not give up the struggle so easily and so suddenly without additional provocation. This girl had a brother four years younger than herself. During his early childhood his father had taken little interest in him, the daughter being definitely his favorite. But as the son turned the corner into adolescence and blossomed out in the direction toward which many of his father's ambitions tended, the father suddenly transferred his chief affections from the daughter to the son. It was as if the daughter were suddenly given to realize that in spite of all her efforts to be a charming woman like her mother, it did not avail to hold her father's interest in her. Her sudden flight from femininity was in part related directly to this feeling of abandonment, as if to say: "There is no use trying to be a woman—it gets you nothing. I had better play the part of a man."

These conscious disavowals of femininity and conscious aspirations for masculinity can be enacted in dress, attitudes, behavior, and speech. But the curious thing is that when such strivings are psychologically repressed, when they can be neither expressed in words and behavior nor recognized and counteracted, they do gain an influence over the physical and physiological processes of the body and do effect changes that can be seen and otherwise recognized. The vegetative nervous system regulates glandular and smooth-muscle activity and is constantly responding to our moods, wishes, fears, and hates with physical reactions. The cardiac, respiratory, perspirational, and other well-known somatic expressions of emotion are accompanied by widespread circulatory and endocrine changes. These, at first, are so-called functional responses, but in time almost any structure may become modified in adaptation.

This means that the woman can, to some extent, say with her

body and her bodily processes what she is unable to say with her lips or in her behavior—even that she would like to discard her femininity and become a man. We know this to be true from both theoretical and empirical evidence. The theory I have outlined at length in *Man Against Himself* and shall not repeat here. But some clinical evidence is to the point. Take the extreme case of those women who are recognized as overt homosexuals. Such women are rarely conspicuous for masculine behavior and attitudes, but physical examination reveals in a preponderant number the presence of firm muscular and adipose tissue, an excess of hair on the face, chest, back, and legs, a small uterus, a contracted pelvis, underdeveloped breasts, a low-pitched voice, and either undersized or overdeveloped external genitalia.* [1]

2

Leaving those women whose repudiation of femininity takes the form of overt homosexuality, let us return to some "normal" women, women who are normal at least in behavior. Who is not familiar with the unattractive angularity characteristic of certain spinsters—the thin, flat-chested, narrow-hipped, neurotic woman? There has been little scientific effort to correlate this masculine body build, the absence of feminine plumpness and body beauty, with the deep stratum of masculine envy which we have been discussing; but popular literature and opinion are not so silent about it.† Some would say promptly that such women are unmarried because they are unattractive. But it is equally tenable that they are unattractive because they are unmarried. Everyone knows how

* Some authorities would not accept this as evidence that an unconscious trend away from femininity was reflected in body structure. They would maintain that these women should be considered as having become masculine through no "wish" of their own, but by the will of God, as it were, or, more technically, as the result of fortuitous germinal changes to which the psychological processes are secondary.

† See Gregory Nicolai, "Psychoanalysis and Beauty," *You*, Dec. 1941-Jan. 1942, p. 13 ff.

much marriage and pregnancy improve the appearance of many women.

Emotional trends are reflected in gestures, attitudes, gaits, and pursuits, and these certainly to some extent determine the distribution of muscle development and fat deposits. Every psychiatrist has seen in his practice many examples of this, in which patients' lives were determined by an effort to reject as far as possible all those things which were characteristic of the females in the family and to imitate as far as possible all the characteristics of the males in the family. I have repeatedly noted masculine legs, thighs, and hips in women patients in whom it was possible to demonstrate that they had, since childhood, consciously or unconsciously, imitated a father's gait, a brother's athleticism, etc.

As for facial evidence of the wish to reject femininity in favor of masculinity, it is well known that neurotic women frequently have hard, tense faces and wear a querulous, bitter, pained expression. We cannot say that such women are attempting thereby to look more like men, but it is significant that an actual change often takes place in the facial appearance of some of these women following psychoanalytic treatment in the course of which conflicting masculine ambitions are renounced. This has been demonstrated to my own satisfaction in several instances on the basis of objective and not subjective evidence. I recall, in particular, one spinster of thirty-five who remained away from home the greater part of two years undergoing analysis. The change in her facial appearance was so striking that it was a matter of general comment among various of my clerical assistants, upon whose judgment I have learned that I can rely in such matters. Furthermore, when this woman went home, she was passed, unrecognized, by numerous lifelong friends. In another instance a girl whose face was quite unattractive changed in appearance so much in the course of analysis that she was sought out by a portrait painter as a special object for posing. As further evidence, I submit that she began to attract male attention and within a year was married.

I do not know why psychoanalysts should feel apologetic about announcing as a scientific fact that some of their patients grow prettier as a result of treatment. Certainly the plastic surgeons and dermatologists have no such inhibitions. Of course we should not minimize the extent to which the result is influenced by external manipulations, by a great interest in trying to look feminine, by a more skilful use of cosmetics. However, no one will deny that the facial muscles express emotion, and if emotion, then also tension and desire; and there is nothing illogical in assuming that if a woman unconsciously wants to look like a man she will to some extent do so, at the expense of her feminine beauty.

Dr. John Rickman of London [2] describes this experience:

A patient in deep depression came for analysis. She was dressed in black and wore knotted round her neck a long scarlet rope of silk; her face was hooded with a large black hat. She wore black gauntlets of shiny kid, but her fingers, which kept up a twisting angular movement, seemed too small for the gloves, so that the thin leather creased and bent as if it were the loose, scaly covering of a bird's claw. Her face was made up in the livid purplish colouring of a corpse; her mouth was curved almost to deformity and was usually drawn in, but it opened and closed slowly as the tip of the black kid claw pulled down the lower lip. Her brow was drawn and her eyes stared intently at nothing. All this while she uttered soft groans, saying to herself "Oh! Oh! Oh!" In the course of a session a commonplace interpretation was made; instantly she changed to a new creature. The angular movements of her fingers gave place to a smooth stroking of her body, the claw turned to a soft caressing hand, the hunched shoulders relaxed, her brow smoothed, her eyes brightened, the hollows in her face filled with smiling cheeks, her expression was radiant. The thought crossed my mind, "Why, my goodness, she is beautiful!"
Reflection shows that in repose (I am not speaking of the expression in melancholy) and even when smiling, which had great charm, the attribution of beauty might perhaps be an exaggeration. My first idea was that my mind followed the quick return of animation, and, possibly in relief of strain, overshot the due mark of appreciation. But to that view another and less psycho-mechanical explanation can be added. For the moment my words—so I then regarded the episode, or so my

unconscious phantasy ran—had brought this living corpse to life. It was a miracle, and the description "beautiful" was applied because that is what we think of life when we expect death, that is what we think when we see signs of triumph over death.

Feminine beauty and feminine popularity are closely associated. I have been interested for many years in the problem of the lonely girl, the girl who consciously desires male company and a lover or a husband but who seems to be unattractive to men. The psychology of these women is explained to them daily by editors of newspaper advice columns and of magazines on cultivating personality and feminine charm. It has been studied also by psychiatrists and psychoanalysts. I do not mean to offer a final answer, but I do want to contribute an interpretation in line with the ideas advanced in this book.

I have noticed that these unpopular girls are frequently either strikingly handsome or the exact opposite. In either case, they may be quite forward with men or excessively timid, but the result is the same: men shun them. Psychoanalytic study of some of these women, both the very homely ones and the very beautiful ones, reveals regularly that they believe themselves unlovable and consider that this is proved by their experience.

If one looks closely into the reasons for this conviction of unlovability, one finds that it is frequently based upon the following tripod: First, such women always have an unconscious attitude of great disparagement of their femininity.* As the result of comparisons made between themselves and their brothers and other males in childhood, they regard themselves as injured persons. Their attitude toward their own sexual organs is one of contempt and depreciation; for them the vagina is only another excretory opening, like the rectum. This feeling is connected with their idea

---

* The general tendency to disparage femininity is universal in both women and men and is related to disappointment in the child's original ideas concerning the omnipotence of the mother. It has other roots, however. An analysis of this little known period of childhood was made by Ruth Mack Brunswick in collaboration with Professor Freud. See note 5 in Chapter 3.

that they have been injured in the region of the genitals, that their normal genital organ was originally like that of their brothers and was taken from them presumably in punishment for childhood sexuality.

Secondly, the consequence of this sense of having been "castrated" * is not only self-depreciation but also envy and predatory feelings directed toward all males. Such women are for this reason described (in psychoanalytic literature) as being *castrative*, although this characterization does not indicate any particular type of activity so much as it indicates an attitude. It is this attitude which contributes to the development of anxiety with reference to men. On the other hand, it increases the feeling on the part of these women that they are unlovable. For surely, such a girl thinks, in a vague, unexpressed way, if any man could know how resentful and predatory I feel toward him, he would not come near me. However, just because she does have such feelings, she often has a strong need to disprove them or to make circumstances disprove them. She will therefore make approaches to men of a type from which the man takes unconscious warning—overeffusive, overtimid, overeager, possessive, threatening, presuming, etc.

The third reason that such women feel unlovable is related not to these more infantile and genital feelings but to the conflict with the mother in relation to the father, the old Oedipus triangle. The peculiar solution made by these women is to assume that competition with men and partial adoption of the masculine role are less dangerous than competition with women. This is the reason that women with strong, dynamic mothers frequently fall into this class.

Now the point of all that I have been saying is that the conviction of unlovableness becomes so strong in such women that they completely resign themselves to it; one might almost say that they try to prove it to be so. It goes without saying that they do

* A technical word introduced by psychiatrists to describe this feeling of genital injury and inferiority—*not* equivalent to the surgical meaning.

this most frequently in behavior. It is toward that aspect that most magazine counselors and the like direct their adjurations. But I think that this unconscious attitude, beginning as it does in the girl's early years, has a tendency to find expression also in her physical structure. A psychological test recently introduced by Dr. David Rapaport and named, after its originator, the Szondi test,[3] bases conclusions about the personality of the person tested on his selections from a set of photographs of some very cruel characters, some homosexuals, some depressed individuals, and so forth. The average person will select as a preference pictures whose originals—though the subject does not know this—have traits quite dissimilar from the subject's own. In other words, he will avoid selecting pictures that represent trends overtly displayed by himself. Persons subject to depression but at the moment free from it will, for example consistently avoid pictures of depressed individuals in the standardized set without having any knowledge about the original of the photograph.

This test—which is more complicated than appears above—has proved extraordinarily useful in detecting latent personality trends in psychiatric diagnosis, and its theoretical significance in the present discussion is obvious. It seems to prove that secrets may be unintentionally revealed not only in transient facial expressions but in permanent physiognomic casts perceived unconsciously by others. Hence, it is not only possible but even probable that women who consider themselves unlovable advertise that fact in some permanent or semipermanent way, thus helping to make their fantasy an objective reality. (I shall not attempt to go into the possibility that this is also expressed in body build, although the tendency of such women to allow themselves to get fat is surely an example of it.)

This would help to explain some homeliness, but it leaves unexplained the psychology of the particularly attractive women who suffer from the same unconscious feelings as the homely ones. I think the explanation here is slightly different though related. The unattractive girl, as I have already said, longs for men to notice her but is left strictly alone. She is likely to blame this on the fact that she is not pretty. "Men cluster around a pretty girl like dogs around a bitch in heat," said a patient of mine one day with bitter enviousness. This remark suddenly gave me a clue as to the meaning of the special development of beauty in some girls who are sexually frigid, according to psychiatric experience. It is almost as if such girls were able to accomplish the same thing by beauty that lower animals accomplish by certain smells: they use beauty as a lure. Now, a lure is needed only when there are dangers to be overcome, and the necessity of using so great a lure as outstanding beauty appears to indicate that there is only one degree of difference between such a woman and the particularly homely woman; at heart these two women are the same. They have the same deep conviction of unlovableness and for the same reasons. But the girl whom we call homely has resigned herself to it and has exploited, if not actually developed, her homeliness; the beautiful girl has not entirely resigned herself to being unlovable, but is stimulated to a special effort to have her convictions disproved, an effort that also involves certain unconscious modifications of her facial and bodily appearance. That this is lure rather than genuine attractiveness is confirmed by the fact, already mentioned, that these women are very often frigid, and in many other ways show a deep hostility toward any particular man among the many whom they take pleasure in attracting.

We should logically expect that the most significant alterations in function or structure related to the repudiation of femininity would be connected with the reproductive organs. Frigidity and vaginismus represent physiological rejections of the feminine role in intercourse and cannot persist over a long period without some corresponding structural changes, such as (at least) the atrophy of unused tissues and glands. Sterility is somewhat comparable to frigidity: it represents the failure of normal biological functioning. That it occurs far oftener in civilized life than in savage, and far oftener among human beings than among animals, should have suggested before now that something in the spirit of our civilization interferes with a process generally regarded as beyond psychological control. Whether sterile women are more likely to be frigid than nonsterile women is difficult to prove, since the actual incidence of frigidity is unknown. It is my impression, however, from clinical experience, that sterility is often associated with frigidity. One patient, I remember, illustrated almost every proposition in this chapter: she was completely frigid, suffered from dysmenorrhea, was sterile, resented all of her feminine activities and obligations, and had her breasts amputated, first one and then the other, on the pretext that she might be developing a cancer in them.

That the emotional life has some relation to this phenomenon of involuntary childlessness (sterility) would appear to be demonstrated by several reported cases in which a reorganization of the psychic life (e.g., psychoanalysis) of a woman results in pregnancies ten, fifteen, and twenty years after marriage. I myself am familiar with two instances of this. Moreover, pregnancy frequently follows the adoption of a child.[4] Regardless of how it is explained, and frankly admitting our vast ignorance on this sub-

---

* A few obstetricians and gynecologists recognize the importance of psychological factors in the highly complex functions of reproduction, although, generally speaking, the mechanical aspects of the process remain their chief preoccupation. Such phenomena as the occurrence of pregnancy following the adoption or the decision to adopt a child are frequent enough to belie the explanation of coincidence for even the most organically minded doctors. Some have gone so far as to postulate the details of the psychological and physiological mechanisms which may underlie this paradoxical phenomenon. For example, it has been suggested that in certain women over-eagerness for a child might be reflected in some obscure hormonic way by an over-activity of the ovaries so that each month a premature maturation of the follicles occurs with the result that ova are discharged which are not yet ready for fertilization. Conversely, when the anxiousness, fear of disappointment or sense of frustration are diminished by psychotherapy, by the gradual reconciliation of the woman to her sterility or by the adoption of a child, a decrease in the pathological emotional acceleration of ovarian function would result in normal ova being discharged and thus the sterility terminated. This explanation may not be the correct one, but that emotional factors influence reproduction seems indisputable. Every ornithologist is

ject there is much evidence at the present time that sterility need not be considered a hopeless condition or one dependent upon peculiar physical and chemical interferences only. The fact that many sterile women are consciously very eager to have a child and bitterly disappointed by their condition does not contradict the thesis that in some of these women, at least, an *unconscious* wish may exist in the contrary direction.* It should be added that this wish may arise from other things besides the repudiation of femininity which I have been discussing. It is probably more frequently based on a tremendous, unrecognized fear. Many women have a conscious fear of pregnancy, but this would not necessarily result in sterility.

Whatever its origin, an unconscious aversion to pregnancy which is insufficient or incapable of producing sterility may show itself in the difficulty and painfulness of pregnancy and parturition. I can say from clinical experience that in some women the degree of discomfort both in pregnancy and in parturition has been directly proportional to the intensity of their resentment at having to live through this phase of their female role. The excessive vomiting of pregnancy is recognized by many obstetricians as a physiological expression of protest and a gesture of rejection. I believe this same protest may express itself in excessive pain prior to and during delivery.

I was very much interested, as I am sure others were, in a series of articles and letters in the *Atlantic Monthly* initiated by an article by a woman (Mrs. Leonore Friedrich) who wanted to have the pleasure of having a baby without an anesthetic. In some of these comments there is implicit recognition of what I am trying to say; namely, that a part of the pain of childbirth may be ascribed to an unconscious resentment of the feminine role. As

familiar with the phenomenon observable in the woodpecker family and in some other birds: if a normal clutch of eggs is, let us say, six, the artificial removal or loss of one of the eggs will result in another being laid to replace it, and this can be repeated many times. It is clear that the female has some *psychological* control over the number of eggs she produces, the stimulus of the awareness of a certain "perfect" number.

one contributor put it, "What is painful and unnecessary in the average childbirth is not due to the anatomy of the mother or of the child, but to the attitude with which the experience is envisaged and met.

Certainly many of the pains ascribed to the non-gravid uterus are definitely connected with unconscious psychological conflicts, often with conflicts of precisely the type I have been discussing. The very fact that menstruation is referred to by so many women as "the curse" or as a sickness of some kind is an indication of how much they resent this manifestation of their femaleness. Pain is only another expression of this protest, an expression coming from a deeper repression, and one which therefore retains a more intimate connection with the vegetative nervous system, and through it with the muscles and glands functioning in menstruation, and through these with the nerves that register the disturbed physiological activity as pain. Every woman knows that what might be called her frame of mind may influence not only the character and comfort of the menstruation, even the date of its appearance. I have seen numerous instances in which this date was shifted as much as two weeks, apparently in order to accomplish some unconscious (never a conscious) purpose.

All this is quite well known to some laymen and some physicians. But there are others who shut their eyes to what is so obvious. They want to believe that pain in the course of what should be a painless physiological process is a result of some structural or chemical disarrangement, some kind of inexplicable internal accident.

But why? What are the reasons for the persistence of ideas of female suffering, and for such a myth as that of the floating uterus, the theory that all nervous diseases are caused by disorders or displacement of the womb? I think we must regard these popular theories as indicating an unconscious recognition on the part of the physicians and laymen that there *is* something wrong with the genitals of many women, something functionally wrong, something structurally wrong. It is a "wrongness" of instinctual de-flection, referred by the patient to anatomical and functional processes which then *do* become deranged. The willingness with which some patients submit to painful local treatment is sugges-tive evidence that they suffer from a sense of this "wrongness" connected with the genital organs.

Whether or not the unconscious depreciation of femininity is as influential as I have suggested in determining the minor modifi-cations of the structure and function of the body, its expression in the acts and attitudes of people's lives is undoubtedly a phenom-enon of widespread occurrence and of profound significance in our present-day civilization. I have already indicated some of the forms this takes, but I want to emphasize that not all forms of flight from femininity lead to conspicuous maladjustment. It is a matter of degree and kind. Complete repudiation of one's bio-logical role (if such a thing is possible) would undoubtedly be accompanied by psychological abnormality; but such complete denial of one's being is very rare. Much behavioristic repudiation is comparatively shallow—that is, it is at a conscious level and is largely conditioned by what is often called a "man-made civili-zation." Some women (George Sand, Rosa Bonheur, Amy Low-ell) have obtained substantial rewards in terms of their own sex through affecting certain mannish prerogatives and characteris-tics. It has often been remarked that a combination of certain so-called "male" traits such as good sportsmanship, good fellow-ship, generosity, and physical courage, with certain so-called "feminine" traits such as tenderness, sympathy, and constancy, make an ideal woman, one more fitted to be a companion to man. On the other hand, as some of our illustrations have indicated, great hostility toward the feminine role, especially toward the opportunity to cherish a man and reciprocate his love, may be cloaked by exceedingly pretty feminine ways.

Many career women lead successful and useful lives, resent the implication that they have sacrificed their womanhood in so doing. They argue with justice that their lives, even in those instances when they are childless and manless, have been conducted along essentially feminine lines, although at a sacrifice of personal satisfactions. Some rebellion against female passivity and physical handicaps, against social restrictions and male jealousy and domination, is a part of the healthy girl's development, and is responsible for such beneficial results as healthier dress, greater social freedom, woman suffrage, better conditions for working women, etc. Women have mobilized to fight such evils as the slave trade, war, and man's inhumanity to man (and to women), as illustrated by the work of Dorothea Dix, Florence Nightingale, Clara Barton, Emmeline Pankhurst, and Jane Addams; and this struggle cannot be dismissed as pathological or unwomanly, although its leaders were undoubtedly considered both by some people while the fight was going on.

3

We have discussed some of the more disastrous and unfruitful ways in which the repudiation of femininity is carried out—the ways that lead to unhappiness, illness, ugliness, sexual maladjustment, loneliness, and a general retreat from life. These are ways in which women frustrate themselves, or react in self-destructive ways to what they feel to be the unfairness of nature. We come now, at last, to the most self-frustrating behavior of all: the aggression of women against men. For no woman is self-sufficient, regardless of her fantasies, her pretenses at masculinity. Though she is, as we have said, the center of the universe, she needs her men. Hence, her acts of revenge against men are in the end frustrations for herself.

What is the nature of these aggressions? It is an ancient theory that women have it within their power to ruin men. And in most of the stories and legends in which this idea has been immortalized, the procedure has been one of abandoning the man to the consequences of his own self-destructiveness. He is, so to speak, permitted or even encouraged by the woman to destroy himself. Eve persuaded Adam to do what he knew to be fatal for their paradise. Delilah coaxed out of Samson the secret which spelled his ruin. Circe let the bestial nature of those attracted to her have its full expression. In 1922 the City of New York erected in City Hall Park a statue by Frederick W. MacMonnies called "Civic Virtue," which represented a man standing victorious above a heap of conquered temptations in the form of women. For nearly twenty years a controversy raged over this statue. "It is a terrible thing," wrote a prominent woman, "to suggest that man symbolizes virtue and woman vice." "But," replied Mr. Mac-Monnies, "the most widely accepted form of temptation is that of a woman. Can it be that the women are angry because some man finally found strength to resist temptation?"

There is a contrasting theme in legend and in history and in popular thinking to the effect that women can *save* men. Lysistrata's behavior was precisely the opposite of Helen of Troy's; she and her women opposed themselves to the self-destructiveness of their husbands. Florence Nightingale battled against incredible opposition from the British government and the British army when she set out to save some British soldiers from unnecessary death. The uncounted millions of women who succor their husbands silently with their love and comfort and service remain anonymous though not unsung. The theme of Wagner's opera *The Flying Dutchman* is that a man loves a woman not for her sake but to save his own soul; in *Tannhäuser* the good woman prevails over the bad woman in the contest for a man's soul.

The implication of these venerable contradictory themes is that women may choose whether or not to allow men to become the victims of their own self-destructiveness. The assumption is that men may act while women remain passive, but the power of a woman remains in her function of choosing. She can choose to favor man's self-destructiveness, or she can choose to favor his spiritual development. The assumption is also implicit that men are more susceptible to the direct action of their self-destructive instincts than are women.

By those who are impelled to minimize the psychological differences between men and women or who insist that, in spite of anatomical and biological differences, there is no psychological difference, these legends are explained away as examples of the well-known tendency to blame someone else for one's difficulties. But if, on the other hand, one assumes that the biological differences between the sexes are related to fundamental differences in psychological structure also, one is justified in examining these psychological differences, and considering the evidence for the notion that women are capable of diminishing or encouraging the self-destructive tendencies of men. Because, if women do have this capacity, their failure to use it constructively must certainly be regarded as an aggression which is also self-destructive for them.

It is exceedingly difficult to be definite in designating which psychological characteristics of women are consistently different from those of men. From the anatomical standpoint, they have the same bones, the same blood, the same bile; from the psychological standpoint, they have the same instincts, the same intelligence, the same inhibitions. Even what we mean by masculinity and femininity are not very definite, in spite of the popular assumption that they are quite definite qualities. We know that there is some woman in every man and some man in every woman. It would be out of place here to review the long technical discussions of the subject contained in psychological and psychiatric literature, but a little experimentation will soon establish the fact. Try to think of some traits that might be said to be characteristically feminine: the love of finery, for example, the propensity to gossip, affection for children, skill at food preparation; they will be immediately recognized as characteristic also of many convincingly masculine men.

There certainly is a prevalent conception that women are by

nature more conservative, more interested in problems of love and less in affairs of strife. A quick conclusion from this would be that men embody the destructive instinct and that women embody the constructive or creative instinct. "Women began the work of the world," writes G. A. Studdert-Kennedy,[5] "and have done most of it ever since. Father was predatory, mother was creative. Father lived by putting things out of existence, mother by bringing them into it. Agriculture, house-building, boat-making, pottery, basket-weaving, leather-work, all of the primitive arts and crafts, were started and for ages carried on by women. . . . Women were the creators. Men were the slayers. This arose out of a deep difference between the male and female nature, the very root of all their differences."

There is something attractive about this picture of the fierce belligerent male protecting the loving creative female, and there is no doubt much truth in it. But it has many flaws, not the least being the careless treatment of the idea of destructiveness. To kill a wild beast that threatens a home, or to destroy weeds that invade a garden, or to grind up wheat or coffee beans so that they can be used for food, is a destructive act, but destructive in the service of creation. On the other hand, preparing an indigestible meal of manufacturing a bomb is an act of creation, but creation in the service of destructiveness. This is true whether the act is performed by man or by woman. The real criterion of the constructiveness or destructiveness of an act is, in the long run, its effect upon the individual himself, and if we turn Kennedy's theory around to read that men are self-destructive and women are self-preservative—which is what it implies—its sophistry immediately becomes apparent.

Yet we feel that there *is* some difference in the behavior of the sexes. We need not idealize women and think of them as the embodiment of love to recognize that biologically they are more closely associated with creation, with conservation, with race preservation, than are men.* One sees the reflection of these biological trends in the behavior of social groups: men fight while women knit sweaters; men kill animals for pleasure and women foster humane societies; men flock to prize fights and women to concerts.

But it is difficult to prove whether these activities are chosen by individuals as an expression of the special interests of their sex, or determined by tradition, custom, and superstition. This becomes apparent if one examines almost any particular example. Dressmaking, like the wearing of dresses, was once the prerogative of men and in some countries still is. A man who can cook or do hairdressing is regarded quite differently by an ordinary bourgeois group in a Middle Western town and by the management and clientele of a New York hotel. Many women are as predacious in hunting or as enthusiastic over prize-fights as any man. Of course one can always say that these are exceptions, but there are so many exceptions that we cannot safely derive any rule from group activities, the earnest efforts of the sociologists notwithstanding. We have to fall back upon hypotheses derived from intensive study of the individual.

The fundamental, inescapable, differential fact is that a woman can bear babies, and a man cannot. But in order to do so a woman must enlist the co-operation of a man. Around this formula clusters all the psychological differentiations of the sexes. Everything else is secondary. It is a direct corollary that men are relatively more self-sufficient than women (although the opposite is often al-

* As Lillian E. Smith and Paula Snelling write:[6] "But there are reasons for thinking that woman does not share equally man's affinity for death. . . . It is probably . . . true that among the polarities of the universe, masculinity and death, femaleness and life, are linked together. And by simple mathematics, qualitative differences to one side, the sex which has to spend nine months in the begetting of each human being would have less time to devote to the service of death, were it equally inclined, than has the sex of whom nine minutes are required. Add to that the thirty years during which by custom woman is harnessed to the cradle, caught in the treadmill of the home, and one sees that, whatever her impulses, she could not have made of herself the effective bondservant of death which man has become."

leged).* Logically, it is women who must pursue men rather than the reverse. This is disguised by an arrangement of nature whereby the males appear very active, driven to the gratification of a physical need. But for the female it is more than a physical need: it is a psychological, biological need without which she cannot perform her primary and characteristic function. Women renounce their envy of men's physical equipment and strength only when they, too, come to possess something and to be "haves" instead of "have nots."

In order to win the co-operation of the male, it is not sufficient for the woman to be passively patient and "wait for nature to take its course." Once it may have been so; it still is, among the wild animals where the competition for attractiveness takes place among males instead of among females. But civilization in "protecting" woman has also handicapped her, and in contemporary society she must compete. She must prove herself lovable—and hence attractive. In order to get what she wants she must give the man what he wants.

It is this that determines the woman's distinguishing psychological characteristics: a relatively greater capacity for receptivity and adaptability.[7] It is the girl who awaits her suitor's pleasure in suggesting an appointment, an expectation, a course of action.

It is the mother who must listen with the proper sympathy and appreciation to the proud or sorrowful accounts of the petty happenings of the day. It is the wife who must endeavor to find some joy in whatever situation her husband's inclinations and economic opportunities force them to live. It is she who must sustain her husband's courage, bolster his ego, and assuage his disappointments, even if only by sympathetic listening. Whether married or unmarried, a woman, far more than a man, must struggle to make the best of every situation. She has all the external adjustments to make which face any man, and in addition she undergoes internal

* Women are, as a rule, more practical and less sentimental than men, which may sometimes give the illusion of greater self-sufficiency.

bodily events which require tremendous psychological elasticity. Menstruation, pregnancy, parturition, and lactation are physical experiences for which there are no male analogues, over which a woman's conscious voluntary control is very slight, but to which she must adapt her whole life, just as she also adapts it to her lover's program.

The psychological effect of this adaptability upon men, or, let us say, upon an individual man, is very difficult to do justice to in a brief description. The dynamic essence of the masculine spirit, based perhaps chiefly on biological functions, has been described as the impulse to penetrate, to make an impress upon something or someone. It is this that leads to clashes between men, this that leads to the happy union of the receptive female and the propulsive male. The sense of achievement that springs from a proper reception of his ideas, his love, his constructive efforts, his genitality, is a *sine qua non* of the man's mental, physical, and spiritual life. It reassures him, but it does more: it affords him an opportunity to give love that is welcomed, and makes him capable of more and more love, and hence of less and less hate and feelings of guilt.

Thomas Mann called attention to Wagner's recognition of this need that men feel for the redeeming or, as we should say, the reconstructive service of women to men. He quotes those lines from the opera of *The Flying Dutchman* in which the hero sings to his sweetheart:

> The somber glow I feel within me burning—
> Shall I, wretch that I am, confess it for love's yearning?
> Ah, no, it is salvation that I crave—
> Might such an angel come my soul to save!

Mann goes on to say that ". . . never before had such a complex thought, so indirect a feeling, been sung or written for singing. The condemned man loves this maiden at first sight; but he tells himself that his love is not directed toward her, but toward redemption and release. She, on the other hand, stands before him as the embodiment of a possible salvation. And so the poor man can neither distinguish between his yearning for redemption and his yearning for her, nor does he wish to do so. For his hope has taken on her shape and he can no longer even wish it to have another. He loves redemption in this maiden." [8]

Now, it is true that in thus protecting or building up the personality of her husband or lover by means of her receptivity, the woman builds her own personality. In one sense it is very flattering to a woman, this feeling that she is necessary to a man and can actually help him to live and to escape death. But she, too, must be helped to live and to avoid death; their contributions must be reciprocal. It is a part of the function of marriage for the partners to supply to each other that amount of support and encouragement which is necessary to assuage the wounds and frustrations encountered in the daily lives of each. Whether the woman has any greater powers or greater responsibility in this direction than the man is debatable. She probably does have a greater capacity for it. But an expectation on the part of a husband that the wife should accept an exaggerated exploitation of this greater responsibility is itself a frustration for the wife, and is not an indication of a mature love relationship where the adjustment is automatic and mutual and where most of the attachment is based upon constructive rather than reconstructive functions.

In a normal relationship the energy of both partners is directed to what they can do together in the present and future rather than to what reparation they can make to each other for troubles of the past. In addition to the somewhat negative need —this need for reassurance, for protection against self-destructiveness—marriage must be based upon a *positive* instinctual attraction. Joan Riviere has put this excellently:[9]

How much does this motive of the need for reassurance about one's own value (one's own freedom from hate, and, therefore, one's lovableness) play a part in the decisions of men and women to marry, and how little in comparison with it does the feeling of love or sexual desire impel them? . . . For true love, as we call it, is precisely a condition in which the two factors coalesce and become indistinguishable, in which ease of mind and happiness are perpetually being derived from the fact that the man or woman is full of a love which can satisfy and fulfill the needs even of another beside himself. A mutual love serves as a double insurance to each partner. The other's love, added to one's own, doubles one's store of love and well-being and so of insurance against pain, destructiveness, and inner destitution; and also, in complementing and fulfilling each other's sexual needs, each transforms the sexual desire of the other from a potential pain and source of destructiveness in him or her, to an absolute pleasure and source of well-being. By this partnership in love, therefore, satisfaction of the harmonizing and unifying life-instincts, the self-preservative and sexual, is gained; and security against the destructive impulses and the dangers of loss, loneliness, and helplessness is increased. A benign circle of enjoyment with a minimum of privation and aggression has been achieved and the *advantages of dependence* are being used to the full.

When the balance between these two elements in the love bond is unequal, when one party or the other is deficient in his capacity to give love, the other partner is imposed upon and unconsciously resents it. In such instances, we speak of a husband being burdened with an overdependent wife, or vice versa.

It is a relative question how much of this dependence one partner can endure. In many instances, either because she is unduly burdened and resentful over an excessive dependence on her husband's part, or because she is unable to sustain even the normal expectation in this respect, the wife will aggressively withdraw her efforts to support a husband emotionally. She then passively "lets the man down." She lets him destroy himself.

Everyone is familiar from personal acquaintance with women who seem to foster, or at least to permit, the self-destructiveness of their husbands. Yet there is always some doubt about it because, not knowing the details, we wonder whether the husband's behavior is what has provoked the wife's attitude or whether the wife's attitude has caused the husband's behavior. Actually, it is always interactive; both things are true. But clinical examples frequently come to the attention of the psychiatrist in which the remissness of the wife is clearly discernible, even by her. I remember a prominent public official who began to involve himself in very serious difficulties about which no one but his wife knew. She disapproved of them and pleaded with him to desist, but to no avail. Finally, recognizing the pathological nature of his behavior, she secretly consulted a psychiatrist who warned her that her husband was displaying symptoms of a grave mental illness and that she should take immediate steps to safeguard him by placing him in a sanitarium for treatment. This she could not bring herself to do. Afterward she could not forgive herself for not having taken the step, nor could she explain why she had not done so, except that she was so exasperated at him that any action she could have taken would have been interpreted by him as revenge instead of as prophylaxis. But her failure ruined her life as well as his; he was sent to prison and their home was broken up. Or take, for example, the all too common picture of a family in which the husband is addicted to alcohol—a drunkard, in short. The drunkard's wife is usually a pitiable sufferer. She must endure neglect, abuse, privation, and humiliation and at the same time try to protect the children, neighbors, her own relatives, and sometimes those of her husband from the knowledge and consequences of his self-indulgence. And yet, in spite of all this, and in spite of the fact that such wives exclaim that they are at their wits' end, that they don't know what to do, that they have tried everything, and so on—in spite of all that, I say again that some of these wives not only permit but actually encourage their husbands to drink.

Why does this sound more strange than the familiar expression "She would drive *anyone* to drink"? Is it because such women so completely deceive themselves? Or is it that our pity overcomes our critical judgment? One can't help feeling sorry for such wives —I have seen too many of them not to have a vivid picture in my mind of the miseries and horrors they live through. But time after time, in my professional experience, a wife could have put a stop to the drinking or compelled her husband to get treatment for the anxiety underlying his addiction had she been willing to take a firm step and refused to tolerate it.

Wives often remove their husbands from confinement against all advice at a time when to do so is unwise because of the prospect of suicide. One of my professional friends was removed against his own wishes and against our advice by his no doubt well-meaning wife, only to kill himself as we had predicted he would. In fact, as I said in *Man Against Himself*, it is this curious refusal on the part of so many relatives to believe that they might be contributing to making a suicide possible which led me to become especially interested in that whole problem. I concluded from my study that people cannot bear to see how close such behavior is to homicide.

Occasionally I am consulted by a parent or a widow who has had the misfortune of bereavement by suicide. They suffer not only from the sense of loss but from the flashing pains of conscience and gnawing suspicion that perhaps they were in some way partly responsible. Such a woman said to me once: "It has been over a year, and I still cannot sleep or eat or work. Our years together had been so wonderful! They were the happiest of my life, and of his, too, I am sure. Why should he have ended them in this way? Was it something that I did? Or something I didn't do? He was always inclined to be a little melancholy and he would get discouraged so easily. I used to have to urge him on and pump him full of courage and reassurance every day, and tell him I knew he was going to succeed. I am afraid I got a little tired of this and let up on it. Sometimes I used to wish he would give *me* a little encouragement—but that was selfish of me. I just let him down. So now I blame myself. I feel as if I were responsible for his death . . ."

There is no doubt about the intensity of the suffering of such a woman. Even while she appeals for reassurance that she surely did everything she could be expected to do, she confesses to a feeling of having failed to do all that she could. She broods constantly, and by neglecting her children, her work, and her other responsibilities, repeats the lapses for which she reproaches herself. This indirect aggressiveness is quite typical of depressions.

One can see in the self-reproaches of the woman just quoted how bankruptcy finally ensues in a relationship in which the emotional support comes chiefly from one side. A man who is so strongly impelled by self-destructive impulses resulting from childhood calamities that he ultimately commits suicide is one who naturally turns to a woman with an urge in the direction of rescuing someone. She appeals to him because she is a rescuer; he appeals to her because she needs someone to save. When, after a period of success, her efforts fail, as they are likely to do, she is overwhelmed with a feeling of defeat. It is like a surgeon, intensely proud of his professional attainments, who operates upon an important patient only to have the patient die. All physicians feel discouraged if they fail, but some are more subjective than others about it, and for one of these to lose the most important case of his career creates no greater trauma than that created in a woman who, with the "saving" impulse, fails in the most important mission of her life. This same intense wish to succeed in saving someone accounts for the tenacity with which some women cling to unregenerate and derelict husbands, and their overwhelming bitterness when they find themselves continuously failing in their elected task. In fact, in some of these struggles the grimness of the conflict is more evident than the devotion.

We might pause here to explain in general why this rescuing function seems so important for some women. The little girl overcomes her feeling of inferiority with reference to her brother when she discovers in herself a quality that she can exploit which often surpasses his abilities: she can be lovable. But she may not receive sufficient assurance of this lovability from the behavior of her father, or subsequently from the behavior of other and more eligible man-objects; and she then not only distrusts her own attractiveness, but also begins to doubt the potency of the male instinct of pursuit, and falls back upon what Freud called an anaclitic type of love—that is, love based on dependency. One may see in her attraction toward the type of man who needs reassurance and tenderness the feeling that she cannot be loved for herself as a woman but must offer extraordinary gifts of strength and security. She promises him a refuge and a haven, thus drawing him to her and demonstrating her extraordinary ability to dispense love. Just as her ego has been so hurt in childhood that she is more than ordinarily impelled to prove to herself that she is lovable and curative, so the man who appeals to her will be one whose ego has been injured in childhood so that he will have far more need to be loved than ability to love.

Now when, in spite of all her efforts, such a woman loses the battle to save such a husband, she feels both grief (loss) and depression (guilt)—guilt because, like all human beings, she feels anger when she has been hurt. The woman quoted above got tired of a one-sided arrangement in which she did all the encouraging and comforting; she resented the necessity of always being strong and of suppressing all impatience. When a woman who has a driving impulse to save someone in order to prove her own lovableness grows weary in such a situation, she cannot rebel openly on her own account nor admit, even to herself, her resentment. But she may rationalize her feelings by thinking that it might be kinder to let a man take the consequences of his own self-destructiveness—not, of course, expecting this to go so far as actual suicide. She can persuade herself that if he is allowed to take the consequences of his own self-hatred and depression instead of having it smoothed away by a solicitous wife, he may suffer enough pain to make some spontaneous efforts to rid himself of the cause of his troubles. Driven to the limit of her capacity for endurance, she withdraws her support like a mother who, provoked by the fretful tossings of her child, lets him go even if he is likely to injure himself, in the hope that he will control his own behavior.

This extreme illustration of how one woman may first retard and then accelerate self-destructiveness in the man she loves resembles such legends as those of Circe and the Lorelei, in which a woman first seduces a man and then lets him destroy himself through his dependence on her. That all such myths carry a seed of psychological truth is well known. The inference is that if woman has a great psychological capacity for receptivity and adaptability, she also has the power to use it both negatively and positively, and that, so far as it *is* a distinctively feminine attribute, she has a peculiar ability to interfere with the course of man's self-destructiveness. I do not mean that she can actually save or destroy men, like the sirens of old, but that she can make her influence as a woman felt constructively or destructively.

4

We have spoken of the fact that one partner or the other may be deficient in the ability to give love and in this case will resent *any* emotional demands or expectations made upon him. This is extremely important because the inability to support even the normal demands of a relationship without resentment is responsible for much disappointment and disillusionment in marriage; it represents at bottom an inability to love. There are many ways of reacting resentfully to the demands of love. Many men and women carry out their aggressive feelings actively and directly, but others use the technique of passive withdrawal, which I have described as being more characteristic of women, or at any rate more dangerous in women.

This is seen in a certain type of martyrdom which is very familiar in daily life. One thinks of those housewives whose chief occupation is drudgery, who drag out a petty, dreary existence with an ill-concealed grudge against life, sometimes lifting a brave tear-stained face to the mildly sympathetic world, but more often gazing wistfully upon the distant purple hills of illusion. Such women have little conscious realization that one of the chief motives of such an attitude is their wish to inflict pain upon someone near them. "See how I am made to suffer!" is but a thinly veiled way of saying, "See how *you* make me suffer!" or "See how I suffer for your sake!" This same martyr attitude is often so apparent in neurotic invalidism, and in physical invalidism as well, that some physicians and many relatives cannot escape the suspicion that it is an important motive in the illness. I shall not labor this point, because I have discussed it and illustrated it in detail in *Man Against Himself.*

No less familiar are some of the innumerable social situations of which women complain bitterly, often with apparent justice, but which upon closer scrutiny prove to be further examples of this same phenomenon. We are frequently invited to shed a tear for golf widows, women whose husbands are so addicted to playing that their poor wives are left at home alone, lonely and neglected. There is no denying that many men play golf compulsively as an escape from responsibility, or as a return to the play days of childhood, or to elude petticoat rule; but it is also true that many women react to such neglect with a kind of indolence which, in substance, is nothing else than an aggressive passivity which carries its own self-punishment. Some women feel that silent acquiescence is the only course open to them in such situations. Resignation, "the courage of the weak," is necessary, they say, because of the insecurity they feel in regard to their husbands.

Nothing illustrates better the underlying hatred in passive martyrdom than this insecurity and fear felt by many women in the fundamental relationship of their lives. For it derives from a secret sense of guilt which makes the self-depreciation a true self-judgment. Such women *do* lack capacity for love—not only for their husbands, but for all human beings other than themselves. The very tactics which they use to "safeguard" their position actually increase their insecurity, for, like all unacknowledged, unconscious aggressiveness, excessive forbearance is self-destructive. These women bring to pass what they most dread by an exaggerated timidity, based not so much on fear of actual consequences as on fear of their own hostilities, smoldering in silence but felt as grievous wrongs. Sometimes the underlying aggressiveness appears more directly, but deflected toward other women. But always the situation is arranged so that the victim can suffer and succumb to humiliating circumstances.

The reluctance of many women to throw themselves wholeheartedly into any community activity, in spite of having a large amount of leisure time, is another illustration of self-destructive passivity. The women who lament most bitterly that their husbands are away from them so much at clubs or on business—the very ones who have the most need for association with other women and for social outlets which would in some degree compensate them for their loneliness—are the ones least likely to join in such activities. They usually decline for no explicit reason, and yet the same women often complain that they have difficulty in making acquaintances and are restricted in their list of friends. This is a typical example of passive aggressiveness, in which the aggressive nature of the passivity is ignored, but the resulting disappointment is exploited as if it were a misfortune which fate or an unkind providence had visited upon them. There is no recognition on the part of such women that this type of self-punishment is related to the extensive guilt they feel about their envy of others, both men and women, who have more initiative and wider interests than they.

Other women make martyrs of themselves by compulsively pursuing so-called pleasures which they do not enjoy—endless rounds of bridge parties or dull teas at which no one says anything interesting or does anything constructive, stuffy dinners given and attended from a sense of duty, a routine which they rationalize by saying they are doing it "to advance my husband" or "to maintain our social position." Meanwhile, they relegate to hirelings such things as the care of their children, from which they should obtain the maximum of enjoyment.

One could extend this list of examples indefinitely, but those I have cited will serve to illustrate how passive techniques are used aggressively and at the same time self-punitively by many women. In fact, this whole chapter might have been entitled "passive aggression," or rather "unconscious passive aggression." I use this revised phrase to distinguish it from the conscious use of this technique in the sit-down strike, in Mahatma Gandhi's program, among the peoples lately conquered by the Germans, and in the practice known as "soldiering." Conscious passive aggression is rarely used by women; unconscious passive aggression is characteristically used by women—not all women, let me repeat, or at least not all women all of the time, though by many women some of the time. Perhaps this is the place to emphasize again that "aggressive" is not the antonym of "passive." In its primary meaning, to be "aggressive" denotes the wish to do an injury to someone or something. All wars, for instance, are aggressive whether they are fought offensively or defensively.

These, then, are some of the ways in which women add to their own frustrations, frustrations already great enough by reason of nature, civilization, and the oppression of men. That these frustrations result in compensatory strivings, success in taking the place of men, and leading men's lives in politics, in sports, in business, and even in foreign affairs—this may be said to represent the most favorable and least harmful reaction. More painful to the man are those innumerable attacks upon his masculinity which the frustrated wife inflicts in the course of the daily routine of life, the things that are discussed in every magazine of popular psychology and in every column of advice to the lovelorn—neglecting, reproaching, distrusting, criticizing, ridiculing, interfering with pet hobbies and habits, playing the martyr and giving the impression of being the victim of the husband's suspicion or cruelty, disappointing him in major or minor expectations, improvidence, tardiness, and so on. It seems invidious to make such a list, which must necessarily be not only incomplete but equally applicable to husbands. Aggression is not the monopoly of either sex. The object of aggression is to hurt, to make unhappy, to destroy; and all the techniques available to a woman who is unconsciously hostile toward her husband she will use against him. He will react to them; they will evoke in him still more pronounced evidences of his own semi-controlled hates, and he will modify his infantile pattern of hostility in such a way as to most comfortably meet and defend himself against his wife's attacks. Because he is bound to her by law, by convention, or by his own passivity, he may remain within the bonds of matrimony, but he will find satisfactions for his frustrated love elsewhere. If he does not, his own self-destructiveness will overcome him: he will develop a neurosis, or a psychosis, or a physical illness. In such a case, his wife's attitude will probably be modified toward him. Her guilt feelings and her maternal feelings will be stimulated, which in turn will result in his exploiting the illness.

The same things may happen to the wife but, being less mobile in our society, she is less likely to find opportunities for compensatory love outside the family and will attempt to make up for this deficiency by overstimulating the affections of her children. It is not that she will love them too much, but that she will displace to them a *type* of love which should be reserved for older love objects, and she will do this in such a way as to conceal the unconscious hostility beneath it. She will burden them with her dependent and possessive love.

But while the adult can react in various ways to the woman's aggressions, the little child has no such choice. He can only submit, and suppress his fear and bitterness, burying it beneath his intimidation, where it incubates for twenty years and comes out ten times stronger. What he didn't dare do once, he later dares to do a hundredfold. Who can look fairly at the bitterness, the hatefulness, the sadistic cruelty of Adolf Hitler without wondering what Hitler's mother did to him that he now repays to millions of other helpless ones? We must remind ourselves again and again that the men by whom women are frustrated are the grown-up sons of mothers who were chiefly responsible for the personality of those sons.

Every normal mother wants her son to be a "real boy" and to grow up to be a "big man." But if one asks a mother just what she means by this, one discovers that her ideas tend to be vague and variable. For example, she is glad to see her son indulge in sports; but if his courage goes to the length of exposing him to considerable danger, she is likely to become alarmed and deplore his adventurousness. She wants him to be self-assertive; but if he begins to defy her, she is likely to threaten and punish him. She wants him to be gallant to little girls and pleased with their attractiveness; but if he goes to the length of satisfying his natural curiosity about their anatomy, she is likely to be horrified and feel herself cursed with a perverse offspring.

In other words, the average mother, disciplined as she is by the stern regulations and restrictions of the social order, is constantly in the position of forbidding her little son to develop in precisely the directions in which his masculine instinct impels him, a development which, in principle, she favors.

Some readers will say, "There are limits to the extent to which instincts can be expressed in society, and the child must be taught these limits." That is quite true. But, owing to the pressure of unconscious hostility in the mother, to her own unconscious resentment toward masculinity, to her own sexual repressions, and sometimes to still other causes, the ideals of society are often only an excuse to justify her in the restrictions she puts upon her child. She is more loyal to the ideals of society than to the ideals of personality development in her child. Smothering a child by anxious concern over every detail of his life, robbing him of all opportunities to express himself naturally and to discover the world for

himself, rebuking his early efforts to explore and direct his dawning sexuality—these are more crippling than beatings and curses.
One mother of my acquaintance punished her son cruelly because
he disobeyed her injunction not to stand up to urinate, when he
went to school and found that the other little boys did stand up.
Another mother made her son practise pushing his ears to the side
of his head and squeezing his nostrils together so that he would
not look so much "like a burly nigger" (as she told him). And
another mother put a diaper on her seven-year-old son and exposed him to the ridicule of her friends in order to cure him of
bed-wetting—this being, of course, one of his protests against her
domination. I could fill many pages with similar illustrations. Such
tactics and attitudes rob the child of that sense of masculinity which
he must have in order to love confidently and live constructively.
And against this robbing and suppressing of his masculinity, as
against all other manifestations of hatred by the mother, the growing boy bears a deep resentment. The state of being curbed and
controlled and wounded by a woman is one which breeds in him
an eternal distrust of that woman and of all other women.

To be sure, this interference with his natural pleasures is probably felt to some extent by *every* child, male or female. But when
the necessities of reality adjustment are forced upon the child with
an aggressive technique that bespeaks unconscious, if not conscious, hostility, it arouses particularly bitter resentment. This occurs especially when the mother's unconscious hostility arises from
her envy of her son's masculinity and a wish to rob him of it. Because she is usually not aware of this, she is likely to effect this by
petty and indirect but none the less effective methods, such as
overprotecting him, keeping him in curls, snatching him from the
company of other boys whom she regards as rough or dangerous,
insisting upon perfect manners, and other effeminizations.

That these devices actually do have the effect of crippling the
masculinity of the boy, every psychiatrist knows from clinical experience. It is the sort of thing that has happened in childhood to

men who consult us many years later because of impairments of masculinity which may show themselves in an unsatisfactory sexual life, or more commonly in various attempts to compensate for an unsatisfactory sexual life, such as alcoholism, hypochondriasis, neurotic illnesses, all kinds of marital conflict, and even actual psychoses. Call them the extreme cases if you like, but they are extremes that indicate what I believe to be an increasing trend of a most malignant sort.

The effect upon a boy who grows up with these buried resentments and intimidations is a reduced capacity to love; this in turn thwarts the woman whom he tries to love, and this thwarting increases her resentments. She is bound to show these in her attitude, and thus encourage him to turn for his emotional satisfactions to business activities, clubs, athletic associations, scientific societies, pool halls, bars, poker parties, and so forth. The brotherly camaraderie of men is not so much a proof that love now prevails to a greater extent than in the bellicose days of old, as an evidence that the expression of love is being forced out of its more natural channels. Much as such men may fear and hate one another, they feel safer with each other than with women. Whether one says that this is because less is expected of them in such company, or because they are anxious to be free from the dominance and surveillance of their wives, or because they are positively attracted to one another, it all comes to the same thing.

The danger of such a solution is that men's destructive impulses are not sufficiently neutralized by this mutual interdependence and sooner or later the hate explodes in the form of a fight with someone, and fights turn into wars. That is illustrated by the course of fascistic countries where masculine association is exalted, and where wars become inevitable.[10]

We are left in a seemingly hopeless impasse: the social and economic structure deprives women of satisfaction in their femininity and antagonizes them toward (male) children; the children reflect this in their subsequent associations with other adults and with the next generation; men turn away from women to the company of other men and thwart women further; men and women unite only to go to war with other men and women. What can be done?

At the close of each of the two preceding chapters I made some practical suggestions as to what could be done, but at the close of this chapter I refrain from doing so because I prefer to focus the attention of the reader upon the more general problem. I have tried to delineate the vicious circle which exists in our civilization, a vicious circle which comes about because we forget our childhoods; rather, we think we forget them, but the body remembers. Repression introduces a screen between experience and intelligence so that we act blindly and do not understand until too late. We are at an impasse only if this vicious circle cannot be broken; but I believe that it can be, and the remainder of this book is a blueprint for ways in which I believe that possibility may be realized. The next six chapters are the "practical suggestions."

Chapter 5. Breaking the Vicious Circle

WHEN a man falls down and breaks his leg, we do not rail at the law of gravity even though we recognize that gravity "caused" the fall. If we are practical and proximate and humane, we devote our attention to putting splints on the poor fellow's leg knowing that in time—after a measure of suffering and disability—he will regain its use.

But if we are more than merely practical, if we are foresighted and intelligent, we shall want to do more than this. We shall want to find out more precisely why this man was overcome by gravity at this particular place and at this particular moment. We may learn that he has fallen several times of late, or we may learn that others have fallen at this same spot. We shall want to examine the man's shoes, his habits, and his nervous system. We shall also want to examine the flooring and the lighting. We may even want to put up a sign saying "Watch Your Step."

Most of my professional life has been spent in applying splints. Some of the injured recover; their legs heal, and they walk more carefully thereafter. But this role of standing by and waiting for the next victim to slip and fall and cry out for help before we rush up with our services is not an entirely satisfactory one for the physician. That is why we have turned increasingly to preventive medicine and public health programs. In so far as we can derive principles from our experience with individuals that can be applied to the public weal, it is our duty to report them and to urge their application. To shake our heads and warn people of the seriousness of breaking a leg is not enough. To cry out, "Watch Your Step!" is not enough. To rush up with a pair of splints is not enough.

The trouble is more fundamental than a mere moment of distraction, a careless misstep for which a warning can suffice as a preventive. Accidents don't happen; they are caused, and chance plays a small part in this causation. This is the conclusion of the engineers of the Public Safety Division of the National Safety Council. It is also the conclusion of the psychiatrist from clinical experience, and the same is true of most human ills, including those to which we are now giving our attention. People never just "slip" into trouble—depression, obsession, anxiety, alcoholism, perversion, chronic illness—all the forms of self-destruction. They *march* into trouble as if by inevitable predetermination. And the psychiatrist is like a Cassandra—he knows what is coming and foretells it. He knows even more—he knows *why* it is coming and how it could probably be forestalled. It is his duty to proclaim this.

The four previous chapters have outlined the vicious circle in which man, time, and civilization seem to be hopelessly involved. The crucial question is: *How can this vicious circle be broken?* What can be done through deliberate planning, through the application of intelligence and scientific knowledge, toward the interruption of this self-perpetuating interaction of resentments? What can the thinking man and woman do to counteract the trend of emotional misdirection which engulfs them and their children no less than their parents and grandparents so that today the world is burning up with flames of hate?

Shall we succumb to pessimism and call this a hopeless task? This is what those do who think in terms of fate, nemesis, the will of God, hereditary predestination, and of economic determination. Some of those who believe in the last theory point to the rigidity of the social pattern and remind us of the power of economic pressure. Men and women, they say, are bound by an artificial structure imposed by a ruling class which holds most of us helpless in its grasp. It will be idle to wave all such persons aside as ultrapessimists, for this they are not. Some of them are ultra-optimists: they have a sure solution. Revise the social order, they say, discard the vicious economic system in which we live, and all these troubles will disappear. Men and women will be free; their frustrations will vanish; their love will flow to their children; and their children, like themselves, will grow up in a happier world where hate is unknown.

I wish I could be as optimistic and idealistic as the Marxians, and those who, less revolutionary in their program, believe that one can attack or treat the social order as if it were a biological entity, and make it over into something better by changing its diet. Both those who believe in changing the system from the roots and the less radical but no less articulate enthusiasts for the theory of "social orientation" are relatively free from the superstition that behavior is determined entirely by heredity. But both make the comparable error of overemphasizing the contemporary environment to the neglect of instinctual needs and childhood personality influences.

It is useless to debate such an issue in the opponent's territory because the discussion rapidly reduces itself to a mere statement of conflicting opinions. He can say, for example, that it is pointless to discuss instincts and frustrations, love and hate, sublimations and gratifications, when the economic situation is such that people are hungry; a man cannot think of loving his wife if he is faced with the terror of starvation. This, I concede, is true for collective unemployment, but not in the particular case. That a man does not have a job does not prove that the economic system is a bad one; it is at least equally possible that his not having a job has some relation to his own incapacities—let us even go so far as to say his own self-destructiveness. Such a reply throws my more extreme opponents into a frenzy of exasperation. They regard it as an evidence of total blindness to the suffering of millions, and class me immediately with those calloused exploiters of labor whom they regard as the archdevils of civilization. It is all true to form, they say. "Freud had no social awareness; psychoanalysis is a bourgeois luxury for the amelioration of the bad consciences of the less insensitive exploiters; doctors generally are a selfish, stupid lot, who do not realize that it is futile to work for a price at patching the wounds of a hundred in a battle which is slaughtering millions."

But no economic order ever arose or ever could arise that did not spring from the imaginations and needs and instincts of the human beings it governs. That the present order is a creation of hate more than of love I freely concede. It was built by a race of men who did not fully understand or know how to control the power of hate. But the cultivation of love in the heart of the individual and in his relations with those about him may ultimately change the economic system in which he and they and others live.

"The problem is therefore presented to the men of science to devise a method of generating friendly feelings in the mass of mankind," said Bertrand Russell. "Exhortation has not proved very effective. . . . I have no doubt whatever that methods could be devised for creating a world in which most men had friendly feelings toward other men, but I think rivers of blood will have to flow before the holders of power will allow such a world to be created, and I am doubtful whether rivers of blood are the right kind of rivers to water the tender plant of human kindness." [1]

At first blush it might be thought that everyone subscribes *in theory* to the desirability of such a program. But in the past few years the political direction of three great empires has been based on the contrary principle—the Nietzschean platform that more hate and less love makes for a better world. We in America, like the peoples of China, Britain, and Russia, cling to our belief in what we call democracy, which really only means that we do not favor pushing people around, that we do not exalt hate, and that we do want to love and be loved. "Rotten," "effeminate," "hypocritical," "degenerate," the fascists call it. But we believe in it. We live by it. We fight for it. We die for it.

It is all the more timely, then, to ask the question: How can we achieve democracy, psychologically speaking? How can we bring about better human relationships? What are the methods of cultivating love and increasing our capacities for it? What are the methods available for harnessing or diminishing our hates?

"The voice of the intelligence is weak," said Freud, "but it is persistent." Knowledge of the truth cannot make sudden and revolutionary changes, but to know the truth can help to make us freer, if not exactly free. As clearly as we can see the truth, it is that men and women for their own unconscious purposes frustrate not only each other, but their children. If some of this is, as we believe, unnecessary, it only requires that it be seen clearly for some of the frustration to be abrogated.

The material of the earlier chapters has implied that if we could provide children with a more consistent atmosphere of affection their frustrations would be diminished in number and in intensity and their emotional security would be enhanced so that their subsequent lives would be freer from ebullitions of aggressiveness. The fundamental principle that the capacity for love and hatred is developed in childhood as a result of parental attitudes and behavior is thus of basic importance. So long as people assume that the hatreds of today depend upon events of only yesterday instead of the events of many years ago, they are futilely entangled in a psychological fallacy. Furthermore, most of the injuries to the child occur while the parent is unconscious of the fact that he is inflicting them, and they are also repressed into unconsciousness by the child, so that he, too, "forgets" them. This creates a *terra incognita*. It is a basic principle of modern psychology that to bring something which has been unconscious into the consciousness of a person, whether it be through education or through psychoanalysis, acts therapeutically by broadening the domain of the ego or, to put it in more philosophical terms, by extending the limits of the region in which it is possible to exercise free will.

I hope this explanation will justify the apparent gloominess of the earlier chapters of this book and prove that they are not so nihilistic as they may have sounded but just the opposite. To become aware of our aggressiveness is not only the first but it is also the most important step in correcting it and thus enabling us to re-place it with love. This, in turn, allows us to stimulate a greater development of love reactions and love patterns in those who are most strongly influenced by us, especially our children.

What possibility is there of diminishing or harnessing the aggressive impulses which have already come to dominate the life of the *adult?* Most of us have passed our childhood and are now battling, on the one hand, permanent hostile structures in the framework of civilization and, on the other hand, permanent structures in our own personalities which give rise to incompletely controlled hatred. What can *we* do about our aggressions?

I was once invited to speak to a group of probation officers. As I sat and looked at my audience before being called upon, I turned over in my mind some pictures of their daily work, that of going about the state of New York checking up on paroled prisoners. I compared this professional interest in probation with the unspoken, unrecorded conflicts which I knew must exist within the hearts of these very probation officers themselves, the struggles with envy and insecurity, the aspirations for success, the hopes for promotion. I asked myself, "Who is there that is not 'on probation'? And against what temptations are we on probation? Are we not *all* on probation against the victory of our own aggressions over our efforts to control them?" The ex-prisoner who is on probation is only an exception who failed glaringly once, or twice, or more, and was caught in his failure, caught, tried, punished, and released, and who now needs reinforcement in his good intentions. His aggressions may escape again; and so may ours.

To the extent that we do manage to control ourselves—to the extent that *anyone* controls the forces of hate which a lifetime of frustrations has aroused within him—how do we do it? How does anyone do it? How do we do it at all?

To answer these questions I think we must review once more the life history of the aggressive instinct:

No sooner is a child born than the self-absorption which characterizes the fetal state must begin to disappear. He begins to respond to the irritations of the outside world, meeting them first with hostility, then with tolerance, finally with affection. Irritations are retreated from or are conquered. The child may make these objects a part of himself, and if he does so the constructive outcome of this process is the result of a modification of the original hostile impulses by the infusion of erotic impulses. There remains, of course, much unexpended self-destructive energy, but in the natural order of things, more and more of the aggressive capacity of the growing child is directed outward. At one stage in his development it far exceeds the capacity of his erotic energies to neutralize it. Hence in childhood and adolescence we observe the manifestations of unabashed criminality, savagery, destructiveness. But after this, in the normal course of development, the constructive energies begin to assume dominance. One sees the development of philanthropic impulses, with reaction against all those traits which seemed to dominate the earlier years, and a deflection of aggressive energy toward objects the destruction of which is in the interests of self-preservation. The little criminal becomes the G-man. The jealous sister becomes the protective nurse. The boy who wanted to chop off his little brother's head becomes a surgeon. One of the children at the Southard School who had been sent for treatment because of his compulsion to burn down his father's garage became chief of the fire prevention program. The fundamental psychological motivation in the choice of all the professions arises at this point of reaction-formation. Reaction-formation is in time gradually infused with more directly motivated constructiveness, motivated not so much by undoing evil as by doing good. Evil itself rather than persons felt to be foes becomes the object of the destructiveness, and the individual is then on the threshold of complete maturity.

In the final stage—if it is successfully attained—there is no self-destructiveness. Internally directed aggressiveness disappears completely, and external aggressiveness is directed only toward threatening or existing dangers. The mature love object, in so far as it is selected for its own sake and not as a symbol of some reluctantly abandoned earlier object, receives the unalloyed affection, protection, and confidence of the one-time child, now the mature adult.

This is the schematized natural history of the victory of the life instinct (love) over the death instinct (hate). All aggressive energy except that small quantity necessary for self-defense against real dangers is turned into useful channels and employed in the services of living and loving. Aggression, destructive energy, is thus effectively denatured, and by a shift in object and modality it becomes constructive. This latter process constitutes *sublimation*, as I view it.*

Freud introduced the term but he was never very explicit in his definition of it, so that various concepts of its meaning exist. In the earlier days of psychoanalysis—before the recognition of the destructive energies—it was used in a loose and variable way, which is still reflected in popular attitudes. The idea came to prevail that if one substituted a non-sexual activity for a sexual activity, this represented a process of *enheightenment*, provided it were socially acceptable. But this idea was based on the illusion of an old and

---

* There is a technical point here. Is it sublimation, someone will ask, to shoot a marauder in self-defense or to man a machine gun against the Japanese? This is certainly aggression in the service of living, and in a broad interpretation of the ideas here presented it might be called sublimation. Technically, it would not be sublimation, however, because the aggressive element is not unconscious. Neither is the aggression entirely unconscious, however, when the rancher shoots wolves that prey upon his flock or the orchardist sprays his trees to kill insects. The conscious realization of the destructive element and the variations in zest with which it is accomplished do not alter the fundamental purpose and therefore the real meaning of the destructiveness, however. The feeling of a need for definitely established constructiveness in the ultimate object of the destructiveness is to be seen in the current demand for a definition of our war aims. Dr. Robert Knight has called my attention to the fact that Sergeant York justified his killing of so many of the enemy soldiers, in spite of his conscious conflict over fighting and killing human beings, by saying that it seemed to be the best and quickest way to bring to a close the organized mass murder represented by the war. The fiercer the fighting, the more intense the temporary destructiveness, the less total destructiveness. This may be a rationalization, but it is one with which most of us would agree.

false morality, according to which anything sexual was something low and vile and hence the replacement of it by something non-sexual was morally superior, more "sublime."

But how is it possible to "sublimate" sexuality when sexuality is already the highest and finest thing we know? What we *can* sublimate is our aggressive tendencies, and it is the infusion of sexuality into them which enables this to be accomplished.[2] A woman, for example, who, deprived of her lover, turns to the profession of nursing as a consolation is making a sublimation, but not of her sexual energies as was formerly thought; her sexual energies are enabling her to sublimate her disappointment, her resentment, her destructive impulses. It is these latter impulses which need elevating. Sublimation is always a compromise; it is better to love than to sublimate but better to sublimate than to hate.

If there were no aggressions to be harnessed, sublimations would be unnecessary. We would till the fields or nurse the sick out of pure love, which is just what many people think they are doing. But hate, like the poor, we have always with us and to master it absorbs some of our supply of love. In some individuals it requires so much that a personal love relationship is impossible. Many who have revered the glorious life of Clara Barton interpret it as the substitution of the love of humanity for the love of a man who died. What they forget is that she repeatedly rejected this lover through a feeling of inadequacy to the demands of a love relationship. (Abraham Lincoln's love history was somewhat similar.)

The normal individual, then, might be described as one who is able to invest his love in a full and satisfying way in certain direct objects—primarily, his wife and children; secondarily, a group of intimate friends, the larger group of society (not vaguely but specifically, in practical humanitarian activities); and, finally, such non-human love objects as are available and meaningful to him. At the same time he will have invested (sublimated) his aggressions in ways which will protect, support, and foster a fuller realization of these loves. As a practical matter, one may say that if the aggressions are well invested, well controlled by a sufficient infusion of erotic elements, well "sublimated," the love life will take care of itself.

Here we have much to learn from the empirical observations of psychoanalysts. As I have related in *Man Against Himself*, the dynamic processes in psychoanalytic therapy can be described as the establishment of a situation in which the aggressions which have failed of sublimation are redirected. They have previously been misdirected either toward the individual himself in the form of self-destruction or toward elements in the environment which were undeserving of such attacks, and they are now temporarily permitted to find expression toward a person (the analyst) sufficiently objective not to retaliate or even to discourage such expressions. Rather, he assists the patient to recognize the inappropriateness of his investments of hate and to enlist the aid of his unfettered intelligence in finding more expedient and controlled directions for his love and hate. Patients first gain the courage to heap upon the analyst a full measure of their scorn, bitterness, resentment, and unreasoning hate, and then, gradually, gain the courage and the insight to direct this energy into more logical, more fruitful channels. The better investment of this hate enables the previously inhibited love impulses to be expressed directly, also, and to aid in mitigating, altering, and fructifying the aggressive energy.

This basic psychoanalytic principle is used constantly in modern psychiatry aside from the use of psychoanalysis as a treatment method. The technical ways in which this is done with patients * need not occupy us here, but the fact that it *is* done is important

* My brother, William C. Menninger, has devoted himself to the study of this problem for years and has classified some of the techniques in numerous scientific articles.[3] In psychiatric practice emphasis is placed on initiating activities which enable the patient to disperse his aggressions in socially approved ways. This method is preferable for individuals who cannot accept deep psychological insight into their destructiveness.

to know since it guarantees the validity of the principle that such a rearrangement of instinctual expression is possible, granted sufficient opportunity and a sufficient degree of insight on the part of the individual himself.

In tracing the final distribution of the aggressive tendencies or destructive instinct, we should make mention of that peculiarly human phenomenon, the conscience. According to psychoanalytic theory, the conscience is an internalized censor, exercising an influence upon the decisions of the ego similar to the voice of the parents and teachers in childhood. A part of it appears to be conscious, and holds up certain ideals; but judging from consequences, it is certain that a larger part of it is unconscious and acts in a punitive, bargaining, often cruel and dishonest way. This is not the place for an extended discussion of the super-ego and ego-ideal, more technical terms for the unconscious and conscious consciences, respectively. But it is important to stress the fact that the power exerted by this disparate portion of the ego is supplied by the aggressive instinct.[4] As I have explained in *Man Against Himself*, it is as if certain criminals in a community had reformed and turned policemen. For this reason, highly conscientious people (for example, Cotton Mather) are so often cruel, harsh, destructive people. They are often even more severe with themselves than with others, although this seems less important to the world. The time will surely come when the supposed virtues of conscientiousness will be more carefully scrutinized and the superiority of intelligence over blind (and corruptible) conscience more generally acknowledged. At present, however, this is too much to expect—the more so when one recalls how religious systems have grown and thrived on the exploitations of a (false) sense of guilt inculcated by a cultivated conscience.

We may summarize, then, the fate of the aggressive energy in the theoretical "normal" person in whom it has been properly neutralized by love thus: Some of it has been completely repressed; some is expressed directly in self-defense or protection of others;

some is expressed in sublimations; some is internalized as "conscience." In the less normal individual we would have to allow for the portion which is directly expressed against others as cruelty, theft, murder, provocativeness, and the like, as well as that which is directed back against the self as depression, neurosis, and suicide.

In the following chapters we shall consider the ways in which the aggressive tendencies may be more expediently directed or, as we can say now, sublimated. These "normal" expedient ways are, as will shortly be apparent, very ancient and well known. They are simply Work and Play. But we must also seek to discover the ways in which love can be better invested, for only to the extent that we love do we live, and only love can combat the trend toward a return to the inorganic silence from which we have temporarily emerged. In support of love, we have Faith and Hope. Thus the keys to the rupture of the vicious circle are Work and Play; Faith, Hope, and Love.

Chapter 6. Work

OF ALL the methods available for absorbing the aggressive energies of mankind in a useful direction, work takes first place. It may
not be the oldest, it certainly is not the most pleasant. But it has a
certain realistic quality which makes it seem the most practical and
obvious of all sublimations. Almost everyone would accept it as
self-evident that we must work in order to live; not everyone believes that we must play in order to live, or that we must have
something to believe in or to love.

Furthermore, the connections of work with the destructive
instinct are close and clear. It is easy to see that all work represents
a fight against something, an attack upon the environment. The
farmer plows the earth, he harrows it, tears it, pulverizes it; he
pulls out weeds, or cuts them, or burns them; he poisons insects
and fights against drought and floods. To be sure, all this is done
in order to create something, for which reason we can call it work
and not rage. The destructiveness is, so to speak, specialized or
selectively directed, and a net "product" is obtained. But even
this product must be torn or cut from its producing matrix by
dint of more labor, transported by labor to other places for storage
or consumption, prepared for use as food or clothing by still
further destructive energy. It is cut, crushed, scorched, torn,
burned, boiled, twisted, combed, exposed to the sun and air for
desiccation. The construction of sheltering granaries requires the
destruction of trees or the splitting and avulsion of rocks and
the reassembly of the fragments into an artificial structure. The
forging of tools or weapons, the making of clothes, even the fabri-
cation and hoarding of money, the symbol of value, require the
expenditure of aggressive energy.

One could carry the illustration further into the realms of mastering the sea and the air, or forcing earth, clay, or metal into molds, or creating energy by burning carbon, or slaughtering animals for food and clothing. In every instance it is the same: destructive energy is applied to a constructive goal through discriminating between the desirable and the undesirable, and encouraging the former by eliminating or suppressing or altering the latter.

The reader may feel a little taken in by the selection of these examples; he may think rather of such illustrations as the work of the housepainter, the seamstress, the lawyer, or the banker—which do not seem to be so obviously destructive. I admit that there is room for argument at this point. Some of my colleagues [1] feel that we must distinguish another element in work, best described as an impulse toward mastery—controlling, re-forming, organizing, directing, etc. They believe that such an impulse is an instinctual striving to use the powers of mind and body and is not motivated by love or hate. But to me this urge to master something, whether it be a mechanical puzzle or a complicated accounting problem or a recalcitrant horse, seems to be indistinguishable in its *essence* from the aggressive, destructive impulse, purposively and expediently directed. To the extent that something is mastered, some kind of resistance is broken down or overcome. Of course the destructiveness of the whaler is different from that of the lumberman, and the destructiveness of the lumberman is different from that of the miner, and that of the miner is different from that of the surgeon; but all of them are working *against* something in an effort to master a situation or a material and to produce something in the end. It is the modification of this destructive energy in such a way as to achieve this creation of something that distinguishes work from wanton destructiveness.

It may furthermore be objected that it is not always love that modifies the aggressive energies in such a way as to make them useful and fruitful. Hunger, the need for protection against the elements, the fear of approaching enemies—these would seem to be the more immediate determinants of the labors described. Man must eat to live and he must work to eat, we are reminded. But this objection loses sight of the broader concept of love that is implied in this discussion, just as the other objection takes too narrow a view of aggression. This is the old stumbling block in the psychoanalytic theory of twenty years ago, a stumbling block that for many years confused even Freud's thinking. For one cannot fruitfully divide the function of love as applied to the fostering of one's own life, and love as applied to the fostering of another's. Love is the reflection of the instinct of life, and the love of ourselves is of the same texture as the love of others; it is the love of life itself. What man does to survive is dictated by the same love that dictates his compulsion to continue the race. The immediate emotional stimulus may be fear, or anger, or curiosity, or cupidity, or the desire for warmth and peace and caresses, but the instinct is the same.

So we shall not linger over these objections. The essential point is that in work, as contrasted with purposeless destruction, the aggressive impulses are molded and guided in a constructive direction by the influence of the creative (erotic) instinct.

Savage man's first work was killing. He hunted and killed men and beasts. Closely allied to this work was worship, which consisted of sacrifice and efforts to propitiate the gods and to forestall *their* aggressions. With the development of social organization, certain important changes took place. Mutual agreements had to be made between individuals for purely selfish reasons, to impose some restrictions upon indiscriminate destruction. According to Freud's concept, it was the father of the primitive horde who ended the rule of complete individualism and by means of his prohibitions directed the destructive energies toward constructive ends. These ends might be considered constructive primarily from *his*, the ruler's, standpoint; they were enforced through his power and for his purposes. True, they also contributed to the personal advantage of the individual members of the group since they enabled them to concentrate destructive energies against foes. But discipline, obedience, the postponement of personal gain for communal good, and the restriction of destruction to certain specified objects were probably initiated by force, and while they afforded personal advantages to the individual they were accepted only with resentment. This resentment against the power of authority is still to be seen in the way in which work tends to be regarded as a necessary evil. Work became dissociated from pleasure to the extent that it became dissociated from individual initiative. The conception of work as drudgery which everyone experiences to some extent, and which some persons experience in a very high degree, is bound up with this resistance to authority. In the course of time, with the development of society, this authority became introjected, and work—which had formerly been a free outpouring of aggressive energies—became surrounded with a certain sentimental, sacrificial halo. It was described as ennobling and considered an end in itself. But it was still *"work."*

Aversion to work does not spring solely from resentment against its necessity. If we ask ourselves just what it is in work that makes for drudgery, some of us might say it is monotony; others might say that it is the entailment of pain or muscular exertion—or the impossibility of seeing tangible results—or its lack of connection with any creed or purpose or the feeling of being exploited by an unfeeling management—or the sense of isolation and lack of congenial companionship. All these factors are probably present.[2] It would be interesting to examine how it came about that some people must do continuously what seems chiefly drudgery, while other people are able to do what seems to be pleasurable and even delightful work, if indeed it can be called work at all. Some anthropologists explain this by the theory that it was originally a question of physical power: men preferred the labor of hunting, and they were stronger than women, so they made the women (and the slaves) do the cooking, the firebuilding, and the other things that they (the men) didn't "like" to do. "Work only tires a woman, but it ruins a man," runs an old African proverb. Others explain the specialization as the consequence of some sort of instinctual predilection, as discussed in the chapter on femininity. Marxians, of course, explain it on the basis of economic determinism and the power of accumulated capital (or, prior to the capitalistic period, some other form of organized power). Psychologists in the past explained it on the basis of intellectual capacity. This theory was very flattering, and—while it remained current—certain stupid but financially successful persons made the most of it. Probably all of these factors have entered into the differentiations in quality of specialized labor. Thorstein Veblen [3] and many others have analyzed this problem in recent years with varying conclusions.

The very multiplicity of theories to explain the painfulness of work suggests that none of them is adequate. We may venture, therefore, to add another interpretation in line with our psychological theories. Perhaps we could define drudgery as that form or aspect of work in which the satisfaction of the aggressive element is not combined with sufficient erotization to give some degree of conscious satisfaction in the work itself. The satisfaction in work may be related to the product, as for example the pleasure an artisan receives from making a beautiful vase or an author from writing a good book. Or it may be related to the approval received from a superior, or the feeling that the work has been done for his sake. Or the pleasure may be derived chiefly from a sense of cooperation, companionship, *esprit de corps*, brotherhood. Finally it may be derived from some erotization of the actual techniques involved in the performance of the labor itself.* I remember a charwoman who used to get a most evident pleasure out of her daily floor-scrubbing. It was not only that she took pride in the

---

* Bernfeld and Hendrick (*ops. cit.*) make much of this last point as the basis of satisfaction in artisanship, craftsmanship, skill in painting, etc.

thoroughness of her cleansing, or in the compliments she received from people who praised her assiduousness: she actually *liked* to swash around in the suds and would attack the dirty floors with something of the vehement pleasure portrayed in the advertisements for Old Dutch Cleanser. Yet what could be worse drudgery for the average person than floor-scrubbing? All of the above are ways in which the erotic instinct can actually neutralize the destructive elements in the work sublimation.

If work is done only by compulsion, external or internal, if it gives none of the pleasures just mentioned, it is felt to be drudgery, and it is not a complete sublimation. "Take, for instance, the housewife's occupation: cleaning and so on certainly bear witness to her desire to make things pleasant for others and for herself, and as such are a manifestation of love for other people and for the things she cares for. But at the same time she also gives expression to her aggression in destroying the enemy, dirt, which in her unconscious mind has come to stand for 'bad' things. The original hatred and aggression derived from the earliest sources may break through in women who make life miserable for the family by continuously 'tidying up'; there the hatred is actually turned against the people she loves and cares for." [4] In other words, the sublimation breaks down.

Although these principles might seem to be almost self-evident, it is astonishing to discover what widely divergent opinions prevail on the subject of work. In an age when billions of dollars are spent in promoting efficiency and increased production, an age when work has been exalted to being the justification of existence, it is almost unbelievable how consistently the basic requirements of work are overlooked. The psychological prerequisite of successful labor is dimly perceived and poorly manipulated even by those for whom it is a problem of paramount importance. Consider the stupid and costly blunders of industry in relation to manpower. The organization of labor against its employers furnishes workers with a closely knit brotherhood and a formidable enemy upon whom they can project all their aggressions. The men in power see this as a menace and attempt to make their position more secure by fighting; but in doing so they are forced to yield ground because of the losses they incur in decreased production. The stiffer the opposition, the stronger waxes the battle, until much of the energy which would otherwise go into production of goods is deflected into personal warfare. That some of this waste is unavoidable is probably true, for the aggressive instinct seems never to be satisfied with entirely impersonal objectives. But that it may be redirected toward other ends is shown by the way in which labor difficulties become unpopular during war when employers and employees unite against a common foe. This is what has happened in England and in Russia; it is beginning to develop belatedly in our own country. The feeling of brotherhood among workers is intensified and their hostilities are directed against national enemies.

Personal psychology has been so discredited in the entire set-up of industry, and the profit motive has been assumed to be so powerful and all-controlling, that satisfaction in work has come to be assessed entirely in terms of wages and hours, not only by employers but by the employees themselves. Yet, from the standpoint of psychology, the recurring industrial and economic depressions might seem, in some degree, the result of profound dissatisfactions and disappointments in work, on the part of both employers and employees. When psychology has been applied to industry, it has too often been patronizingly used as an aggressive tool to perpetuate or feebly patch certain obvious evils. We pay only lip service to the idea of increasing production and profits by constructive reorganization of workers and redirection of aggressions, and both sides look hopefully to the government for redress and support.

An extraordinarily important study of a small group of workers in the Western Electric Company was made by some psychologists.[5] For five years productivity was checked daily and compared with all sorts of conditions affecting the employees—their health, their working conditions, their home conditions, their attitudes, and their general morale. Of the many conclusions the most pertinent to the present theme is the fact that no matter what changes were made in working conditions, in management techniques, in hours of labor, etc., if the change was made with the manifest purpose of benefiting the workers, efficiency and production were immediately and markedly stimulated. Reducing this to the simple terms of our thesis, we would say that, prosaic though it may sound, fostering the affection of workers for an employer is more important than any specific concession or regulation, because it permits more complete sublimation of the aggressive impulses which otherwise "leak out" in the form of resentment against the employer.

Economists do not deny that disturbances in industry are based on fundamental human conflicts. The dynamic nature of these conflicts is a legitimate study for psychiatrists, but these have confined themselves largely to the study of individuals and to neurotic attitudes toward work in the individual. The inability to play brings some persons to the psychiatrists; the inability to work brings many more. It is from the study of these that the general principles enunciated above were derived. Some case illustrations may make them more convincing.

2

The function of work in the management of aggression was very clear in the case of Alan McLore. He was born in a poverty-stricken Scottish home, but left his family and came to this country at the age of fourteen because there was insufficient food for all of the children. By dint of persistency and hard work, he obtained a B.S. degree, and by gradual stages became one of the technical advisers to a large tire-manufacturing company. Here he came to be held in high respect by the management and the workers; the former recognizing his ability and the latter appreciating his honesty and friendliness. He was an indefatigable worker, arriving at his laboratory very early in the morning and often working late into the night, although this was not required of him in his contract nor expected of him by his superiors. He had held this position for twenty years when I first saw him.

The ostensible reason for his seeking psychiatric advice was his depression. He was sure that there was nothing either in his private life or in his work to account for it. He was happily married, he was fond of his children, and he had complete economic security. He liked his work and was, as I have said, successful and appreciated. In spite of all this, he woke up each morning feeling very much fatigued. He went to work reluctantly, doubtful of his ability to solve the problems before him, a doubt which was not supported by past experience. He felt incapable of turning out as much work as he should. To be sure, as the day wore on, his fatigue diminished rather than increased, but he felt constantly obliged to force himself to work, and he noticed all sorts of interference with what ought to be smooth and almost automatic performances. For example, he thought he could not set up his laboratory equipment satisfactorily and would get his assistants to do it; he could not dictate letters and would have to write them in longhand, only to be dissatisfied with them and tear them up. He could not read his technical journals and found himself increasingly turning to what he had previously regarded as light and trashy literature. He began to be obsessed with the fear that he was obtaining money (his salary) under false pretenses—that he wasn't worth it. Then physical symptoms appeared, and he began the rounds of various physicians who attempted to link his depression and work difficulties with some physical cause. He was treated for gastric ulcer, high blood pressure, glandular disorders, allergy, prostate enlargement, and many other things, none of which treatments did him any good.

Any psychiatrist will recognize this picture. It is the sort of thing for which patients constantly go to doctors, to religion, to faith healing, or on trips. For such a patient is never depressed about what he *thinks* he is depressed about, nor sick in the way he thinks he is. He does not know what he is depressed about; he only knows that he feels badly and cannot work. Sometimes he thinks he is depressed because he cannot work, only to be told by the psychiatrist that he cannot work because he is depressed.

The full explanation of such problems is this: Such people suffer from prodigiously strong aggressive impulses which, by long-time training in self-discipline, by persistent application, and by meticulous compliance with the demands of necessity, they learn to manage by means of complete absorption in work. Almost invariably they do not know how to play; they regard recreation as something trivial, even wicked; they do more work than economic necessity dictates and accept less compensation for their work than it deserves. They have a meager, unsatisfactory love life which they do not enjoy. On the other hand, they drive themselves to overwork and think they enjoy it. Indeed they do enjoy it more than they would enjoy the anxiety that they would suffer if it were not possible for them to express their aggressions in this way. This kind of work, however, is not a true sublimation; or perhaps we should say it is not all sublimation—it is partly compulsion. By compulsion I mean that it is no longer an automatic and comfortable conversion of the aggressive energy into useful channels; it is partly a neurotically determined attempt to over-exploit this device and thus to overtax it. The trouble with the device is that it never quite suffices; and unexpressed aggressions gradually accumulate and are aggravated by the resentment incidental to the overwork until they threaten to break through into consciousness. These persons are characteristically unable to express this aggression directly, and so they turn back upon themselves the excess of aggressive energy. This state of affairs makes itself evident by suffering (depression, physical ills), by self-effacement, by self-abnegation, and in a particularly vicious way by actual interference with the previous method of cloaking the aggressions, the work sublimation.

Such breakdowns in a previously workable pattern probably arise not only because of accumulating unexpressed aggression but also because of some unperceived emotional disturbances to which such persons are particularly vulnerable. Although Mr. McLore had always been greatly admired by his superiors, his equals and his inferiors, he was so busy working that he had no very warm friends among any of them. In fact, he seemed so wrapped up in his work that he was not taken into the confidence of the management as much as he should have been or as much as he wanted to be, but he was the last man on earth to complain about this neglect. He had not even permitted his resentment to enter into his consciousness more than slightly. It is a great pity that he was unable to allow it to come not only into consciousness but to vocal expression, since in the light of subsequent developments there is no doubt that he would have been given more than he had even hoped for.

What brought things to a culmination was a change in the policy of the company which involved a shift in the direction of Alan McLore's researches. Intellectually, he approved of this change, but felt slighted at being told about it only after it had been decided on. He felt that this had been done without a sufficient consideration of whether or not he would be able to function successfully. He interpreted this as an indication that he was not fully appreciated, and supported this idea with the fact that his salary had not been increased in ten years, although the company had made a great deal of money. He had never said a word about this, either; but, as he afterwards learned (when he had been brought to the point where he could discuss his feelings frankly with the vice-president in charge), he had been a victim of his own silence, since the management had characteristically assumed that he was satisfied and did not expect any increase. In fact, he had several times said this very thing, and such was his reputation for honesty that no one suspected he was actually being dishonest with himself on this point.

One can see how incorrect it would be to say that such a man was unable to work because he was depressed, or depressed because unable to work, and also how incorrect it would be to say that everything could have been straightened out by a salary increase. He was absolutely incapable of accepting an increase—it would only have made him feel more than ever that he was not earning what he was paid. The nucleus of the problem was that for this man the sublimative function of work was overtaxed. The feeling of not being appreciated and of not getting his deserts began, of course, in his childhood which had been a very hard and bitter period. For some years a successful method of sublimating these resentments held them in check and incognito; ultimately they became too strong and threatened to overwhelm the protective barrier. It was then that the emergency defenses of depression, self-depreciation, and physical illness were called upon—and this is what we see as the illness.

When from time to time I read in the *New Yorker* the profile of some successful man, who by dint of hard work has risen above a modest station in life to great wealth, power, and influence, I think of the many case profiles that I have known in my practice which ended in a different way. After similarly achieving success, they have attempted to retire, to reap the fruits of leisure, only to collapse physically or mentally, and often to proceed to an untimely death. Nothing shows better than this phenomenon how necessary work is for psychological reasons quite apart from economic reasons.

I recall, for example, the case of Sam Snow. If I were to tell the literal truth about him, he would be recognized by many readers, and in disguising his identity I shall have to detract from his actual accomplishments. But when I first saw him he was propped up on cushions on a chaise longue in a luxurious hotel suite. His face was distorted with pain, pain which many medical consultations had failed to relate to any organic pathology. Nurses and servants at his beck and call hovered about. Relatives, some of them anxious, some of them bored, some of them frankly antagonistic, had adjoining rooms or were in touch with him by telephone and messenger.

I had heard of Sam Snow, his extraordinary accomplishments in business and finance, his shrewdness and wisdom and wealth, and I was ill-prepared to see such a pitiful specimen of a man. When I came into the room he extended his hand wearily but greeted me with almost childish wistfulness. He began immediately to describe the incredible suffering he was experiencing. He placed his hand on various parts of his body. In vague but very emphatic terms he attempted to convey some idea of the pain that he was suffering. He assured me that no one realized what he had been going through, that his pulse was racing, his heart was about to burst, his bowels were "clogged-up," pain shot through his chest like a knife, his limbs were tingling as if they had been struck by a club; he was about to have a mental breakdown from pain that no one believed he actually suffered. A score of doctors had seen him, but none had been able to relieve him. A famous clinic had studied his case and had pronounced it (as he repeated over and over) the only one of its kind in existence. A great New York specialist had called Mr. Snow the sickest man he had ever seen.

I learned that in spite of his constant preoccupation with his "nervous breakdown," "unendurable pain," and imminent death, he ate well, smoked big cigars regularly, watched the clock so as to be in the bathroom for a bowel movement at precisely eight o'clock on the dot, and immediately afterwards began begging for a laxative, and then for other medicines. If these were not forthcoming he grew very much provoked, and inflicted his petulance upon all who hovered about him, insisting that they were not trying to help him, did not want him to get well, did not believe that he was ill. After great urging he could be persuaded to go out for a short walk but would spend most of the time clamoring to return to his apartment.

I could give a great many more details of this picture, combining as it does elements of comedy and tragedy. The impression that the layman gets from such cases is that of malingering and fraud. But this man was not fraudulent—he was indeed one of the sickest men I have ever seen, though his sickness was not organic.

Sam Snow was sixty-two at the time I saw him. He had manufactured more (let us say) agricultural implements than any other man in the world. Besides factories in many of the civilized countries of the world, he owned coal mines, lumber yards, virgin timber forests, and I do not know what else. I suspect that he himself had only a general idea of the precise extent of his possessions; as a matter of fact, he was not at all interested in them.

As a boy he had been forced to leave high school to go to work, and got a job at nine dollars a week on a delivery truck. In a short time he was made shipping clerk, then foreman of another department in the plant, and so on and so on. He worked very, very hard. He never participated in any sports or developed any hobbies; he did not even develop any social life. He married almost in haste when he was about twenty-seven and was divorced by his wife a few years later. After his marriage he worked even more diligently, was so seclusive and silent that his associates began to call him "Silent Sam," a nickname which he kept for the rest of his life.

From this point on, his rise in business was like that of many other tycoons. To every new development or new task he applied prodigious energy and intensity. Owing to his lack of educational background, which he felt keenly, he resolved to study Latin and Greek, and acquired a reading knowledge of both. In the course of establishing branch plants in France he made an intensive study of the French language so that in six months he was able to read French newspapers and books as easily, he claimed, as he could English. He learned German and Italian also. Because the manufacture of a certain chemical product was related in an important way to his business, and because he had never studied chemistry, he decided that he must know something about that and plunged into this pursuit so intensively that he became a fairly proficient research chemist and obtained a patent on a chemical process that he discovered. He was always very proud of his physical strength, although his physique was not outstandingly good; he refused to use automobiles to go to work in or even to survey his properties, and frequently walked thirty miles in one day. He did not know what fatigue was. At the age of fifty-three he took up golf and by dint of characteristic application and persistency became skilful enough to play in the low eighties and twice made the eighteen holes in seventy strokes.

Many other such astounding accomplishments could be mentioned, but my intention is only to convey the idea that even his play this man turned into drudgery. He had to work at everything and work hard. It was his ruling passion to master things. In the matter of golf, for example, I was told that he practised the use of the mashie for ten hours a day for twenty-one days without a break, without touching any other club, and without leaving the spacious front lawn of his estate. He bought five hundred golf balls and stood in one spot and worked away patiently until he had perfected the stroke.

His nephew told me that he remembered that as a little boy, when he went to see his uncle, he was very much terrified because, while the uncle was generous and definitely interested in the lad, he would immediately begin plying him with questions about his history, arithmetic, chemistry, or whatever happened to interest Snow at the moment. Then he would nervously exhort the boy to "get busy" at one or another of the sports available on the estate, and if he demurred at such vigorous play his uncle would become disgusted and call him a "sissy."

It was this man who had attempted to retire from active work at the age of fifty-eight. He turned over the management of most of his businesses to various of his older employees and set out to put into action some of the plans he had long been making for his old age; but none of them worked. Golf began to bore him. His country estate was already groomed and decorated to perfection, so that there was nothing more to do with it. He could find no one his own age who was equal to the mountain-climbing he enjoyed, and he did not like to go alone. He had been so busy working that he had very few social friends, and he did not know how to entertain, being opposed to drinking and to games of chance. He had traveled all his life in the course of his business and felt restless and uncomfortable when away from home. Time hung heavily on his hands.

Then he began to get sick—not seriously sick at first, but with minor symptoms that preoccupied him and drove him from doctor to doctor and from hospital to health resort to be "put in shape" for entering upon the program of leisure and retirement which he had looked forward to all these years. But, instead of growing better, he grew progressively worse. He found fault with every doctor and with every treatment suggested. He became increasingly irritable, gloomy, obsessed with the idea that his heart was about to stop or that his body was being riddled with ominous pains. Convinced that his children were unsympathetic, he would stay in a hotel when he was not in a sanitarium, writing dismal and reproachful letters to them, the purport of which was that he was a very sick man, almost at death's door, and that his family evidently did not care at all and probably even hoped he would die so that they could be rid of him and have all his money. If relatives came to see him and spoke encouragingly or urged him to go out, he accused them of being blind to his infirmities; if they stayed away, he accused them of being neglectful. All the tremendous energies which had constructed a gigantic commercial empire were now engaged in a melancholy civil war with no peace in sight.

I am sorry I cannot report that Sam Snow's aggressive energies

were redirected by psychiatric techniques to satisfactory sublimations—in short, that he got well. A man who has struggled with
such terrific aggressions and who managed them only by dint of
enormous sublimatory efforts and domination of himself and
others had eventually reached the place where he could no longer
continue at this rate and was more and more in danger of being
overwhelmed. It was too painful and dangerous for him to face
this. He preferred to continue to run away.

3

The average person may suppose that when patients come to a
sanitarium for the treatment of what appear to be relatively mild
maladjustments, the great problem is how to keep them busy,
how to fill their leisure time. It will probably astonish many,
therefore, when I say that the great problem in every well-con-
ducted sanitarium is how to get the patients to do *anything!* The
place may offer ten times as much to do as the average patient can
bring himself even to attempt; but, despite all the efforts of the
medical director, the medical staff, the nursing staff, and the
therapists—despite schedules and regulations and exhortations—
some patients manage to evade with an uncanny skill every opportunity for amusement, recreation, exercise, constructive craft work,
and all the other devices so carefully planned for them. At the
moment I am thinking of a rather characteristic example—the son
of the president of a large manufacturing concern. Although the
patient had an older brother, he expected ultimately to succeed his
father as head of this business. However, when he reached the age
of thirty-five he had never stuck consistently at any task. Several
times he had worked briefly in the executive offices of his father's
plant, but he soon became irritated at what he regarded as his
father's bad management and either engaged in sharp arguments
with his father or abandoned his duties for an alcoholic debauch
or an extended loaf in California or Florida. He came to the

sanitarium for treatment because of severe headaches which were recognized by his physicians to be emotional in origin and related to his terrific rage against his father—a rage which, while not entirely unjustified at times, was scarcely becoming in this indolent son.

It was easily recognizable that his indolence, like his headaches, was the result of an emotional reaction of fear and hate directed toward his father. But it was interesting to see how this attitude was carried out during his sanitarium residence. Although he was very anxious to get well and worked earnestly and co-operatively at any treatment that was immediately supervised by the physician —including, for example, his psychoanalytic interviews—everything else about the sanitarium he considered negligible. Time after time he reiterated his eagerness to get well and to go home. For many months during his treatment it was only rarely that he would turn his hand to doing anything constructive, even when urged by the physicians to do so for his own health. He would walk five or ten miles a day for exercise but would not lift a spadeful of dirt or make a single puppet; he would play tennis occasionally but he would never roll the tennis courts. He would play bridge until he had a blinding headache, but he would not set up a bridge table or manage a tournament for the pleasure of the other guests. Although his education needed supplementing in many particulars, he refused to attend any classes. During the first ten months of his stay he spent altogether only four hours in the craft and carpentry shops.

Toward the end of his treatment, when the energy locked up by his inhibitions began to be released, he began to take increasing interest in the very things he had so long avoided. It is a frequently observed paradox that when a patient really begins to take full advantage of the opportunities of psychiatric treatment he is approaching the time when he is able to give it up and return home.

Exceptional cases often illustrate a phenomenon more vividly than do more representative run-of-the-mill cases. Perhaps three-fourths of the patients who come to psychiatrists are suffering from an incapacitating impairment of their satisfaction in work or their ability to work. In many it is their chief complaint; in the case of a woman I shall call Mrs. Scoville Mayer, it was practically the only complaint. Let me quote from her first letter:

> I am by profession and inclination a fiction writer. For a dozen years I have followed this with happiness and extreme satisfaction. I have written and published a dozen novels and several hundred short stories. Now I find myself in the distressing position of being no longer able to write, though actually I have never been so well equipped for the job nor so desirous of accomplishing it.
>
> What my family physician actually thinks about it I have no means of knowing, but he has told me to travel. A good portion of my adult life has been put in doing just that, and I am very fond of it so that it is not an unpleasant prescription. But I have given it a thorough trial and I still cannot write; yet my mind generates the same amount of energy that in past years went into a tremendous production of word-age, the difference being that now it somehow stays inside and I suffer from what I can only describe as a tension that is at times quite unendurable.

Her letter goes on to describe some of the various types of treatment to which she has submitted. A thorough examination of Mrs. Mayer showed that she had very high blood pressure but no other physical symptoms. So far as she knew she had no anxieties or other "mental" symptoms except the tension she had described and her depression at being unable to use her talents.

In order to give a clear picture of just how she felt at this time I want to quote from something she wrote subsequently describing it:

> I had possessed a clear, direct thinking mechanism. I could look over the immediate situation, realize it at a glance, see exactly what was to be done, and set about the doing of it. I could do a number of things at once. By which I mean I had organizing ability. I could think ahead, take things in as a whole, arrange them in my mind, and set them all

into motion. I had been quite contemptuous of those poor, ineffectual people who could only stumble from one thing to another, and never more than one thing at a time.

As a means of destroying egotism, my experience was unsurpassed. My inability to accomplish a task was stupendous. And I was so bewildered by it. I struggled so hard to regain my old competence. My struggling was so useless. As useless as everything else.

I could not spread a blanket over the couch without a great deal of difficulty. I could not handle it. It seemed literally possessed of a vicious life of its own, that was stubbornly opposed to my will. I could not prepare a simple luncheon unless I started very early and worked very, very hard.

The simple act of sewing a button on a shirt assumed for me colossal magnitude. And that is how it was. I worked desperately for an hour and a half to thread a needle, pick up a tiny button, place it against a piece of material, insert the needle, draw it through, repeat the process—

I cried in sheer desperation and rage because I could not accomplish such a simple thing. And at the end of the day, and long before, I was exhausted to the point of despair.

Instead of giving a running account of this woman's childhood, I shall describe what happened in the course of her contacts with me. At first she was just as helpless as she describes herself. She was pleasant and co-operative but quite unable to give me any consistent explanation of her volitional paralysis. After a few days, during which she had roughly sketched the main outline of her life, she told me that her mind was preoccupied with a name which meant nothing to her but which kept recurring over and over. It was "Horatio." She had thought of "Horatio at the Bridge" (really "Horatius"), of "Horatio Alger" who wrote so much, of "Her ratio" as possibly referring to her failure to accomplish as much as her brother, who was also engaged in creative work. But none of this was very convincing. Suddenly she expressed herself as strangely disinclined to talk and asked if she might have a pencil and paper. I gave them to her and she began to draw strange lines and figures and scribblings without paying much attention to what she was doing. Presently she began to write some short sentences in a large, childish script that was not at all like her natural hand-writing. When she had finished a page of this and was about to leave, I asked her to read it. She did so with considerable bewilderment since what she had written made no sense to her whatever, nor could she identify the handwriting.

The next day she came in and we discussed the curious phenomenon of her automatic writing of the day before. She said that it was a new experience for her, although she had read about it; she was rather pleased that she had been able to write anything at all, and she thought she would like to try it again.

I have many hundreds of pages of the manuscripts which she wrote in my office in this peculiar way during the next few weeks. From these I shall cite only two or three passages which will serve to illustrate in a somewhat skeletal way the nature of her work inhibitions. On the third day, after some rather vague material that I shall omit, her writing went on to describe a very severe illness which she had apparently had as a child and during which she was highly feverish and delirious.

And those street-cars ran through my brain Every seven and a half minutes I could hear them coming I could feel them coming coming coming rushing toward me roaring toward me—grinding on the curve running straight into my brain I wanted to scream maybe I did I don't know I don't believe I did I do not scream any better than I cry I wish I could scream I have screamed in my mind many times but never outloud when the Dr Blank raised the curtain that time Oh why did he do that The light hurt my eyes when it was down and he stood there looking at me lying unconscious on the bed unconscious I Oh no I knew everything I heard them I saw them I saw him and I didn't like his white clothes then he reached over and shot up the curtain that awful white sunlite came in It was like Knives through my eyes It was torture I screamed and screamed and screamed but no one heard me It was all inside inside inside Don't stop me don't stop me Let me write please let me write I shall never live long enough to write all I wish to write but please please let me write Don't make me talk Just let me write Let me say what is inside my head Let me write it Let

me write it There's something there that means something This is foam
Let me write it see what is underneath Something is underneath Don't
tell me Let me find find it I wish to find things for myself Only then
am I content I should like to have been an explorer If I were a man
perhaps I would have been because I like mysteries I like to untangle
knots I always untangle Knots in Scoville's fish line I am very good at
it Oh God I'll never be able to write all I want to but I know the
secret of untangling Knots Everything must be kept loose Hold the
line loosely Keep it from tangling and then it is easier . . .

Day after day Mrs. Mayer continued to come in and untangle
the knots through using this automatic writing instead of talking as
most patients do. The essentially important material that developed was that as a child she had been very much disparaged by
both parents, had turned to writing and elocution as methods of
self-expression only to have her parents ignore her accomplishments. They told her she was no good at them and ought to turn
her attention to simpler domestic matters. Apparently her chagrin
and rage had reached great heights, and she had had fantasies of
killing her mother, toward whom she felt more hostile than her
father. In this connection it is interesting that many of the short
stories with which she had later won commercial success had been
built on a fairly fixed pattern: a "bad" woman who seems to
be a good woman is ultimately exposed as the villain who killed
the victim or else was herself the victim. The interpretation seems
obvious. Mrs. Mayer gradually began to realize that her great
success in writing was not only self-vindication but was to a certain
extent a defiance of the disparagement and the disapproval she got
from her parents and a method of "killing" them. But perhaps the
way in which it actually began to appear in her material would be
more convincing.

One day, a week or two after the first session, Mrs. Mayer wrote
for a time, then did some aimless scribbling for about fifteen minutes. This material turned out to be a series of boxes containing
such sentences as these:

Love Murder Murder Love

Love murder murder murder murder

Love should not be killed

Then, in a more adult handwriting than she had previously used, she wrote the following very significant passage describing the mixed emotions she had felt toward her mother:

I always wanted her to love me and she never did. She always thought more of someone else than she did of me I never really pleased her because I did not have curly hair She thought more of others than she did of me She thought more of my cousin Mabel than she did of me She thought more of my sister than she did of me I cannot continue to care for people when they do not care for me My Mother did not care for me She never believed in anything I did She did not even believe that I was sick She never cared that I was ill She did not care that I suffered so she did not care she never cared she never cared for me and I loved her so much I thought her so wonderful I thought her so beautiful She always seemed very beautiful to me but she never really loved me. If she had she would not have pushed me away when I came to kiss her good night If she had loved me she would not have done that She would have believed in me She would have cared when I was ill and suffered So but she didn't care She thought I deserved to be ill because I had done so many wrong things Everything I had ever done was wrong and my illness when I suffered so was my punishment for doing everything wrong. She was not sorry She did not care She was glad She was glad I suffered so She laughed at my suffering I knew she laughed though I did not really see her but I knew she laughed I lay in bed and suffered so and she was glad and laughed at me and I came to hate her because I loved her so much and she never cared for me I hated her and wished to kill her I would have killed her if I could because she never cared for me.

I regret that discretion prevents my giving more of the details of this very interesting and dramatic illustration of work inhibition; I can only say that, having written this material about her-self (and much more not quoted), *none of which she had con-sciously remembered before she had written it,* the patient felt vastly relieved; her blood pressure fell from its previous high point; she became increasingly uninterested in any subsequent treatment, decided to return to her home and resume her work, and did so without further ado. A year later she sent me a copy of a book she had just published.

What does this case go to show? Several things, perhaps—the unusual use of automatic writing in therapy, the relief of physical as well as mental illness by a process of recollection under au-thoritative auspices, the after-effects of certain infantile traumata. But it is cited here to illustrate again how the harnessing of ag-gressive energy in work may break down so that the aggressive energies threaten to emerge directly and destructively; this then requires the erection of emergency defenses—costly, last-minute barriers against exploding. We recognize these defense measures as symptoms of illness; the more significant "illness" is the inabil-ity to work, to sublimate; and the genuine, deeper illness is the uncontrollable excess of hostility.

Women have special difficulties in regard to work. In our social system idleness is not such a reproach to women as to men, and women, more shamelessly than men, look forward eagerly to be-ing emancipated from the necessity of labor. Work is not visualized as a fulfillment for women, and aggressiveness is supposed to be drained by some mystic process from all their overt activities. Prosperous middle-class women are often patronized if they choose to do their own housework, although some of them recog-nize consciously that housework serves to neutralize their hostili-ties. Women lack both a defined objective and an organized co-operative sisterhood. This is well demonstrated in the case of housemaids, a problem which admittedly is handled cruelly and clumsily. Too often the employer-employee relation has a strictly

personal basis without benefit of social considerations. Many
women use their maids as targets for their hostility.

We are accustomed to say that women as workers are less creative than men. How much of this is due to faulty education and
attitudes we cannot estimate exactly, but certainly the pleasure that
women manifest in expressing their aggressions in active labor
during wartime when the men resume their traditional role of
fighters indicates that women, even more than men, waste great
potentialities in ordinary times through lack of an adequate framework in which to utilize them.

The constant arguments as to whether married women should
work outside the home, and whether when they do they are taking away men's jobs, will certainly have a very different coloring
after the war, but the heat generated by these arguments shows
the profound confusion that exists regarding woman's function
and her proper sphere of labor. It is a field in which scientific
principles have been relegated to a subordinate place in favor of
various economic and social theories, theories which come and go
in the sweep of world events and changes in custom and prejudice.

4

Another index of our lack of scientific thinking in regard to the
function of labor is our colossal ignorance and neglect of the
problem of vocational choice. Here is one of the momentous decisions that cast the lives of human beings in fixed though diverse
channels. Perhaps next to the choice of a marital partner, it is the
most important and far-reaching decision made by the individual.
(A place of residence is important, as are a standard of living and
a selection of friends, but these things often depend immediately
upon the mate and the vocation chosen.) Yet the subject of vocational choice has had all too little scientific investigation and is at
best the field of only a few specialists. Both in literature and in
psychology there appears to be a tacit assumption that one's voca-

tion is something almost foreordained, something determined by chance and circumstances—or, to give them their more sophisticated titles, by economics and the social pattern. One inherits a family interest in a business or a profession, or acquires one by inspiration, or happens upon an opportunity which he exploits. For some years the large problem of unemployment has reminded us that for many persons there is no choice, but only the possibility (sometimes not even that) that they may find an opportunity to exchange muscular contractions for food.

It may not be entirely futile to study the choice of vocation in this very group of persons who appear to have no choice; we might learn something from the study of them, just as we learned something of the nature of the erotic inhibitions created by our civilization from the study of members of that large group of unhappy persons who are unable to find a mate, and who have resigned themselves to celibacy. However, many difficulties face us here. For one thing, such unemployed persons are for the most part beyond our reach psychologically. They are too wholly convinced of their victimization at the hands of fate to be able to co-operate in a study of the internal reasons for their unemployment or their economic maladjustment, even if they were given the opportunity.

It is singular how little support psychiatry and psychoanalysis have given to those commendable efforts in the direction of vocational education which a few specialists have put forth.[6] If one has occasion to observe in a young adolescent about to be graduated from high school his struggles over a choice of college and, particularly, over his course of study in that college, one cannot but be grateful to those who have made some effort to put at his disposal a survey of the complicated activities of life in which he will soon be forced to participate in some capacity or other. It would seem as if there were some taboo on the subject that makes us so loath to accept it as a necessary part of education. Not only we, but also the educators, are at fault in this respect. A survey of educational and vocational opportunities is seldom afforded a student until too late to be of much practical value. It was only a few years ago that colleges introduced orientation courses, and for the most part these served to orient the student with regard to knowledge only but not with regard to practical activities. Most of the high schools of the country have no courses in vocational guidance, and in none of them, so far as I know, is such a course compulsory. Even in those where it is offered, it seems to be presented in such a way as to be of value to only a small percentage of the students. Of course, no vocational-guidance course in high school or even in college can hope to explore *unconscious* reasons for vocational choice, either in general or in particular. Furthermore, as one wise teacher put it to me, how can one expect the secluded and protected teachers in such institutions to present even the known realities about worldly professions and occupations?

Of course, there is some extenuation for this lack. One might assume that to high school students who are unable to afford further education the question of vocation is largely a question of opportunity and chance. On the other hand, for those who can afford to go to college, the entire college career might be looked upon as an orientation in vocational possibilities. Sometimes it works out this way, but all of us have seen cases in which a vocation must be decided upon before the student has gone far enough in college to know much about the world, past or present.

What is there about the practice of medicine, for example, that appeals to the young man as a vocation? The college or high school student has no very accurate idea about what the practice of medicine is, and he makes his decision largely on the basis of certain conceptions that are more or less illusory. Among the advantages that attract the young man or woman to medicine is probably the traditional dignity and social rank of the medical man. Some of this is perhaps unrealistic, but for the most part it is based upon a long tradition and a sound one. There are certain financial and social accruals that can reasonably be expected if one has obtained a legal prerogative for selling professional advice and services. Furthermore, this promised economic security is of an independent variety—"the doctor is his own boss," so they mistakenly think.

Such features of a profession probably have a wide though very superficial appeal. Banking has, or at least did have, more social prestige and better financial rewards than medicine and requires much less training and, theoretically, less intelligence. The practice of law permits an equal amount of independence and has more opportunities for personal exploitation.

Then, in certain instances, there are the purely fortuitous circumstances of family tradition or special opportunity. In many countries it is the custom for the son to follow the trade or profession of his father, and we know that even in America there is some tendency in this direction. How much this is to be ascribed to the special practical advantages which it makes possible, such as the inheritance of a practice, and how much to the psychological factors relating to the son's attitude toward the father must vary in different instances.

The wish to please one's parents, to live up to their ideal or ambition, is frequently a strong conscious determinant in the selection of a life work. The mother who wants her son to be a minister, the father who wants his son to follow in his footsteps, are familiar contemporary figures. The son may comply because he desires to please his parents or because he fears to displease them. If his psychological maturity is somewhat greater, he will comply or not comply because of more external and objective reasons, not excluding the actual inspiration that he may have found in the profession of his father or that of some father substitute.

But we know that beneath the conscious and therefore more superficial determinants there are unconscious motives which strongly influence any decision. Among these, in the case of vocational choice, one must undoubtedly include the unconscious reac-

tion of the son to his father's attitudes. Where the conscious identification with the father in the selection of the father's profession
will appear to be positive, there will be negative valences in the
unconscious and vice versa. In other words, a son may select his
father's profession, or one that the father wishes him to follow,
ostensibly because it flatters and pleases the father; but unconsciously such a son will often be motivated strongly by the repressed impulse to compete with, eclipse, or supersede his father.
Similarly many a son who disappoints his father by what appears
to be an aggressive rejection of the parental hopes is unconsciously
deterred by love of the father, or by the fear of entering into competition with him. It reminds one of that parable of Jesus about
the two sons, one of whom said quickly and politely, "I go, sir. I
do your bidding," but went not; while the other said, "I will not,
I refuse to obey," but did.

In a somewhat different way the unconscious attitude toward
the mother, particularly the mother who has definite opinions as
to the preferable vocation for her son, likewise influences his choice
by very reason of her attitudes, sometimes in one direction, sometimes in another.

All vocational choice ought therefore to be considered from
three preliminary standpoints: (1) Have the parents indicated any
preference? (2) Is the son inclined toward or away from the particular preference of the parents? (3) If the father's preference is
something other than his own profession, is the son's inclination
toward either the father's own profession or his preferred profession, or is it opposed to (away from) both? These questions should
underlie the more usual investigation of personal qualities: preparation, prospective financial return, etc.

In this digression concerning the motives that determine the
selection of various types of work, we may seem to have lost sight
of our original thesis; namely, that one function of work is the
sublimation of the aggressive impulses. The unconscious gratifi-

cations outlined as important for the selection of medicine or any other vocation represent not the energy, aggressive or otherwise, which is vocationally invested, but rather the internal criteria determining the direction in which the energy is turned. If a hostile force attacks a city, the citizens will spring to arms in defense of it. Even the criminals of the community might be willing to join in. One could say then that the aggressive impulses of the citizens of that community had been externally stimulated by the feeling of need for security, the defending of their city. However, a similar belligerent defense might be stimulated merely by more or less groundless fears of the possible approach of such an external menace. This would be an aggressive reaction in response to an internal stimulus. Similarly, when I say that the need for a feeling of greater security is one of the motives impelling the selection of a certain profession, I mean that this is one of the ways in which the aggressive energy is stimulated and indicates the objective toward which it is, in a refined and disguised way, directed.

It will be a long time before we arrive at a comprehensive analysis of the unconscious motives involved in all the various specialties of human labor, but what I have outlined here is sufficient to illustrate the possibilities, based on the original postulate; namely, that the destructive instinct may be modified by the sublimating effects of the erotic instinct into the constructive activity of work. When the doctor administers quinine for malaria or arsenic for syphilis, he is using a refined type of aggression, displaced from its original unconscious aim and directed toward an actual, dangerous foe. And just as the doctor combats disease and the agents of disease, so the teacher combats ignorance, the lawyer crime, the economist poverty, and the minister vice. Nor does this leave out of account the creative artist who combats ugliness, monotony, and boredom. These, too, are enemies of mankind. And in all of these activities the worker, by using his aggressive energies to save others, is saving himself.

5

So specialized is the work of civilized men that it may be difficult in some instances to see how a particular task fulfills the formula that I have outlined. As man tends to rely more and more on his wits and less and less on his muscles, the nature of work changes from physical to mental, and mental work seems to have less potency in this direction of saving ourselves through dispersing our aggressions. I cannot improve upon the words of an editorial writer in the New York *Herald Tribune,* who has this to say on the subject:

One of the many expressive old English words long gone—more's the pity—from ordinary vocabularies is "swink": meaning to do hard muscular work. Chaucer used the word frequently and evidently knew that the act does not necessarily depress the spirits:

"And many a ribaud [laborer] is mery and baud
That swinketh, and berith, bothe day and night,
Many a burthen of great might."

Undergraduates at Yale who soon will have their first experience of swinking, when they will begin to dig ditches, chop wood, cut brush and toil at similar labor as part of wartime physical training, need not be commiserated. Man is still basically a muscular and motor animal. Habitual denial of this fact in sedentary living, in the long run and in most cases, produces ill health or, at least, malaise.

There are many substitutes, to be sure, for the active muscular life of earlier and simpler days. . . . Recreation of body and soul in athletics has taken the place of chores and town-and-gown fighting; all to the good the adaptation and change, if at times somewhat overdone. But there are still satisfactions in productive hard labor that those who have exercised their muscles only in games know not.

The voluntary striated muscles of Yale men who are men will rejoice when they take hold of the pick and shovel, the ax and the brushcutter. Before they have gone a yard in the ditch they will instinctively begin to spit on their hands. A few hours of this swinking will quiet the nerves that among undergraduates, as among us all in recent years, have been overexercised at the expense of relaxed muscles. More power to them as they swink for God, for country and for Yale!

Whether by "swinking" or by more attenuated methods, the work of the world remains to be done; it is "necessary." But its necessity stems from two realms, the economic and the psychological. Its economic necessity makes work a means to an end, important for what it produces; its psychological necessity makes it an end in itself, important for what it does. To work without protest "is the only way to make life endurable"[7] because work absorbs aggressions and shapes them into useful forms, thus tending even in its most humble and obscure forms "to beautify and embellish the world."[8]

In any circumstances, therefore, work is necessary and work does us good; but does work give us pleasure? Is it, as Marcus Manilius claimed, "a pleasure in itself"? Around this question revolve problems of world importance—problems of labor legislation, labor organization, vocational choice, public policy, personal adjustment. It is certainly no such open-and-shut question as many blandly assume. It is all very well for Tertullian to say, "Where our work is, there let our joy be"—for Carlyle to ask, "What is the use of health, or of life, if not to do some work therewith? . . . Blessed is he who has found his work; let him ask no other blessedness"—for Emerson to record that "When I go into my garden with a spade, and dig a bed, I feel such an exhilaration and health that I discover that I have been defrauding myself all this time in letting others do for me what I should have done with my own hands." The fact remains that Tertullian, Carlyle, and Emerson were not compelled to spade up gardens or dig ditches or lift stones or plow furrows; they did as much of these things as they enjoyed and under no external compulsion; they ceased when they became weary; they accounted to no one for the product and to no one for their time. It is all very easy to say in theory that work is one of our pleasures; human experience refutes this as often as it confirms it. Those who rhapsodize about the joy of labor are likely to be persons who are not obliged to do much of it.

There is no evidence that work is in itself pleasurable; the question is rather: In what circumstances is it pleasurable? These circumstances include certain external conditions and certain internal conditions. *Externally* there must be a minimum of compulsion, an opportunity for comfortable group feeling with fellow-workers, absence of intense discomfort or fatigue in the performance of the work, proper provision for interspersed rest and recreation periods, a realization of pride in the product and a conviction that the work is useful and appreciated. *Internally*, there must be relative freedom from guilt feelings connected with pleasure and from neurotic compulsions either to work or not to work. The latter are carried over from the childhood era when work is a method of dealing with reality, not elected by the child but acquired by him from his parents. So long as his thinking is governed primarily by the pleasure principle, the child sees no necessity for work except the parental compulsion. If his introduction to reality has been accomplished with sufficient smoothness and grace, he will appreciate those tools which enable him to deal with it productively, but the technique of teaching a child to work is something we know very little about. We only know that most children are so clumsily taught that they seem to have learned more about how not to work than about how to work. Not methods so much as attitudes need to be taught.

When my daughter Julia submitted for her Master's degree at the University of Kansas a thesis proposing that work and play differ substantially only in the attitude taken toward them, she thought she was partially refuting my theory that work and play differ essentially in their relation to reality. The subtle implications of this "refutation" pleased me very much; she had intuitively perceived the truth that much of the distaste and weariness associated with work comes from within and that the motive power of both work and play is the same.[9]

Chapter 7. Play

AFTER work, play is the most universal method of safely disposing of our aggressions. One of the oldest theories about play is that it is a method of "blowing off steam." Schiller described it as the "aimless expenditure of exuberant energy." [1] Even William James, who was wise enough to propose work as a moral equivalent for war, did not see that play *also* is a moral equivalent for war, and joined Schiller in writing of the expenditure of energy as if in some way or other the human being were an over-fueled engine. If this were true, jumping up and down in the center of a room would be just as useful as any form of play.

The curious thing is that so many people tacitly accept the notion of play as something "aimless" and hence unnecessary—a luxury available chiefly to children and to prosperous adults. Not so long ago it was condemned even for children. Harry Emerson Fosdick quotes from the rules of an American school in 1784 as follows: "We prohibit play in the strongest terms. . . . The students shall rise at five o'clock in the morning, summer and winter. . . . The students shall be indulged with nothing which the world calls *play*. Let this rule be observed with strictest nicety; for those who play when they are young will play when they are old." [2]

Popular attitudes have changed to some extent since then, but that play actually serves some useful function is still not subscribed to whole-heartedly by most people. For evidence of this one need only observe the reactions of the public to the information that in certain penitentiaries prisoners are permitted to play; there is likely to be a general outcry that such prisoners are being "pampered." Those who do not join in this protest are often deterred by humane and sympathetic motives rather than by any scientific convictions that it is important for these prisoners to play if their lives are to be reconstructed and society further protected.

Yet John Eisele Davis, who has devoted his working life to the use of play as a therapeutic device in the treatment of the mentally ill, declares that it "enhances the sense of self-respect and personality worthwhileness, produces readjustment upon a higher reality level, establishes a foundation in skills upon which more constructive psychic adjustments may be made, assists in the substitution of wholesome objective activities in place of morbid subjective creations . . ." [3] He quotes Carr as saying, "Play is a better stimulant to growth and development than work because it meets nature's demands in a natural and timely way."

To be sure, there have been scientific voices raised in support of the theory that play is a necessity! Over two hundred years ago Lord Kames, a Scottish philosopher, declared that "play is necessary for man in order to refresh himself after labor." [4] Professor Lazarus of the University of Berlin [5] held that play was more restful than complete idleness and served to recuperate and restore the fatigued individual, which seems trite enough now but which is, of course, the exact opposite of the surplus-energy theory of Schiller, Spencer, James, and others, which has had and still has wide vogue. Some scientists have gone so far as to declare that play is necessary for the development of higher intelligence. [6]

The nearest approximation to a psychoanalytic theory of play was first proposed by Aristotle, although neglected by most writers since then. He said that in play the emotions "become purified of a great deal of the distasteful and dangerous properties which adhere to them." *

It was Freud's theory that this "purification" of the emotions

* Groos went back to this when he wrote his two celebrated books on *The Play of Animals* (Appleton, 1898) and *The Play of Man* (Appleton, 1901), arguing that play is an instinct.

takes place when an unpleasant or dreaded course of behavior is rehearsed or re-enacted in a form or situation lacking the dangerous elements. In this way we obtain a mastery of the situation and get revenge against external reality for its threats against us.[7]

It might seem desirable to attempt a definition of play—not a dictionary definition but one that takes into account the psychological principles involved. We might define it as pleasurable activity in which the means is more important than the ostensible end. This clearly differentiates it from work, and is in line with our hypothesis that, like work, play is an end in itself, an opportunity for the discharge of aggressive energy in not only painless but actually pleasurable forms, energy which would otherwise be repressed at a definite psychological expense or else expressed in harmful ways. Play acts out timelessly in pantomime, symbol, and gesture the unfulfillable aggressive and erotic wishes of the players. I say unfulfillable, although the fantasies of some play are actually realized later, as, for example, in the little girl's play with her doll.

Play differs from work in four respects. In play (1) the means rather than the end is the important thing so far as the player's avowed and conscious purposes are concerned; (2) pleasure in the activity is more regularly conscious; (3) the activity is consciously dissociated from the restrictions of reality; and (4) the aggressive motives are more obvious. I should like to discuss each of these.*

(1) That play activity has no important ultimate objective differentiates it sharply from work. A man plows a field with the conscious intention of planting grain which will yield him bread upon which he may subsist; he plays golf not for the purpose of

* I do not say that these are the only respects in which play differs from work, but they seem to me to be the four most important ones. The literature contains many other differentiations. See Harry A. Carr, "The Survival Values of Play," Investigations of the Dept. Psychol. and Educ., Univ. of Colorado, Boulder, Colo., 1902; and S. A. Britt and S. Q. Janus, "Toward a Social Psychology of Human Play," J. Social Psy., 13:351-384, 1941.

transporting a ball from one point to the other, but for the satis-faction of mastering and exhibiting the peculiar and difficult proc-ess by which he does it. According to our own theory, this differ-ence is more apparent than real, because we have already assumed that work actually does have a psychological function quite apart from its ultimate product. In some forms of play there are impor-tant ends in view; for example, in collecting postage stamps or art treasures. Nevertheless, in the main this is a distinction tacitly but clearly recognized by everyone. It is acknowledged when we use the word "play" reproachfully; when, for example, we say that someone is making work out of play or play out of work, we mean that he is putting the wrong emphasis on the question of means versus ends. This leads us to the next point.

(2) It is the general assumption that one enjoys play more than one enjoys work. This is not always or necessarily true. Many people appear to enjoy work more than they do play, but they are regarded as neurotics, eccentrics, or geniuses. I have seen all three, but it is my impression that they most often enjoy work so much just because they cannot enjoy play. On the other hand, it is true that some people are so normal, so to speak—so free from the necessity of retreat from reality and the temporary surrender of repressive efforts—that they can and actually do find almost complete satisfaction in work, and need relatively little play.

(3) But for the average person it is certainly true that play is more pleasurable than work, and the question why this is so is not hard to answer. In the first place, play enables one to return to those pleasurable intervals of childhood when one could do just as one pleased. For the time, one is free from the dominance, the restriction, the surveillance, and the command of the parents or their representatives in adult life (although, of course, he must—even in play—adhere to the rules of the game). Furthermore, in play one can let down his disguises. He does not have to wear the dress-up clothes of polite society. He does not have to assume a friendliness he does not feel or maintain a maturity and dignity

that put some strain on his self-control. He does not have to obey either the time-clock or the traffic lights. If he wants to take a piece of wood and call it a king and ascribe to it great authority and move it about on a chessboard he may do so, and he will find others who will make the same assumption and indulge in the same fantasies. If he wants to take a somewhat larger piece of wood, whittle it into the semblance of an airplane, and imagine himself a manufacturer, he may do so. If he wants to take a still larger piece of wood and use it to strike with all his might a quite innocent ball, he can do so with the consciousness that the harder and more viciously he strikes the ball, the more he will be applauded by some of his playmates and feared by others who are playing against him. There is no necessity for pulling punches, no necessity for being hypocritical.

Furthermore, play permits the opportunity for many miniature victories in compensation for the injuries inflicted by the daily wear and tear of life. This is a comfort which some egos sorely need. In competitive play there are also defeats, to be sure, but the saving grace of play is that a victory is a victory and a defeat is not defeat—for, after all, "it was only play." The way that men who are only moderately successful in their business become highly proficient golfers is ordinarily interpreted as an example of the way in which the impulse to play undermines business success; but sometimes it may rather be an example of the necessary assuagement of a sensitive ego injured by the defeats of business life and restored by great victories in the play life.

This element of reality denial can be seen in every form of play. Much play is timeless, and time is the greatest tyrant of all realities. The very word play has come to mean make-believe, a temporary assumption made for the purpose of the game—an actor, a symbol.

In play we can fall back upon those principles of magic for which there is an eternal longing in the human heart. Persons and substances take on miraculous powers and virtues. They may be made to vanish, to reappear, or to be transmuted. By a touch of the hand, the utterance of a single word or the contact with a pre-established "base," fundamental changes in status are accomplished. With the aid of magic all the dreams of fairy tales can be realized in play: giants slain, treasures discovered, kingdoms acquired, distance annihilated, dragons destroyed. The laws of the prosaic workaday world are replaced by an entirely new order.*

It will occur to scarcely anyone to question why it is so necessary for us to abandon temporarily our strict loyalty to reality and fall back upon magic and make-believe. Life is hard; reality is stern; civilization has added heavy burdens to the already great difficulties of living and loving. For this reason we can assume that the more complicated civilization becomes, and the more intense and elaborate the machinery of living is made, the more necessary it will be to create that temporary retreat from reality which we call play.

(4) The most important value of this unrealistic nature of play is the opportunities that it affords for the relief of repressed aggressions. It enables us to express aggression without reality consequences: we can hurt people without really hurting them; we can even kill them without really killing them. "It is all in play." We say that we do not really mean it, although this is not quite true. We do mean it, but we know and our victim knows that it has no dangerous consequences and he can therefore tolerate it and (usually) forgive us. Of course, if he is very intuitive and very sensitive, he will know too much for his own comfort, and we call him "a poor sport." He may only be too good a psychologist, like Pagliacci and Hamlet.

It is this function of play as the expression, in thinly disguised

* The principles of magic in the thinking of primitive man have been elaborately discussed by Frazer in his incomparable *The Golden Bough* (see the abridged edition, Macmillan, 1942, pp. 11 ff.), and in the psychology of modern man by numerous psychoanalysts (see Freud, *Totem and Taboo*, Dodd, Mead and Co.; and Reik, *Ritual*, Norton).

form, of the aggressive impulses that I should like to emphasize. Let us analyze some of the typical kinds of organized play among normal children. It is sufficient merely to name some of these. One of the most popular organized games is some variety of the pursuit and capture of one group of players by another—"Cops and Robbers" or, more recently, "G-Men and Gangsters." In these and others like them the acting out of aggressive impulses is obvious. It is a little less obvious in such games as "Hide and Seek," "Drop the Handkerchief," "Pussy in the Corner," "Blind Man's Buff," or simple "Tag" in the variations in which the object is capture. In such group games as football and baseball, the aggressive element is obvious enough, although more refined in the latter, where physical violence is displaced in its direction from other human beings to a ball which can be struck, intercepted, thrown, etc. The baseball acquires magic properties after it has been struck so that the player, instead of hitting a second player with it, has only to touch him with it for the second man to be "out" (dead). It is true that in football there is some direct attack on the ball in the form of kicking, and this is one form of violence which the rules of the game forbid players to inflict upon one another. In soccer, hockey, and similar games the object receives all the blows and contacts, and force is seldom directed against other players except by accident.

Frequently, as we all know, the aggressions and hostilities which the games are supposed to absorb break through the repression into consciousness, and quarreling ensues. This applies not only to child's play but to adult play as well, and not only to the physical forms of play we have been discussing but to the more symbolic contests such as table games.* The animosities that frequently flare up in the course of card games are so well known as to need no comment, but even in a completely civilized and wholly

---

* Boxing is regarded as a form of sport, as are bullfighting, gladiatorial combats, and hunting; but these would fit into my definition of play only to the extent that they are not actually destructive.

friendly game there are many subtle indications of the disguised battle which the game really represents. I think this was most impressively brought home to me once in the clinical history of a woman I saw professionally. She was extremely skilful at bridge and played it frequently. Upon a certain occasion, at a time in her life when she was for various reasons rather heavily burdened with anxiety, she attended a bridge party in her mother's home and entered into it with her usual intensity. In the course of one rubber she bid a little slam in clubs and made it. Almost immediately she was overwhelmed by a headache and had to go to bed; by the following day there were definite signs of depression, which became increasingly severe. While she had been playing her club suit, the thought flashed into her mind that she was "winning with clubs," and this rapidly transformed itself into the thought that she was using clubs upon her opponents and that in winning she was actually clubbing them to death. This thought was so absurd that she tried to dismiss it, and it was as a result of this conflict that she developed the headache and then the depression. Now, it would be quite unsound to draw too many inferences from this one episode, because one might well suspect that this woman's interpretation was an afterthought, or at least that it represented only the complications of an already sick mind. I should not dispute this were it not for the fact that investigation showed that this woman happened to be an exceedingly avid bridge-player who took every game with great seriousness and played skilfully, swiftly, and humorlessly, and was always distressed if she didn't win. Her aggressive bridge-playing was in contrast to her generally restrained and decorous bearing and was a matter of comment among her friends. Bridge was definitely her method of fighting, the only one she used, and one in which the aggressive impulses ultimately broke through the sublimated disguises. One of her opponents on that particular day was a woman who, for various reasons, represented the patient's mother, and it was in connection with her mother that she had always had the most serious conflicts. I cannot estimate how convincing this is to the reader, but the experience enabled me to understand better the aversion that some people have to bridge and the fascination it has for others.

In poker there is, of course, no attempt to disguise the aggressive element. Poker is a fighting game, a game in which each player tries to get the better of every other player and does so by fair means or foul so long as he obeys the rules of the game. He may bluff or lie about his own strength, the object of the game being either to frighten the other players into believing that he has greater strength, or else to prove it.

Chess is a more highly symbolic game, but the aggressions are therefore even more frankly represented in the play. It probably began * as a war game; that is, the representation of a miniature battle between the forces of two kingdoms. Incidentally, it was a favorite recreation of some of the world's great military leaders, including William the Conqueror and Napoleon. As Ernest Jones [8] has put it in a very competent study of the psychology of chess, it is plain that the motive actuating chess-players is not only the conscious one of pugnacity that characterizes all competitive games but also "the grimmer one of father murder" since the goal of the game is the capture (immobilization) of the King. Chess has frequently been prohibited by kings, bishops, and others because of its warlike import, and John Huss, when in prison, deplored having played chess and thereby having given way to violent passions.

This is not the place to discuss the finer points of the psychology of chess, beyond saying that all agree that it is a highly sublimated battle in which the aggressive patterns characteristic of different

* According to an interesting story, the game of chess developed in India among the Buddhists, who believe that war and the slaying of one's fellow-men for any purposes whatever are criminal, and who invented chess as a substitute for war. There is also a Burmese story to the effect that chess was invented by a Talaing queen who was very fond of her lord and hoped through this distraction to keep him out of war. (S.T.J.G. Scott, quoted by Ernest Jones.)

personalities are clearly discernible in the nature or style of play adopted. As every chess-player knows, there are the strong attackers, the strong defenders, the provocative players, the cautious players, the attack-from-behind players, the so-called classical and romantic styles, etc. Some players are particularly skilful in the use of the Queen, others are particularly fond of the pawns (the underdogs), and so forth.

I should like to anticipate some objections that may arise in the reader's mind regarding this theory as applied to certain types of imitative play; for example, the almost universal interest of little girls in dolls. "This," they will say, "you certainly cannot call aggressive; it is the childish form of the maternal impulse; it is undisguised love." Women who speak thus are recalling their childhoods too fondly and with much more distortion than they realize, or else they are observing with kind but not very keen eyes the behavior of their daughters. What they say is partly true: the little girl does treat her doll as if it were a child, but she bestows upon it not only love, but, unless she is exceedingly inhibited, also hate. She treats it as she herself has been treated (which means that she punishes the doll as she has been punished), and thereby avenges herself upon her mother. Or she treats the doll as she wishes her mother had treated her—another form of revenge on the mother. Sometimes she treats the doll as she would like to treat her brothers and sisters, which is even more likely to be aggressive.

But there is a more significant sense in which playing with dolls is an aggression against the parents. The very fact that the little girl plays with dolls at all—which the mother takes to be such a sweet and natural act of imitation—is in the child's unconscious an aggression against the mother. It is an aggression in that it is a way of saying, "It is I who should have the children, not you." It is the same kind of aggression in play form which one immediately recognizes if the son puts on his father's hat, as if the Crown Prince were playfully resting the King's crown upon his own head. Little girls like nothing better than to put on their mothers' dresses and frequently do it surreptitiously; this has the same unconscious motive. It is a way of saying, "Mother, you are no longer necessary; I am a big lady now, and it is I who should have the long dresses and the babies, not you; you can be dispensed with." If we did not know empirically how children unconsciously and sometimes consciously wish to have their parents disappear into limbo—die, in short—these might seem to be fanciful theorizings of a very unpleasant sort.* It is much more comfortable to look upon such child's play in the more superficial, conventional ways, but if one really wants to understand what play means, one cannot be satisfied merely with what is pleasant.

The same thing is true of little boys. They love to play with blocks, building towers or houses with them, and they find a great fascination in toy trains or toy automobiles. If one watches carefully how they handle these blocks, what they do with these trains and automobiles, one soon realizes that the most violent, destructive fantasies are often acted out with them. Such forms of play have been carefully examined by Melanie Klein [9] of London and Homburger Erikson [10] in this country. The latter has shown that even when college students are given toys—toy automobiles, toy houses, toy furniture, and the like—and asked to construct dramatic scenes for possible use in moving picture plays, the arrangement they make of these toys sets forth in quite easily discernible ways their own destructive trends. The typical theme used by most of twenty-two Harvard students was an accident in which a little girl was the victim. Thirteen put in the center of the scene an automobile accident or an arrangement that prevented one. Erikson [11] has elsewhere shown that the play of the Sioux Indians is similarly based upon the conflictual situations in the child's life, using as symbols not the actual participants but animal totems, particularly buffaloes and coyotes.

* Richard Hughes in *The Innocent Voyage* (or *High Wind in Jamaica*, in England) brings out very clearly the aggressiveness and cruelty of children's play. The book was criticized for its "lack of sentimental illusions."

Another common example of children's play which on the surface appears to be benevolent and nonaggressive is the "doctor game," which has been studied by Simmel [12] and other psychoanalysts. One child plays the part of the patient, another child the part of the nurse, another the part of the doctor. The patient's relatives and other participants may be added to complicate the game, but as a rule it is limited to the three players. The patient is, of course, sick; the doctor comes to minister to him—to examine and treat him. The ministrations may be limited to the most innocent and superficial attentions, or they may proceed to the point of genital inspection. In the latter case, if the parents learn of it, they make a great to-do without realizing the harm done by such signalization of sexual curiosity. The whole point of the doctor game is the erotic fantasy of being the victim of a powerful man who has access to all parts of the body, with a concomitantly acted hostile fantasy directed against the parents' prohibitions.

One could go much further in analyzing these and other forms of play, but such analysis belongs in a more technical treatise. I have the uncomfortable feeling that what I have said is not very convincing to those who are unfamiliar with the deeper elements in child psychology, unfamiliar also with those unconscious tendencies which are repressed. Play is a method of carrying out these aggressions in forms socially acceptable. One is likely to be disturbed on discovering the aggressive elements concealed in the play by the erotization. One ought rather to be happy to learn that it is possible for the erotization to handle the aggressions so completely and successfully.

2

I have not attempted to differentiate play into group play, competitive play, imitative play, and the like because I have preferred to put the emphasis upon the fundamental principles underlying play of all forms. Attention must be called, however, to what would appear to be an important differentiation—between participating play and vicarious play. Vast numbers of Americans get their greatest play satisfaction through passive identification with active participants, as in watching a baseball or a football game or a wrestling match or a motion picture.

Turel [13] argues that great mass demonstrations, a feature of the modern dictator states, symbolize men's passivity, their acceptance of the feminine role. He cites the ancient Olympian games and the Roman gladiatorial fights as forerunners. The spectator crowd is passive, sensually excited, but does nothing, renders no help. Only with betting at horse races and other similar sports does the spectator take any risk or share any of the danger in the "game."

There seems to be some moralistic feeling that hobbies and recreation do us "more good" if we "work" at them (that is, expend energy and endure some pain, danger, or fatigue). This may be due, in part, to the conscience restriction that pleasure must be earned; but it may also be an intuitive recognition of the valuable function of play in releasing pent-up aggressions harmlessly. People who do not play are potentially dangerous. Spectator sports have been used by political dictators as a means of unifying great masses of people and inflaming them for a common purpose. But in defense of the spectator role it should be said that many people are almost entirely debarred from active competition of any sort because they feel weak or inferior, or fear retaliation. Such feelings are usually inculcated by drastic prohibition of all aggressive impulses in early childhood and are therefore difficult or impossible to overcome in later life. Passive participation is the *only* outlet which such people can permit themselves and it is for that reason all the more necessary to them. They would like to dance or to swing a bat, but they feel unable to do so and become "balletomanes" or "fans." Sometimes these inhibited persons do play games, but they cannot be successful at them. In any competitive sport they almost invariably lose, though they are quite unaware that what defeats them is their fear of losing love by overcoming an opponent. Since the need to achieve active aims by passive means is considered typical of the feminine role in life, the onlooker may be described as temporarily accepting a feminine attitude.

But the function of play is to furnish an outlet for those impulses which are denied by reality, and among these is the desire to be fed, gratified, and entertained without effort. This would be considered dishonorable in working hours but is socially permissible in play time. This vicarious play lacks some of the physical satisfactions of direct play but the emotional satisfactions are similar because of the great power implicit in the mechanism of identification. This is most clearly discernible in the drama. The vicarious pleasure in observing others in the play performance is itself empirically among the most satisfactory recreations, probably because it is so explicit in expressing particular conflicts arising from aggressive impulses.

Hugo Münsterberg, who was the first psychologist to become enthusiastic over the value of the cinema for the mental health of people, regarded the silence of the screen as one of its greatest assets, because, as he said, each person can then within limits put into the mouths of the characters the words that he himself would like to say. Time and experience have shown that the cinema's identification value is not determined by the silence of the screen, since this value is achieved just as readily with talking films, as well as with stage drama.

When participation in the drama becomes a profession, it is, of course, no longer play but work; amateur participation is, however, a form of play which is for some people particularly gratifying. One psychiatrist [14] was so impressed with this from his study of amateur dramatics in Vienna that on coming to this country he developed a psychiatric hospital in which the creation of and participation in dramatic pieces constitutes the chief therapeutic method. There is no question that some patients are greatly benefited by the opportunity to enact their aggressions and their conflicts in a form which is clearly labeled "play," and by this means gain the courage to face them consciously and deal with them in more rational and less crippling ways. The use of the drama and other forms of play has been studied by various of my associates [15] and I should like to summarize some of their findings. I think I can do so best by quoting from a detailed description of the use of one play.

The plot of the play, *Man Submerged*, concerns a man who thinks women have the easier part to play in the day's routine. He offers to remain at home and keep house while his wife goes shopping. He is interrupted throughout the remainder of the play by salesmen, gossipy neighbors, borrowing friends, and even his own son, who disturbs him in his housekeeping. Thus by means of comedy and humorous situations, the husband learns his lesson—that the woman's lot is not always so easy as it looks. . . .

The lead for the play was found in a young man whose illness had been diagnosed as a neurotic depression with alcoholic tendencies. His participation in the play seemed to supplement his psychotherapeutic treatment in such a way that he was able to gain insight into one of his chief conflicts. Upon reading the play he immediately recognized that the plot turned on what was for him a painful subject—namely, passive feminine wishes. He saw that his own conflict was one which many men have; in accepting the part he said that he felt that acting out might provide additional information useful in understanding his own makeup. He apparently received considerable gratification from admitting his passivity publicly and making it a humorous predicament, within the safe confines of a play. He showed intense interest in the play from the beginning. He memorized his part immediately, was faithful in attending play rehearsals, met characters for special practice hours; in fact, he gave up many activities to rehearse with others. He insisted that all properties be on hand and in their proper order. . . . For his own part he insisted upon a frilly apron instead of a tea towel as had been suggested. By acting in the play this young man was able to assume a feminine role in a socially acceptable manner.

The part of the "borrowing neighbor" was that of a woman who was aggressive, interfering, and meddlesome. After much coaxing, a patient of about forty-five years of age accepted the part. She had dramatic ability, and was in reality anxious for the part, but wished to be urged. At first she was critical of the part and of the other members of the cast, but as the play progressed she became more interested and put much of her own expression into it. She did excellent work on the stage, showed no stage fright, and repeated her lines in such an exact yet humorous manner, that she received more applause than the rest of the cast. Upon seeing her psychoanalyst after the play, she said, "I felt I was at home." With this opening the analyst was able to point out that the part satisfied her deeply repressed wish to carry on the same type of aggressions portrayed on the stage. The woman was angered by this and maintained that she was merely acting, that she had heard neighbors at home talk in that fashion, that all the fun had been spoiled by the doctor's remarks. Actually she meant that she was angry because she recognized the nature of her aggressions. Through further talks with her physician she was given insight into the aggressive wishes which produced her depressions.

A young lady about twenty-five years of age took the part of a saleswoman. She had entered the hospital in an almost catatonic stupor, had been in the institution seven or eight months, and was making a gradual, consistent recovery when this small part was offered her. She accepted the lines without urging and had little difficulty in learning them. At rehearsals she needed constant reassurance because she had a great deal of fear of hostile reality which had been a factor in her illness. Two or three days before the play she became noticeably depressed and seemed to lack confidence in herself. The night of the dress rehearsal a large hat which partially shaded her face was secured for her, and she then seemed more confident. The night of the final performance she presented her lines well and showed little or no fear. . . . By means of this reality success she gained added confidence in herself.

The above explanations and examples indicate how dramatics may have a distinct value as a therapy in a mental institution. This simple farce provided outlets for the unconscious needs of the patients that participated and for those who witnessed it. . . . Some patients gained further insight into their own problems, and thus were able to further their own recovery . . . other patients who participated only as members of the audience received some benefit from identification both with characters in the play and with actors in the play, their fellow patients, who had made this contribution to the social life of the hospital.

I have cited this illustration at length because it is much easier to illustrate the therapeutic use of play in the case of the drama than in the case of the many forms of recreational therapy that are used in the modern psychoanalytically oriented psychiatric hospital. All the forms of play discussed above are selected according to the needs of the patient. The basis of such treatment is the theory that these patients are people overwhelmed by their own self-destructive impulses, and that these impulses are self-destructive instead of externally aggressive because the contemplated investment of the aggression externally has been too dangerous. One might say that patients become mentally ill when all their sublimations fail them, when they can no longer work or play. Consequently, they must be taught again to work and play, and it is often easier to teach them to play than to work. This is a principle of psychiatric treatment which is more and more recognized to be fundamental.

Finally, we come to those most refined and stylized forms of play—dancing, art, and music. These modalities have both active and passive aspects. One can enjoy them by participation or by seeing or hearing them. That they constitute play in the sense that they enable people to live out unsatisfied, instinctual urges in a way not hampered or restricted by reality considerations is obvious. The puritanical objection to dancing on the grounds that it represents a thinly disguised sexual relationship was intuitively correct in its interpretation and quite logical if one premises that sexuality is something evil rather than that it is an expression of the best impulses within us. Similarly music and art afford a deep erotic pleasure which is probably related psychologically to satisfactions antedating sexual pleasure in its more limited sense; the child obtains satisfactions from hearing and seeing as well as from feeling, and music and art constitute the highest pinnacle which pleasurable hearing and seeing can achieve.

Parenthetically, we ought perhaps to consider the pleasure derived from smooth, rapid movement through space such as is experienced in skating, skiing, tobogganing, airplaning, and even automobiling. I am not prepared to analyze these exhaustively, but I suspect that some of them, such as skating, combine elements of erotic pleasure with athletic satisfactions related to the pleasure of activity and a sense of power in the overcoming of gravity, air resistance, etc. There are also, of course, the elements of novelty and rhythm. Some psychoanalysts have emphasized the relationship of these pleasures to the pleasures obtained earlier by the child in being carried or moved by his parents in a way vastly transcending his own feeble powers of locomotion.

As for the idea that sublimations represent the fate of certain highly transformed aggressive impulses, we must admit quite frankly that the aggressive element in art and in the forms of sport I have just mentioned is usually difficult to recognize, the erotic (creative) elements greatly predominating. This is why I have postulated that the arts must constitute the highest form of play.*

3

Thus far we have been somewhat vague in defining the reciprocal relationship of work and play. I doubt if this can be done arbitrarily on a psychological basis alone; too many economic and sociological and physiological factors enter into it. But the psychological values of both work and play cannot be omitted from consideration by those who do social planning. They should not be neglected, they cannot be—but they constantly *are*. For example, if it were economically possible, beginning tomorrow, to relieve every man in the United States of half his present work requirements (or, rather, his work opportunities) without decrease of income, the nation would be in peril. It would be absolutely impossible for the great majority of these people to utilize the suddenly acquired leisure in any psychologically satisfactory

* I recognize, of course, that there are aggressive uses of music and aggressive ways of dancing.

way, i.e., in play. *Some* of the energy thus released would undoubtedly be taken up with play, but most of it would be expressed in direct aggressiveness or in some form of self-destructiveness. People would begin fighting, drinking, and killing
themselves and one another.

I do not say this arbitrarily; it is a matter of observation that
this has occurred time after time in individuals and in groups, and
it is exactly what we should expect theoretically. Most people do
not know how to play well enough to fill such heavy requirements
upon sudden demand. They think they want to play, they think
they want more leisure time so they *can* play, but they cannot play
when they do get the leisure. This is not merely because their
time is preoccupied with other things—work, for example; nor
is it because of lack of skill and technique. It is due rather to an
inhibition of interest in play. A very interesting study was conducted by one of our associates at the Menninger Sanitarium, the
director of men's occupational therapy. He compared the hobby
interests which had been spontaneously developed in the earlier
life of certain maladjusted patients with those developed by a
group of supposedly normal and at least fairly well-adjusted ones.
The well-adjusted were found to have pursued nearly twice as
many hobbies as the maladjusted.[16] In our work with psychiatric
patients we are constantly impressed by the fact that they are deficient in the capacity to play, or at least that they have never been
able to develop balanced recreational techniques.

Some of those who advocate more and more leisure for everyone recognize the danger entailed in leisure unprofitably occupied.
They point to the fact that our public playgrounds, public swim-
ming pools, local and national park facilities, our high school
music education programs, and numerous other new phenomena
of American life are encouraging developments in this direction.
I should like to add my enthusiastic endorsement of these; I do
not think there are nearly enough of them. Everything I have
said about play as a useful means of absorbing aggressions should

lead us to encourage training in how to play—how to play in many different ways and under many different circumstances.

On the other hand, it should be pointed out that no one can learn to play all the time because no one *can* play all the time without suffering adverse consequences. I have seen, professionally, a good many wealthy play-boys raised on the theory that work was something determined by economic principles and that since they were immune from economic pressure they could spend all their time in learning to play and in playing. I have never seen one of them make a success of it. Many such play-boys actually turn their play into work; most of them develop neuroses, depressions, or antisocial trends. What they are doing that looks like play is actually a working out of neurotic conflicts or strivings, as is shown by the fact that the pursuit has lost most of the pleasure motive characteristic of real play. This is very conspicuous in the lives of certain women whose husbands' incomes make it possible for them to have more leisure than they know what to do with. Their attempts to "play" (at bridge, for example) become laborious treadmills of compulsive activity. One little girl in a progressive school expressed the same idea when she asked, "Do I *have* to do as I please today?"

Thorstein Veblen [17] made the distinction that some play comes under the heading of conspicuous waste, while other play is a disguised fulfillment of the instinct of workmanship. The former he felt carried with it a justifiable and inhibiting sense of guilt, but the latter, being constructive, carried no such burden. In this distinction he was, I think, too rationalistic and too unpsychological; we know empirically that for some people an unconscious sense of guilt attaches to anything which is pleasurable, and it is this neurotic sense of guilt that does the inhibiting, even more than conscious, rational considerations.

Our Puritan tradition has been blamed as a deterrent to the frank enjoyment of recreation, but behind this and much more powerful is the fact that play is so strongly determined by the pleasure principle, which actuates children and which is controlled with difficulty by the disciplined adult personality, that there is a sense of guilt attached to it. In play we are more truly our natural selves than in our work; yet for this very reason we feel a threat to the civilized superstructure of the personality in the act of play. It is too tempting, too unrealistic. And of this sense of guilt, the larger part comes from the voice of the conscience, an echo of parental prohibitions which are displaced to society, the government, and the voice of science. If, therefore, those who stand in the position of parental figures to society formally sanction the indulgence, it loses a part of its burden of guilt.

Hence it was very wise of counselors on civilian morale to include among the earliest exhortations that they addressed to the American public the advice that we should work as hard as we can, but hold on to our hobbies. For such advice is, in the light of psychiatric experience, very sound. If the proper direction and encouragement of play can be therapeutically useful it can also be prophylactically useful. If it is good for sick people it is even better for well people. We are all subject and liable to the disease of disturbed morale—demoralization—and one of the best antidotes against this is to be found in recreation.[18]

There seems to be a general idea that recreation is all right if one doesn't take it too seriously. My belief is that much the greater danger lies in not taking it seriously enough. If people do not take it seriously enough, the reason may lie not so much in prejudice as in ignorance. The question just what play does for the individual is not yet fully answered; neither is the question why some people learn to play and some do not. These and many other questions relating to the psychology of play deserve the attention of the best scientific minds.

In this analysis of the function of play in human life, I have not intended to be exhaustive. I have only tried to indicate why I believe it to be true that work and play are—as Dr. Richard Cabot put it in his book by that title—*What Men Live By*. I have tried to show why both work and play are necessary, not only from the economic standpoint, and not only from the social standpoint, but even more urgently from the psychological standpoint. I have tried to show why work is necessary for the integrity of the human spirit, and why play, which we speak of so tenderly as recreation, really re-creates. Work and play make it possible for us to live and to love, because they help to absorb the aggressive energy which would otherwise overwhelm us.

Originally, as we have seen, there was no distinction between work and play because each man did what he felt to be necessary. Today what one pleases to do and what one feels it necessary to do are so largely determined by what economics and organized society will permit him to do that the distinction becomes increasingly sharp. Perhaps some of the best work in the world today is done by people who make little distinction between work and play, people for whom all work is play. Among the ancient Hindus the Cosmos is called *Lila*—"a play of the creator for whom work and play are identical." But people who can be completely independent of conventional attitudes are rare indeed, and we cannot hope that any such attitude will become universal. We can only hope that both work and play will achieve increased dignity and respect at a time when the principal preoccupation of men's thought and activities seems to be not work nor play nor the love of one another which work and play would facilitate, but, instead, fighting and destruction.

Chapter 8. Faith

FAITH does not lend itself readily to definition in psychological terms. It might be said to be a conviction that a wish will be fulfilled, a confidence which exists unsupported by adequate proof in reality. We may believe in things without employing faith; for example, we believe that the earth is round because we were told so by our teachers. But we do not need to continue to hold this belief merely upon faith; we are given access to many visible proofs of it. The good teacher encourages the child to test knowledge for himself and to verify it with his own senses. Curiosity leading to exploration and discovery of the natural world is no longer considered a sin, but a virtue. It is the incentive of science.

There are many fields of human life, however, which are not accessible to scientific testing, so that we are all constantly obliged to exercise faith. We cannot measure the sincerity of our friends' love for us but we do have faith in it. Friendship is based on a combination of proved belief and unproved faith. So far as it is based on actual testing of the friend in many situations and on our observations of the way he reacts in these experiences, it is belief based on reality testing. But so far as it is confidence unsupported by experience, it is faith, as illustrated, for example, in sudden violent friendships and love at first sight. If we observe lovers closely, however, we can see how weak the faith is, how prone the lovers are to jealousy and misunderstandings, and how a continual process of mutual testing goes on until an equilibrium of conviction is established.

The faith represented by practices and attitudes which we call religion can neither be proved nor disproved. Of religion Freud said that unsupported hope, the desire for wish-fulfillment, was

189

too prominent a factor in its motivation. The members of one religious faith can always see, in other forms of faith, elements so fantastic, so improbable, so incompatible with everything we have laboriously discovered about the reality of the world that they seem frankly delusional. These are hopes which have become parts of a faith. But since there is no way to discipline the reality of a faith it can easily merge into the pathological and become in essence a kind of psychosis. Freud wrote: "Where questions of religion are concerned people are guilty of every possible kind of insincerity and intellectual misdemeanour. Philosophers stretch the meaning of words until they retain scarcely anything of their original sense; by calling 'God' some vague abstraction which they have created for themselves, they pose as deists, as believers before the world; they may even pride themselves on having attained a higher and purer idea of God, although their God is nothing but an insubstantial shadow and no longer the mighty personality of religious doctrine. Critics persist in calling 'deeply religious' a person who confesses to a sense of man's insignificance and impotence in face of the universe, although it is not this feeling that constitutes the essence of religious emotion but rather the next step, the reaction to it, which seeks a remedy against this feeling." [1]

In the final words of the last sentence Freud implies that religion derives from fear, and he relates that fear to a realistic comparison of man's own puniness with the immensity and power of the universe. In so doing, I think Freud forgot for a moment his own psychological theories and accepted at face value a conventional interpretation of the function of religion instead of a psychological interpretation. There is everything to make us believe that man's chief fears are not of the immensity of the universe but of the malignity of his own aggressive instincts. Freud's skepticism hinged on his lack of conviction that religion could in any realistic way mitigate the sufferings inflicted by the outside world upon the helpless individual. It disregarded the fact that religion may conceivably act as a very real defense against the threat of internal danger. In the same book Freud says, "The true believer is in a high degree protected against the danger of certain neurotic afflictions." But he goes on to explain this with the statement, "By accepting the universal neurosis he is spared the task of forming a personal neurosis."

The position I have maintained throughout this book is that the problem of life is the problem of controlling and directing aggressions. If religion enables us to do this realistically, it is no illusion and not a neurosis. To be sure, we have to take some things "on faith," but as various philosophers have shown—for example, Morris R. Cohen[2]—science itself asks us to take a good deal on faith, including the human ability to arrive at knowledge of the truth. Our question is not one of weighing the content of religious faith and determining its illusory character. It is rather, "Does religion foster life by inspiring love?"

Many people feel that religion does do these things, that it enables men to live more peaceably together, and to be more happy and more constructive. If this be true, there is some justification for the position of those religious leaders who attempt to make religion an obligation, even though in so doing they contradict themselves; for faith cannot be enforced from without. But it is also a fact that many people do not believe that religion absorbs aggressions, but believe rather that it actually stimulates and cultivates them; in short, that it does more harm than good. So while its defenders point to its benefactions—the schools it has established, the education it has fostered, the hospitals it has founded and still maintains, the saints it has inspired to give their lives for what they believed, the ideals it has held up, the gospel of love it has (sometimes) preached, and so on—its opponents point to an equally long list of serious offenses: to inquisitions, to pogroms, to exploitations of the ignorant, to exaltations of the bigoted, to persecution of dissenters, to suppression of free thought and education.

To be sure, the Church * is not religion. But if religion functions in the way its defenders believe, the institutions in which its tenets are crystallized should certainly not be characterized by qualities antithetical to its essential spirit.

One of my psychoanalytic colleagues has analyzed it thus: [8]

One institution, evolved by humanity as an aid, broadly speaking, in controlling hate and egoism, has existed since immemorial times—I mean religion—however inadequately the various forms of it may have fulfilled the task. The "desire for goodness" originally (in our baby-hood) stirred greed and aggression as well as love and tenderness in us. In the early forms of religion this association was still apparent; "good-ness," the God, was killed and eaten as well as worshipped and adored. There had been several religious movements aiming at a separation of these two tendencies before the Christian era; the one that emerged as Christianity, and became one of the great religions of the world, was very largely a supreme endeavor to dissociate all aggression and greed from love. It attempted this by exalting altruistic love to an ideal, but at the same time by denying the reality of many problems that are part of the soul's life—of man's psychology. His aggressive and sexual impulses, if their existence was not altogether denied, were despised and condemned, or ignored. This denial is not peculiar to Christianity, nor have the best interpreters of that religion subscribed to it. It was and is a general tendency in man to deny and ignore what he fears in himself; Christianity, however, adopted and in some ways specially represented the tendency, thus encouraging and maintaining it.

But aggression and sexuality, being integral parts of human nature, are bound to function, for either good or ill, while life lasts. If the attempt is made to deny their rights and exclude them from participation in life for good, they must flow into channels of hate and destructiveness. In such forms as persecution, rapacity, asceticism and pharasaism—the inevitable accompaniments of such a dissociation—they forced their way back into the life of religion and harassed the lives of men. More-over, because Christianity limited goodness so largely to an altruistic attitude in the emotions and *within the mind,* and denied the importance of the external material world, the aggression it denied also had to find

* Many scientists justify religion on a pragmatic but essentially non-religious basis. For example, Dr. Adolf Meyer, the eminent psychiatrist, considers the Church important as "an agency of adult education which can be made as liberal as you like." (Personal communication.)

its outlet in a *personal* way, e.g., in proselytism and persecution against the beliefs, and ultimately against the persons, of men and women. Aggression had no opportunity for expression in the impersonal ways which offer great constructive outlets for it: in the intellectual sphere, or against nature in practical enterprises, such as exploration or experimentation. These worldly fields of effort were regarded as valueless and thus dissociated from goodness. The important beginnings made before the Christian era in the direction of impersonal knowledge, physics, astronomy, mathematics, physiology, etc., were brought to an end by this indifference to the physical world (animate or inanimate) and its truths, and by this denial to man of the constructive exercise of his aggression.

There is an obviously close relation between religion and psychiatry, or at least between the minister and the psychiatrist, and a large area in which they find themselves in complete agreement. Essentially, both are trying to do the same things: to make people more comfortable and to save them from evil. Many details of their work are similar. They both depend upon enlisting the intelligence and through it the emotions. They both use verbal techniques and employ their own personalities to accomplish their results. They both recognize the value of the confessional catharsis. Psychoanalysis agrees with religion that as a man thinketh in his heart so is he, and that guilt attaches almost as much to aggressive wishes as to aggressive acts. For both psychiatrist and priest, love is the greatest thing in the world, whether one calls it God or an instinct.

The fundamental difference between the religious leader and the psychiatrist is probably the difference between St. George and Sir Galahad. Ernest Southard used to say that the good work of the world is divided into the destruction of evil and the promotion of good and that it takes one kind of person to do one of these things and another kind to do the other. Those who hold up ideals and seek to inspire us are like the knights who spent their lives seeking the Holy Grail. Thus, "It would seem that there are dragon-slayers and Grail-hunters. There are those who would prefer to be St. George and others who would rather be Sir Galahad. . . . Nor should we wish to swerve these zealots of the Grail from their goal. . . . But evil is easier to perceive than good is even to conceive. . . . We should, therefore, take advantage of this ingrained destructive trend and endeavor in the first instance to destroy definite concrete, and observable evils rather than to construct indefinite, abstract, hardly conceivable good. Let the proximate task of evil destruction be accomplished and the ultimate task of constructive goodness will shortly follow. The formula might run 'Get the Grail, but first slay the dragon.' " [4]

Certainly then the Grail hunters should not quarrel with the dragon slayers or the Sir Galahads with the St. Georges. There is, nevertheless, a certain mutual suspiciousness. Some psychiatrists justify their skepticism toward religion by pointing to the fact that so many of their patients (i.e., unhealthy minded people) are preoccupied with religious concepts. William James dealt with this fallacy in his *Varieties of Religious Experience*. It is not only philosophically possible but sometimes demonstrable that a psychotic person perceives truth—at least *partial* truth —more accurately and more keenly than a sane person or even that same person when sane.*

But to return to religion and psychiatry; it should be said that some psychiatrists have sought to obtain an understanding of religion through the analysis of the psychology of the religious leader. I have presented my own observations regarding this in my chapter on "Religion" in *The Human Mind*. I tried to show that people strongly urged in the direction of influencing others religiously are often impelled by a need to convince themselves, as it were. This is similar to a phenomenon frequently observed

---

* Naturally I do not mean by this to support the popular idea that the psychiatric patient is saner than his physician. I mean that he often does see *some things* correctly although entirely out of proportion. A man who has made a failure of his life will sometimes realize this first only after he has become mentally sick, but then he will see it so vividly and with such despair that he will be unable to see the possibility for salvage.

in children; namely, that of telling fantasies with great earnestness to other children and even to adults in the hope of convincing themselves by convincing these other people. The child himself wants to believe it is true; he originally thinks it is not true,
but if he can persuade others to believe it is true, then he himself
can believe it.

What is it of which the man of religion wants to convince himself by persuading others? In terms of Christianity, for example,
what really is "the gospel"? Without submitting my conclusions
to a theologian, I believe it could be said to be something along
this line: "Doom threatens mankind. But there is a way of salvation. There is Someone more powerful than we are who loves us.
He loves us in spite of experiences which might tempt us to believe that He does not love us. He has given us proof of his love
(the good things of life, the example of Jesus). He has tried to
show us how to live so as to get the greatest possible happiness
out of life (the teachings of Jesus, or the Buddha, or the prophets, the moral law, the inspired writings of the Bible). He can
be appealed to in times of trouble (prayer) and He will be with
us to the end. 'And there shall be no death,' but we shall go to
live with him."

The only proviso in all this is that we must follow the prescribed rules and regulations. But what *are* the rules and regulations? And there, of course, is exactly the rub. According to the
Roman Catholic church, they are vastly different from the rules
and regulations as interpreted by the Methodist church or the
Christian Science church, or the Buddhist church, or Islam. If
one were inclined to be cynical, he would say that this was the
"joker" in the whole business. Up to this point the program is
impeccable. But if no one knows for certain what the rules and
regulations are, it all becomes an absurdity.

Recently some theologians have made an increasing effort to
get together on this very obvious point of conflict. Jewish rabbis,
Protestant ministers, and Catholic priests have co-operatively en-

deavored to find ways in which to reconcile their theoretical differences. They have tried to present a "united front"—ignoring the fact that even should they succeed, there would remain many millions of Orientals, some of them equally religious, equally intelligent, equally desirous of what religion can give them, who see no convincing reason for exchanging their religion for an Occidental one.

One could probably express the agreed position of rabbis, ministers, and priests by saying that in the last analysis man can be saved from his own aggressiveness by faith and love. But by faith some of them mean faith that man can be saved by faith—a discouraging pronouncement because faith cannot be consciously willed. That he can be saved by love, however, is a more tangible challenge. This is so obviously in line with the whole theory of this book that it cannot be ignored. If religion can increase the amount of love in the world or decrease the amount of hate, it is exactly the program which from scientific studies we have concluded is likely to improve the lot of mankind. If religion can be interpreted in this way, the objects of religion and those of many scientists are precisely the same. Science is likewise seeking for ways in which to make it possible for man to live more comfortably, more productively, more peacefully, more happily.

2

To study people's motives does not impugn their accomplishments, but it may serve to establish a common denominator for several apparently different—even opposed—professions. Since I have already indicated that some religious leaders, whom I have studied, are what they are not because of their faith but because of their lack of it, which necessitates overcompensations, I propose now to submit some of the nonrational reasons why scientists become scientists and show that basically these reasons are the same as those that motivate the religionists.

Primitive religions ascribed illness to the distavor of the gods. As theology became more sophisticated the doctrine of sin was elaborated, and sickness was then often ascribed to sin. The pointed discussion of Job and his friends on this subject and later that of Jesus and his disciples * reflect the currents of thought which prevailed in the infancy of our civilization. With the mounting prestige of empirical science, based on its practical achievements in harnessing nature, the original sin-sick theory has dwindled in importance so that among contemporary religious groups only the faith-healing cults still frankly espouse it. Modern medicine might be said to have been born from the dogged determination of a few Jobs to repudiate the general hypothesis that sin is related to disease.† Intrepid thinkers increasingly surrendered their dependence upon theological theory and turned their eyes to the observable results of the interaction between physical environment and biological tissue. To observe, to measure, to correlate, to tabulate, to resubmit these data to experimental observations—this came to be a method of procedure called "scientific." Its practical fruitful-

* ". . . He saw a man which was blind from his birth. And his disciples asked him, saying, Master, who did sin, this man, or his parents, that he was born blind?

"Jesus answered, Neither . . ." John 9:1-3.

† The traditional conception that mental illness is due to sin, to sinful thoughts and sinful feelings and intentions, continued throughout the centuries and even into the rationalist XVIIIth and the scientific XIXth. The great psychiatric reformers Heinroth and Reil are illustrations in point. Heinroth (*Psychologie*, 1827)—despite his many sound ideas on mental hospitals—and Reil (*Rhapsodieen*, Halle, 1803)—despite his keen intuition—both believe that a mentally sick man is a sinful, weak man, and that his mental health depends upon his spiritual virtues. As Zilboorg points out (*A History of Medical Psychology*, Norton, 1941, p. 289), Reil sought psychiatric wisdom from philosophers (Kayssler, Hoffbauer) and from a minister of the Gospel (Wagnitz). The great liberal movement which began as far back as the fifteenth century is far from completed. In 1492, Pietro Pomponazzi (G. S. Brett, *A History of Psychology*, Macmillan, 1921, 2:159-163) once said to his students, "Reason cannot prove that the soul is immortal. Is the soul separable from the body? Experience never shows us that separate existence. What is the life of the soul apart from the body? There is no material for an answer." This was one of the earliest efforts to divorce psychology from religious metaphysics. The effort has not yet fully succeeded.

ness began to justify it almost immediately, so that those who had been disappointed in the results of prayer became elated over the effects of digitalis. What was called science thus began to capture the loyalty of many who had once depended upon religion. For it seemed that this new method, science, could bring about relief from suffering and the postponement of death with far greater certainty than could communion with the soul, confession to a priest, or prayer to an unseen God. It was not impossible, in such circumstances, to renounce even that last trump card of religion —the promise of life after death to compensate for the brevity or the misery of life preceding death.

In this way the physician took over one of the chief functions of the priest and left the latter to the development of morals and philosophy and the reorganization of religious functions. In doing this the physician was motivated in part by the wish to save himself: his own personal need for something more dependable, more palpably effective, than religion pushed him to the search for the laws of "science."

But what is it that the scientist would save himself (and others) from? The obvious answer, of course, is from pain and from death, and hence from disease. But what is this "death"? Surely not merely biological cessation, for no human being can, in the deepest core of his nature, conceive of nonexistence or imagine its occurring to him. Not even death as portrayed by the early Christians (or the earlier Greek, Roman, or Hindu theologians) as a transition into a new kind of living; this ought rather to have been welcomed. Such concepts are intellectual products and the fear of death is an emotional state, a dread of some vague awfulness which must be translated back into terms of childhood experience. The fear of death, of the outer darkness, the end of everything, even hell—these all refer to the child's anticipation of being overwhelmed by aggressions and (hence) deprived of all love. Lovelessness to the child means rejection, and the end of all life, the end of all hope. The later observation that motility seems to leave some human beings revives this childhood horror added to by the mystery and solemnity of the adult's attitude toward "death." Furthermore, everyone sooner or later experiences pain, often intractable pain, and from this, too, he seeks relief.

When the theological doctrine prevailed that pain, disease, and death are related to sin ("the wages of sin is death"), it was logical to direct prophylactic measures against sinfulness. For some centuries medical science scoffed at this theory, and related pain, disease, and death to external invasions of the body and to idiopathic physiochemical alterations. But today, after a long digression, we have in a measure come back to the sinfulness theory. For, in repudiating this theological tenet, modern science had reverted to the philosophy that man is the hapless prey, the potential victim of solely external forces, which is the philosophy of primitive man as well as of the helpless child; whereas to conceive of disease as related to sin recognizes the partial responsibility of the individual for his own fate. Instead of referring all danger to the outside world, or to the devil, it acknowledges the presence of danger from within. In the infancy of the child, as in the infancy of the race, the dangers from without *are* more vivid and more powerful, so much so that they justifiably produce an enormous sense of helplessness and fear. Such feelings would be overwhelming if it were not possible to obtain some antidote. The protective power and love of the parents are such an antidote, and, until the child becomes disillusioned in his fantasies of parental importance and omnipotence, this antidote is effective. Sooner or later, however, the disillusionment comes. The parent himself dies, disappears, or in some other way betrays his vulnerability. Then confidence has to be displaced to some more dependable bulwark. Depending upon the degree of intelligence, this may be the magical charm, a hallowed idol, a conceptualized deity, an ecclesiastical ritual, or a philosophical system.

Of these the one that now recommends itself most practically and convincingly to some of us is that philosophical system which we call science. Many put the same faith in science that others put in religion, the same faith that we all once put in the comforting arms of mother and father; they cannot let themselves conceive of any inadequacy of science, just as the deeply religious man cannot conceive of defects in his God. Today one may laugh at magic and express doubts about a Supreme Being with impunity, but it is worse than heretical to cast suspicion upon science: it is impious, blasphemous. Yet only a few hundred years ago it was the existence of God that dared not be questioned, although magic was suspect; and, a few hundred years before that, the influence of magic was universally accepted.* I remind the reader of this not to cast any doubts upon our present-day religion of science, but to indicate how it is one of a series of steps in the evolution of human thinking in the direction of finding a substitute for the protective function of the parents.†

But if it is true that science serves so efficaciously in this function of protection against anxiety, the logical question might be, "Why does not every human being seek to become a scientist?" It should not be forgotten that the great mass of people have not yet accepted science in the role that I have outlined. Most people still put far more confidence in religion than in science, and this includes a good many intelligent people. The suffering multitudes who go to doctors are driven by custom, advice, desperation, and numerous other motives in addition to mere conviction. At the present time do the citizens of the United States depend upon

* In 1765 Sir William Blackstone, the famous English jurist, wrote that "to deny the actual existence of witchcraft and sorcery is to contradict the revealed word of God." In 1915, the Jesuit father, Herbert Thurston, wrote in *The Catholic Encyclopedia* that "the question of the reality of witchcraft is one upon which it is not easy to pass a confident judgment. In the face of Holy Scripture and the teaching of the Fathers and theologians, the abstract possibility of a pact with the Devil and of diabolic interference in human affairs can hardly be denied." (See Ralph H. Major, *Faiths That Healed*, Appleton-Century, 1940.)

† See Smiley Blanton, *Faith is the Answer*, Abingdon-Cokesbury, 1940. I am indebted to Dr. Samuel W. Hartwell for the clinical observation that in many children the belief in God is developed as an aid to the child in his struggle to become emancipated from his human parents, and for this reason agnosticism tends to make the emancipation of the children more difficult.

prayer * and right living, and faith in God—or on army tanks, guns, and bombers? This would seem to contradict what I have just said, to suggest that the mass of people do accept science. Perhaps I should qualify it and say that they accept science in its destructive applications; they are far more reluctant to accept it in its constructive applications.

A part of the public's distrust of science is due to ignorance, but some of it is justified. Medical science long shut its eyes to certain data which are as empirical, as definite, as real as the effects of digitalis upon the heart. These data were rejected not because they were unobserved, but partly because they could not be measured and statistically recorded, and partly because of unacknowledged resistances to the investigation of them which make it taboo. Because the theory that sin results in disease involves certain intangibles, it was rejected completely as being outside the legitimate realm of science, which was a grievous error. It would have been more scientific, in the accepted sense of the word, to examine the concept of sin for the purpose of ascertaining what truth was concealed behind this vague but powerful idea. (It is only fair to add that many religionists have fanatically opposed such an analysis and have pronounced it impious.)

Long before science had discovered the details of the transmission of malaria, it was common knowledge among the "unscientific" that it had something to do with bad air. Instead of continuing to ignore completely the proposition that bad air caused malaria, a few thoughtful and slightly unorthodox scientists eventually attempted to discover what it was in air that was bad and why it was called bad. And they found out. They did not find out everything. We do not know to this day, for example, why some

---

* The whole subject of prayer is worthy of more detailed psychological study than scientists have given it. Dr. Samuel W. Hartwell has suggested that prayer, as practised by strong believers, is a healthy psychotherapeutic experience because it enables them to verbalize certain conscious introspective reflections and half-conscious wishes under circumstances of intimacy and faith which rarely prevail in interpersonal relationships.

people are immune to mosquitoes and are rarely bitten by them. If one proposed that certain animals may attract or repel certain other animals by the deliberate production of certain scents, no one would find it hard to accept; yet a speculative psychoanalyst would probably be ridiculed were he to propose that human beings can repel or attract other animals—including mosquitoes, let us say—by the production of certain chemical products in the perspiration, not entirely detached from nervous system control. It is too early, therefore, even to suggest that some people invite the infection by malaria while others resist it. But it could be.

We might go a little further with this correlation of sin and aggression, in theological terms, and say sin was specified to mean such things as blaspheming the Holy Ghost, rejecting the authority of the Church, and breaking the Commandments; it is not difficult to interpret the blasphemy, rejection of God and the Church, and infraction of the Commandments as an expression of a son's rebellion against parental authority. According to psychological theories, the aggressive tendencies of the child are, as we have seen in the earlier chapters of the book, directed against the authority of the parents and entail a wish to supplant them. But to supplant and replace the parents would mean to throw over the advantages derived from being dependent upon them. This is the basis of the conflict which results in repression.

Religion solves that conflict by setting up an authority too great to be destroyed, too kind and benevolent to be hated. The people who can accept religion naturally and devoutly without troubling doubts are those whose early experience was such as to make this plausible. Usually a person with an unswerving belief in a God of justice and goodness is one who was blessed with a loving and incorruptible parent—although occasionally one sees the opposite phenomenon: a person whose parents were so unsatisfactory that the child early formed the fantasy of an imaginary good parent whom he subsequently identifies with the historical conception of God. Unfortunately, many people who espouse religion are not of this pattern. They are troubled by misgivings, hounded by a sense of sin, given to compulsive rituals and ceremonials, and prone to strong intolerance. Such things represent their great uncertainties and ambivalence toward authority. As we have already seen, all children have ambivalence toward their parents and wish to receive gifts, affection, and protection with a minimum of reciprocal obedience. Out of fear they conceal the animosity they feel towards their parents, or try to provoke and then placate them. These attitudes are reproduced in religious patterns of behavior.

One of the automatic devices that modern man has incorporated into his psychology in order to control his aggressiveness, his innate sinfulness, is the "conscience." This phenomenon has always been far better understood by religion than by science. Here is one of the places in which modern medical science is most glaringly unscientific. For the effects of the dictates of the conscience upon the person are just as evident as the effects of a bullet or a poison, although one must look for them in a different way. The conscience not only forbids certain satisfactions—it threatens and even demands the infliction of punishment. The extent to which the person is driven in his frantic efforts to allay the demands of a relentless conscience I have analyzed and described at considerable length in *Man Against Himself*. I there pointed out that the conscience is corruptible; that it is susceptible to accepting bribes, compromises, substitutions, and many other forms of automatic pacifications. Sometimes these work and sometimes they do not; if they do not, acute anxiety and serious maladjustment supervene.

"For it must needs be that offences come," the Bible says, and it is confirmed in this by scientific observation. But what is the "woe" that follows? Reality consequences, yes, to some extent— but also conscience consequences, conscience pain. For many of the offenses are *only in fantasy*, only *wishes* to offend, wishes to hurt. When a part of the second chapter of this book appeared in a magazine, the letters received by the editor clearly showed how difficult the average person finds it to believe that such emotions are universal. Nothing could be more eloquent testimony to the power of repression than this fact. Many readers evidently preferred to believe that *occasional* children with preposterous parents have *occasional* episodes of relatively mild disappointment and chagrin; it seemed incredible to them that every child has more than a few moments in which the only reasons why he does not swiftly dispatch his mother or his father or his brother or his sister or the whole lot of them are at first his lack of physical strength and later the deterrent of conscience fear.

To be sure, if one were strictly rational, no atonement for fancied aggressions would be necessary, and the only sensible atonement for actual aggressions would be restitution. But we cannot expect such normality, such objectivity, to characterize either the unconscious psychology of individuals or the rituals of institutions. And among the devices which have come to be used by men in Occidental cultures particularly are those of atonement by sacrifice or by suffering and sickness, and confession of guilt to an externalized representative of the conscience.

But there is still another device for placating the conscience which is frequently discernible in human beings—less frequently in modern religious ritual, although common in primitive religious practices. It is known as the mechanism of *undoing,* and it is particularly observable in the unconscious motivation of persons who are impelled to try to save others.

What a physician actually does in treating a patient is to *undo* certain processes which have resulted in what is called disease. In his therapy, not only is he carrying out the objective purposes of the healing art, so far as the disease process can be undone, but he may also be symbolically undoing injuries in the patient for which the latter unconsciously assumes some responsibility. This is understandable if we consider that the fantasies of childhood can be unconsciously re-enacted in adult life, or, if of a guilty nature, can be atoned for in adult life by this undoing process.

Fantasies of rescuing, restoring, or making whole are well known in the psychoanalytic investigations of the unconscious mental life of many persons. They are usually clearly referable to guilt feelings incurred during childhood by fancied aggressions against love objects of that period.

Time after time we see the occurrence of bitter hatred toward a brother or parent, fantasies of injuring or killing him, and then a submergence or disappearance of these fantasies and feelings, and their replacement by acts and sentiments of greatest tenderness toward these or substitute persons. Often these acts of reparation are manifestly overdone. We see an older sister sacrificing her life in the most futile and needless way in an effort to help a younger brother, a brother whose most heinous offenses she forgives; in her childhood, this same brother was the object of her greatest bitterness and hostility. He was her mother's favorite, he replaced her as the central interest of the home, he was a male and had prerogatives denied to her. He was the devil of her childhood life. But years later she is the angel of his adult life. She attempts to undo all the injuries which she conceived of inflicting upon him in childhood. That she is never successful only stimulates her to greater efforts. Such people get sick when the now beloved but once hated sibling becomes ill; their dreams are of rescuing the captured or the drowning or the assaulted. Over and over one hears and sees enacted the principle of "I must undo (and thereby atone for) this wickedness of mine."

The professional work of physicians, ministers, priests, nurses, social workers, and many others corresponds to this formula. Physicians and nurses concentrate upon the undoing, as it were, of physical damage; ministers and teachers, upon the undoing of mental or psychological damage; social workers, upon the undoing of social damage. There are practical advantages in this subdivision of labor and there are undoubtedly reasons why a given person is more inclined to see and wish to repair one type of injury than another; but actually it is impossible to separate physical, mental, and social pathology.

Perhaps, too, before leaving the illustration just mentioned, we should make a distinction between the neurotic behavior of such a woman and sublimation in the professional labor of the ministry, nursing, science, etc. The crux of this distinction is the extent to which the mechanism as applied actually does avert self-destruction. The sister described, who ruined her life for her brother, was obviously self-destructive; but the man who, driven by childhood guilt over the hatred of his sister or brother, becomes a physician and ministers to thousands of other substitute sisters and brothers is not self-destructive in his solution.

We have spoken of a search for security in an attempt to solve the riddle of destroying and replacing the authority of the parents and still remaining dependent upon them, and the motive of mitigating guilt feelings, as among the determinants of the predilection of some for finding *modi vivendi* in religion and science. We come now to another motive which is again referable to the psychology of childhood—the motive of curiosity.

It is easier to recognize curiosity as a motive in the scientist than in the priest or the minister. It is significant that historically and educationally medicine begins with anatomy. For most medical students anatomy remains throughout the four years the central core of medical education. But for every child, also, anatomy is for a considerable period of his life the central core of things to be learned. His own arms and legs, ears and nose, fingers and toes, are called to his attention and are given names. But there is one thing in which his parents and teachers seem reluctant to instruct him, especially if he is a boy. Everything else is pointed out to him, explained to him, even submitted to him for examination. His mother's body remains the mystery of the Sphinx.

The child makes his own explorations, usually with considerable hazard and often followed by punishment. He acquires certain astonishing and terrifying information about the different construc-

tion of some of his playmates; but he still remains in doubt about
the person who interests him most and always has interested him
most, the person he is closest to and knows the least about. All
this is made worse, far worse, when he discovers, with or without
misleading information from his parents, that he once came from
his mother's body and that other children come from their mothers' bodies. This renders the already puzzling mystery infinitely
more complicated. He has fantasies, as we all know, of having
come out of her abdomen, of having passed from her bowels. The
fascinating obscurity of those hidden external parts of her body
is only exceeded by the inconceivable intricacy of her insides. Not
all children remain in such confusion and not all children become
physicians, but for some of them curiosity about these mysteries
remains the secret driving force of their lives. They search their
schoolbooks for information; they scan the dictionary and the
Bible; they find a fascination in pictures of human beings; secretly
they are always looking for the same thing—usually, of course,
without finding it.

As such children grow older, they abandon hope of having their
questions answered even by the printed page. They become interested in pets, which they examine carefully but furtively; they
cut open dead animals; they dissect frogs and turtles and scrutinize
the cleaning of chickens by the cook with intense fascination. They
take clocks apart to see what is inside. Then comes a period in
which it becomes proper to abandon childish curiosity and childish
interests and to begin to think in terms of adult interests. Adult
interests are actually just the same as childhood interests, and as
soon as the now grown-up child has become used to speaking the
new language he reverts to the same topics. If his inhibitions are
not too great, he may satisfy himself by more direct investigations.
But even these do not entirely satisfy. There remains a driving,
insatiable curiosity to know what is *really* on the inside. The only
sure, direct method of finding out is to study anatomy.

One might speculate, upon this basis, that those who actually do study anatomy and become physicians are more direct and less turned from their original purpose than those who deflect their curiosity to the study of the anatomy of other mammals or even to the structure of rocks and chemical molecules. One could go still further and assume that something of the same curiosity lies back of those now highly symbolic investigations of the nature of the universe which characterize philosophers and to some extent theologians. For the psychoanalyst there is a striking similarity between the quest for "the nature of God" and the similar quest for knowledge of the nature of the mother's body. If this seems too prosaic, it is only because of our artificially suppressed sense of values; I see no reason why we should regard the nature of God as any more sublime or dignified than the nature of the human body and the functions of the mother's womb. I will go further and say that philosophically I doubt if there is any difference.

3

To recapitulate, we have suggested that in the deep unconscious motivation of both the man of religion and the man of science, one can probably find with a fair degree of uniformity certain determining trends related to their professional ideals of saving others. Among these are: first, the wish to relieve the anxieties of childhood by allegiance to a belief in the infallibility either of a God or of a philosophy or of a technique (science); secondly, the search for a solution of the problem of conflict with authority; third, the need to assuage the unconscious guilt arising from long-repressed hostility toward various members of the childhood family by the psychological process of undoing; and, finally, a glorified curiosity about the human body, particularly the mother's body and the great mystery of creation.

We come back at last to the question posited at the beginning of this chapter: Does religion help in the mastering of aggressions and in the promotion of love? The answer certainly must be that

it serves to do so in much the same way as does science. As a matter
of fact, religion has been used much more than science for this
very purpose in the past hundred centuries. After all, science as
such cannot be said to have been born until a few hundred years
ago.

Whether or not science is a better method than religion may
seem to be a purely academic question. The scientist is bound to
think it is, and the deeply religious man is bound to think the contrary. The medicine man and the priest are both endeavoring to do
the same thing: to help other people to live and to save them from
dangers which to some extent actually exist, but which to a larger
extent are the projections of internal hostilities. For some people
one method will be more effective; for other people, the other
method. As a scientist, I must acknowledge the prejudice of the
scientist. So far as science is able to exploit the existence of universal law by subjecting its hypotheses to a process of trial and proof,
it seems to me to be more trustworthy. The concept of the supernatural which is invoked by religion disturbs scientists because it
violates a fundamental scientific premise. Argue it as you will,
there is an irresolvable contradiction in the assumption that any
person knows more about the unknown than any other person
does, and also in the assumption that there can be exceptions to
the laws of nature. Laws admit of no exceptions. For the explanation of these apparent contradictions, the man of religion has
recourse to an internal reality and a subjective experience which
he can express only in mystical and symbolic language. But this
is not the language of science, and hence the scientist tends to
repudiate it. He cannot tell whether religious authorities conceive
of the supernatural as an unexplored extension of the natural
order (as many modern religious leaders believe), or whether they
think of it as a great counterforce, opposed to the laws of nature
as the scientist knows them. The believer invokes as his authority
a power whose very existence—as far as visible proof is concerned
—depends solely upon the faith of his followers. This very faith

is cited as proof of the existence of God, but to the scientist it is proof only of the human need for reliance on some power outside of and greater than man. So far as this faith represents a confidence in the integrity and intelligence and idealism of a human leader, it is subject to analysis under scientific psychological laws. This same willingness to accept authority and help from a superior figure and to ascribe virtues and abilities to him beyond what he actually possesses is characteristic of the situation that often develops between patient and physician and other individuals in pairs and groups. Psychoanalysts call it transference. It is love even more than it is faith—not love of God, as it is often called, but love of a man who represents a parent. Yet we know that religious groups who consider this phenomenon the mainspring of their energy, and try to formulate what might be called an intellectual theology, soon lose power and enthusiasm. It would seem that the element of the supernatural is essential to effective religion. And this element is anathema to most scientists, because they cannot distinguish it from superstition.

But even scientists have their private superstitions, and the more important practical quarrel of scientists with religion is that it so often tends to emphasize the negative side of human behavior—to encourage passivity, compliance, the endurance of misery, the denial of joy, subservience to outworn methods and to unworthy authorities. It cannot be denied that intuitive truth has often been perceived and proclaimed by great religious leaders long before it was demonstrated by science; but the fact remains that many of the lesser religious leaders who claim the same authority are less gifted, and for some such leaders the temptation to exploit the credulity and wistfulness of the ignorant is irresistible. The intuitive perception of truth becomes confused with the selfish gratification of personal objectives. The will of God is invoked not only to say that men should love one another, but also to say that men should hate and kill one another.

It was in the name of God and religion that Saracens killed and were killed in Asia and that Torquemada tortured and executed thousands of defenseless fellow citizens in Spain. And it was in the name of God that Luther, righteously indignant regarding the peasant rebellion in 1525, wrote:

> For a prince and lord must remember in this case that he is God's minister and the servant of His wrath (Romans xiii), to whom the sword is committed for use upon such fellows. . . . If he can punish and does not—even though the punishment consist in the taking of life and the shedding of blood—then he is guilty of all the murder and all the evil which these fellows commit, because by wilful neglect of the divine command, he permits them to practice their wickedness, though he can prevent it and is in duty bound to do so. Here then, there is no time for sleeping; no place for patience or mercy. It is the time of the sword, not the day of grace. . . . Stab, smite, slay, whoever can. If you die in doing it, well for you! [5]

In other words, religion can act and has acted precisely like a dictatorship, because both of them subscribe to the same principle: that it is not necessary to prove things, but only to declare them and to invoke supernatural power or a wished-for destiny as the supreme authority.

With such presumptions science cannot hold. Science demands that *only* what has been demonstrated, what has been subjected to re-examination with a minimum of observational bias, be accepted as belonging to the kingdom of truth and reality. To the scientist, loyalty to reality is the highest virtue; under a dictatorship, it is a crime.

All of this diminishes not one whit the magnificence of character in those Grail-seekers who are inspired to hold up ideals for their fellow men or to minister to them with friendliness, sympathy, and affection. Nor does it reflect in the least upon the mental healthiness of those who hold to their religious faiths.

If, to anyone, religion means reverence and affection for the created universe and its creatures, the wish to get the most possible

out of it for human beings by the scientifically tested rules of
living and the acceptance of the greater wisdom of certain inspired
leaders as guiding principles of life—if this is what is meant by
religion, I could not distinguish it in practice from science, nor
withhold from it equally high allegiance.

In recent years numerous writers [6] have sought to reconcile the
differences between psychiatry and religion. Referring to Freud's
declaration that religion is a symptom of the lingering childishness
of the race and that religious beliefs are illusions fulfilling "the
oldest, strongest, and most insistent wishes of mankind," Vlastos [7]
grants that there is such a form of religion, one that confirms man
in his childish ways, "releasing him from the natural world . . .
into a supernatural world that guarantees his dearest wishes against
frustration, reinstates him in the center of the cosmic stage, and
relieves him of responsibility to change himself and the world."
It is the religion of magic, and magic is exempt from the ordinary
checks of reason. Such religion is indeed the opium of the people.

But there is another form of religion, Vlastos insists, which is a
man's "complete, single-handed, whole-hearted surrender to the
Sovereign power, order, and goodness" and which he finds in
"that reality that creates, sustains, and outlasts his own life and
every life." To come to terms with this reality, to discover our
oneness with it, to find its meaning—this is the religion of mature
faith.

"From the vantage point of such a faith [Vlastos continues] we
may look back on Freud's indictment of the religion of our time,
and find there not an enemy, but an unexpected ally. Freud has
supplied us with the means of validating the faith of high religion.
The root of childishness is egocentric craving for omnipotence;
its fruits are illusion, fear, irresponsibility. What has passed for
religion has been often an elaborate device for protecting and exploiting childishness. So far Freud was right. But there is another
religion that is not an escape, but a determination to face reality
without illusion and without fear, find its Sovereign Good, and

gives oneself to it in humility and trust. To give one's life away to what one knows to be of highest worth, not only for oneself but for all mankind, is the most mature experience open to man. It can help him face death and tragedy undismayed. It possesses the secret of life everlasting."

Chapter 9. Hope

IT IS a curious thing that of the triad Faith, Hope, and Love, so little has been said in defense of Hope. On the contrary, there is a tendency to depreciate hope as a human weakness, a narcotic to dull the senses of humanity to the miseries of existence and the inevitability of death. That "Hope springs eternal in the human breast" is usually said pityingly; hope is a "sweet flatterer" (Glover), and "Fortune's cheating lottery" (Cowley); "the miserable have no other medicine but only hope" (Shakespeare); "hope is the fawning traitor of the mind, while under color of friendship, it robs it of its chief force of resolution" (Philip Sidney); "hope is the worst of evils, for it prolongs the torment of man" (Nietzsche).

This tendency to undervalue hope may be in part a use of a familiar device for sparing ourselves disappointment, the refusal to believe in favorable possibilities. In its extreme form this is a neurotic symptom frequently encountered in people with pronounced inhibitions. If accompanied by superior intelligence, such a neurotic pessimism can be very brilliantly rationalized, until one is almost persuaded that he is listening not to a neurotic but to a sage. Schopenhauer is the outstanding example, but there have been many minor Schopenhauers. If the rationalization is more clumsy, such people are known merely as cynics, alarmists, croakers, or misanthropists. Neurotic optimism, the sanguine dauntlessness of the "cheerful idiot," is much easier to recognize for what it is and to discredit accordingly.

"Nevertheless," as Ernest Jones has put it, "deep analysis constantly shows that even the philosophic pessimism about life is bound up with internal inhibitions of enjoyment and self-content

which, from their origin and fate after analysis, can only be regarded as artifacts in the evolution of the individual. And we
find, further, that impairment of the natural zest of life . . . is
more often the result of such internal inhibitions than of externally
inflicted misfortune, however severe and however lasting." [1] Convincing as the logic of the pessimist is, and though his dismal pre-
dictions appear to be justified by unhappy world events or even
personal events, the penetrating study of the pessimist regularly
reveals that his pessimism is a pose and that, like every other
human being, he is at heart spurred on by hope.

In scientific circles there is a determined effort to exclude hope
from conceptual thinking, first because of the general obloquy of
admitting any psychological concepts into materialistic and fanatically empirical science; and second, because of a fear of corrupting
objective judgment by wishful thinking. But all science is built on
hope, so much so that science is for many moderns a substitute for
religion. It is true that hoping and wishing must be excluded, as
far as possible, from experiment, but Brown,[2] McLean,[3] and other
scientists and students of methodology have demonstrated that in
most productive scientific work hypotheses, conscious or unconscious, precede the demonstrated facts, and that new ideas, the perception of new relationships, spring from the unconscious. Man
can't help hoping, even if he is a scientist; he can only hope more
accurately. "Everything that is done in the world is done by hope,"
said Martin Luther. "No husbandman would sow one grain of corn
if he hoped not it would grow up and become seed; no bachelor
would marry a wife if he hoped not to have children; no merchant
or tradesman would set himself to work if he did not hope to reap
benefit thereby."

Hope is a consciousness of the realizable wish, and the wish has
become the foundation of psychology, just as the concept of force
is the foundation of physics. For a long time psychology was a
static descriptive science in which sensation was the unit; something
was sensed, perceived, and reacted to. Why this series occurred no

one undertook to explain. Descriptive psychology has gradually been replaced by a dynamic psychology in which the movement, the motive, the purpose has become the primary preoccupation. The unit of such motivation, Freud called "the wish," which Holt,[4] Lewin,[5] and others have shown to be identical with numerous other technical terms in psychology and co-ordinate with such physical concepts as the attraction of gravity. It is a course of action which some mechanism of the personality is set to carry out whether it actually does so or not. "In an organism which is about to perform overtly a course of action in regard to its environment the internal mechanism is more or less completely set for this performance beforehand."[6]

It is not a mere figure of speech to say that the birds that fly north in the spring *hope* to fly south again in the fall, or that, flying south, they hope to reach their winter quarters. What difference is there between the hope of the nesting bird to see its eggs hatched and the hope of the human mother to bear a healthy child? Not only from season to season but almost from hour to hour hope sustains us with this promise of better things to come and the necessity for working toward them. This is not just a spiritual quality, nor is it some great illusion of nature; it is an empirical psychobiological factor in living.

The reader may infer from this that I make little distinction between hope and instinct. It is a fashion at present to eschew the word "instinct" and to substitute any number of essentially equivalent terms; nothing is gained by this except an illusory impression of progress and modernity. I would say that hope is the consciousness we have of forces within us, whatever they are called. What we feel the need of, we will bend all efforts toward obtaining; hence it is "the mighty hopes that make us men."

Thus modern psychologists have come to agree with Solomon that "as a man thinketh in his heart, so is he." There is no such thing as "idle hope"; the thoughts and hopes and wishes that we entertain are already correlated to the plan of action which

would bring these about, even though the whole project is ultimately renounced as too difficult or too dangerous to carry through.
The saying that "anticipation is better than realization" recognizes the fact that the experiences of the personality in getting
ready for an event are often so vivid and so galvanizing that the
actual realization becomes a minor part of the whole. This essential identity of hoping, wishing, purposing, attempting, and doing
is a little difficult for the practical, common-sense man to grasp,
because for him it makes a great difference whether a thing is executed or only planned or only hoped for. There *is* an external
difference, to be sure; and there is an internal difference, too. But
internally, psychologically, from the standpoint of *motive*, there
is no difference. There is a difference in the *fate* of the impulse,
the degree with which it is correlated with reality, inhibited by
internal fears, supported by other motives, etc.—but the motive
force is the same.

It is interesting to see how intuitive and psychological the law
is in this respect, clumsy and unpsychological though it is in others.
The law recognizes that the intent to kill is more serious than
the act of killing, in that murderous assault that fails of accomplishment is more seriously punished than accidental manslaughter.
The law punishes the intention rather than the act. (Of course, the
law considers only *conscious* motives.)

Freud did not ignore the well-known fact that many wishes are
not translated into action. It was his great contribution to psychological science to show that dreams are precisely what our
language implies—our unspoken, unrealized wishes (hopes); and
to show, too, that the specific meaning of the dream language
can be discovered and used to understand a patient's behavior and
symptoms. Our dreams and our hopes do tend to come true!
Freud classified the conscious formulation of hoping and wishing
into that which is done in accordance with what he called "the
reality principle" and that which is done only on the basis of the
"pleasure-pain principle." To paraphrase this, all hopes arise

within the individual; only some of them are realizable in terms of external reality. As a result, every person has two worlds in which to express his hopes—a world of internal reality and a world of external reality. Growing up consists in amalgamating these two worlds to a considerable degree, though never completely. Longfellow well said that the thoughts of youth are long, long thoughts; they are a long way from the hard facts of life as we adults know them. For the little boy there are giants and ogres and witches and sugar mountains and Santa Clauses; when he grows up he does not renounce these fantasies, but he modifies them—there are villainous men in business (or in Washington), wicked women such as his mother-in-law, bonuses and prospective oil strikes to make him rich overnight. Adults who cannot give up the predominant wishful thinking of childhood, who continue to live in a world of their own split off from the real world, are called schizophrenics. The delusions of schizophrenics, like the day-dreams of children, are hopes and wishes. They are not "untrue" hopes or wishes. Admittedly they do not correspond to the world as *we* know it, and therefore they are untrue for *us;* but they are true for the schizophrenic person, and they determine his behavior, his joy, his real life. The pessimist, unlike the schizophrenic but like all neurotic personalities, has both an internal and an external world of reality, but he is unable to reconcile the two in a way that will bring him normal satisfaction.

The hopes we develop are therefore a measure of our maturity. In the process of fusing inner and outer reality, and thus making hope correspond with accomplishment, the child becomes more and more practical, which is to say that he begins to test reality and finds out which hopes can be realized and what restrictions the external world places upon them. He discovers physical laws, economic laws, social and biological laws, and among his discoveries are all the evidences that after a while we cease to have any hopes and any pleasures—in short, that we die. He never quite believes this for himself, but he is practical enough to make plans against the contingency.

Another thing he discovers is the fact that what has happened has happened and cannot be changed, that he cannot relive his life, and that many of his hopes must therefore be renounced.

He may arm himself against these two crushing blows to his hopes in his two worlds: in the world of internal reality he retains his belief in his own immortality and that of his loved ones by a belief in life after death, and in the external practical world he anticipates his immortalization in his progeny. This is why we say that children are the hope of the world and the Kingdom of Heaven.

2

"Yeah it's been a poor day," said the taxi-driver as he drove me up Lexington Avenue. "I doubt if I'll total more'n five dollars—and that's gross, you know. Rain don't help us as much as you'd think. You see people have gotta budget. You know what I mean? The weather is bad so they plan to stay in. They budget. I don't blame 'em. My wife and I hafta budget. How else could we live? Lord, we've got kids, and you can say what you please, kids are expensive. I'm tellin' you.

"I've gotta boy in high school, and he's gotta have clothes, ain't he? Kids look at kids—don't they? At that age, you know. But can I crab? Ain't he the best in his class? All A's last term. *He* won't grow up to be no taxi-driver! I've gotta girl, too—she's only ten but she's comin' along. She's a good kid. And a little fellow— two years old. Awful cute! I wish I had more. But they cost money and no foolin'.

"But that's all right, I've got nothin' to complain about. I've got the kids, ain't I? Just like payin' income tax—you know what I mean? If you've gotta pay one you're glad you got one to pay, ain't you? *I* ain't—I mean, I ain't got *that*, but I got kids, and what else is there to live for? I ask you.

"Take me, now. What kind of a life do I have? On the street all night and sleep half the day, and the kids get home from school about when I leave. The baby jabs her thumb in my eyes to wake me up. Her mother thinks it's cute. Well, it gets me up anyway. I see 'em all a minute, and I have my breakfast or whatever you call it, and then I'm out again.

"But I figure it don't make no difference what kind of a job you got if you can earn a little and keep the kids goin', and satisfy the ol' lady. That's what I mean, though. If you love your kids you got somethin' to live for and you've got somethin' to work for. These fellers that ain't got any kids, I don't know what they keep fightin' for. I wouldn't. Hell, it ain't worth it. Kids is the only real hope we got."

He was silent a few minutes as he negotiated a difficult corner, and I looked idly through the cab windows at the hustling throngs of people. I wondered to myself how my driver's philosophy would strike most of them. Suppose, I thought, his next customer is a merchant. How would a merchant react to the theory that children are the purpose of living? These people rushing by me on the street—would a merchant look at them as parents and children, or perhaps merely as potential customers?—and the more of them the better. If he were an employer, I suppose these people would all be potential employees and a guarantee against labor shortage. If he were an employee himself, perhaps an insecure employee, all these people would be merely competitors. If he were a politician, I suppose they would represent votes. To the men out of work sitting idly and hopelessly on park benches, the crowd must represent the enviable and lucky ones who monopolize the restricted opportunities for converting labor and natural resources into a livelihood.

The taxi-driver interrupted my reveries. "Because," he asked, "what else is there, honest? Why do you go on livin' if you don't have kids? They don't ask to be born, do they? We bring 'em here, it's up to us to take care of 'em. Didn't somebody take care of us? You know what I mean?"

I was a little sorry to see my driver's hedonism developing a flavor of obligation, but I was getting out of the cab now. I went up to my office with his words repeating themselves in my mind.

On my desk was the morning mail. I opened a letter from a colleague:

I would like to have you see a 16-year-old girl, the daughter of rather prominent people in this community. I have known them for a good many years. The patient's mother was a very pampered baby among a large family of children. She married well; her husband is successful but very passive in his family life. When the mother discovered that she was pregnant with the present child, she was greatly distressed and came to me wanting an abortion. When I refused to encourage her she reacted by a violent display of temper which she repeated toward her husband and others and continued for weeks. She made threats of suicide and caused her husband and others a great many uncomfortable and unpleasant moments. I don't remember the details of this very well any more because, of course, it was about 17 years ago.

I mention this because it was in such sharp contrast with the mother's behavior subsequently. She put on what seemed to me to be an exaggerated display of motherhood. She refused to wean the baby until it was well past 16 months old. She fussed over the child constantly during infancy and early school days.

When Mary [the child] got into high school she began to be increasingly queer. At first she was just unsociable and eccentric, but recently she has begun running out of classrooms impulsively, making queer remarks to passersby on the street, and laughing in a queer way. They called me in to see her, and I recognized immediately that she would have to be institutionalized, and am therefore writing you.

It seems to me rather clear that the mother had a prodigious hostility for this child, which the child seems to have sensed in spite of the fact that the mother tried to cover it up. We may soon have two patients on our hands.

I recalled the taxi-driver who thought people had nothing to live for but their children, who wished he had more children even though he couldn't afford them. I thought of this mother, who was obliged (?) to have a child that she later hated and mistreated. I wondered what her own childhood must have been like, what her frustrations had been, what curious distortion of her point of view had brought about the tragedy in her home that contrasted so sharply with the joy in the taxi-driver's home.

While pondering these questions and reflecting what I would say to my colleague in reply to his letter, I was interrupted for my first appointment. It was with a patient I had not seen before. She was an obviously well-to-do married woman who came because she was depressed to the point of suicide over a love affair in which she was entangled. It was, she said, the only worthwhile thing in her life, the only thing she wanted, the only thing that would make her happy, and yet it seemed impossible. I asked her if she had children. Yes, she had one, a little girl of eight. But she did not feel it was right to spend much time with the daughter because they were too antagonistic to one another. She could not "cope" with the little girl, the governess could do it much better; so mother and daughter spent only a few minutes each day together, before the child had supper (alone).

Some hours later I was talking to another woman at the opposite end of the economic scale. She, too, had been on the verge of suicide and had been taken in by the police for having attempted it. She had discovered herself pregnant for the tenth time. Her husband was out of work, she had seven living children, the total family income in the past three months had been less than $100. About the only thing these two women had in common aside from their psychiatric consultant was the wish not to have a child.

I thought again of the taxi-driver. What powerful counterarguments to the theory that we live for our children and that our children give us hope to live!

What is the answer to this? Are children a blessing or a curse? Is it true that this must depend upon the individual parents, and, if so, what are the criteria that determine it? If our world is to get better, it will surely be through the influence we bring to bear upon the next generation, that is, upon the children. But do we want these children? Does our wanting them or not wanting them make any difference?

To raise such questions or to attempt to answer them is to do something very irregular, even—in the eyes of some—blasphemous. Having children is "just nature," and many believe that we should not attempt to apply intelligence to that which is natural law or the will of God. But it seems to me that if we are not utterly pessimistic, if we do have some hope that our children will do better than we did and that their children will do better than they, we are obliged to give some thought to the circumstances under which children come into the world.

Consider the great masses of people on the plains of China, or in the slums of New York, or in the prisons of every state in the Union, and ask yourself how many of these people were the deliberate and considered product of their parents' love. How many of these struggling units of society were the children of parents who planned for them and hoped for them and waited for them with a greeting of joy and welcome? How many of them were the children of parents who produced them only by accident, who resented their conception and dreaded their arrival, consciously or unconsciously hating their existence because it threatened their own, took food from the mouths of an already frantic and miserable family? What effect had this on the emotional life of the child? What are the psychological consequences to the child of being unwanted and unwelcome—of being looked upon by its parents as a punishment for indulgence in a sin?

We must admit that sometimes even the unplanned-for, unwanted, unexpected child may stimulate enough love in the parents to overcome their initial hostility toward him. This we shall discuss in more detail below. But often the parents are unable to suppress or repress their hostile feelings completely. They may fool themselves and others, but they do not fool the child. The child senses that he is not wanted, and the joy and promise of his life are blasted from the very start by this realization, dim and unverbalized though it may be.

Far more important than the dramatic examples in which the hostility of a mother ruins the life of an unwanted child are the more general effects of repressed maternal hatred. Where one child reacts to this with an acute mental illness, dozens of children react to it in more subtle ways by developing self-protective barriers against the inner perception of the feeling of being unwanted. This may show itself in a determined campaign or in a provocative program of attracting attention by offensive behavior and even criminal acts. Still more seriously it may show itself as a constant fear of other people or as a bitter prejudice against individuals or groups through deep-seated, easily evoked hatred for them. The rage of the southern poor white against the Negro suspected of some dereliction is referable to the hate he feels inwardly at having been himself, like the Negro, unwanted. The same is perhaps true in the case of Germans and Jews and in many other situations which give opportunity for the expression of hatred in the denial of the feeling of being rejected. The importance of this factor in the psychology of war is even greater, in my opinion, than the economic factor arising from the increase of population. This is why I say that from the purely scientific point of view, *planned parenthood is an essential element in any program for increased mental health and for human peace and happiness.* The unwanted child becomes the undesirable citizen, the willing cannon-fodder for wars of hate and prejudice.

By planned parenthood I mean parenthood entered into willingly, with adequate preparation for the strains and sacrifices it imposes, with sufficient means and equipment to give the child a healthy start in the world without depriving others of the actual necessities of life. It means, too, sufficient psychological maturity and understanding on the part of the parents to endure the dependency of the child over a period of many years. Of course, every thinking person approaches parenthood with some fears, but these are quite different from the acute protest with which many children are received today, often quite justifiably. I have said a great deal about the mother's responsibility for cultivating in her children the love that will bring about a new order, but we cannot hold her to this responsibility if the physical, financial, and psychological burden laid upon her is far beyond her capacity to bear. The children of the future do not "belong" to their parents alone: they are the concern of every one of us; they are *literally* the hope of the world.

Psychological science concurs with the Roman Catholic Church absolutely on the point that for the highest welfare of the parents it is necessary to create children and to love them. But not all parents are capable of obtaining the highest welfare or of entering into so responsible, so difficult, and (as my taxi-driver said) so expensive an obligation. It is a *reductio ad absurdum* to attempt to force this responsibility on people in the face of reality obstacles—unmitigated poverty, advanced physical illness, a conscious aversion to parenthood.

Economists may differ as to how many people could survive comfortably in our world under optimum social conditions, but they would all agree that with things as they are nearly every country in the world seems to have more people than it can find room for and that the great majority of this population leads a marginal or submarginal existence. In this twentieth century since Christ, most people are miserable most of the time, and many of them from sheer hunger.

In such a world, where neither the children themselves nor their parents will their birth, why do unwanted members of society continue to be born? Who is it that wants them to be born, only to starve slowly or be used to kill off one another or to live out a pitiful life of misery and despair? Is it society? Does society really need them? Is it the government? Does any government want more soldiers, or more consumers, or more taxpayers, even at the expense of individual suffering, frustration, and despair? Shall we blame it on nature, on the blind forces of instinct, the unregulated response to the breeding season, or the incidental consequences of legalized contiguity between a hapless male and female in whose dim intelligence there is often but little grasp of either the present or the future?

These questions are seldom asked, seldom answered. That it is all "the will of God" sounds like a pious evasion; if it is the will of God for men to multiply like rats and lice until some of them starve to death, it must also be the will of God that rats and lice should multiply without restraint. If it is for the purpose of national defense, it must be equally justifiable for *all* nations to enter into breeding contests so that the products bred may be shot or blown up or drowned in action. But who is it that really *wants* more people on earth, regardless of the quality or the happiness of those people? Intelligent merchants don't want them; relief agencies don't want them; medical clinics don't want them; even the Associated Farmers of Southern California seemed not to want them so much after the consequences of their appeals for a labor supply were dramatized in Steinbeck's *Grapes of Wrath.**

This blind compulsion toward increasing the population has in part an historical explanation. In the days when America was an unexplored colonial empire, and even in those later days when the West was still a frontier country, there was some point in seeking an increase of local population: there was more work to be done than there were workers at hand to do it. It became the custom to cry out like the man from Macedonia for someone to come and help (and incidentally to reap the benefits of helping). That this appeal was often made with a shocking disregard of

* This urge for an increase in the local population is not limited to California. It has become the function of Chambers of Commerce and certain evangelical newspapers and real estate companies all over the country. Some few cities achieve both size *and* culture, but the notion that those two achievements are in some way interdependent is a fallacy based upon the secret ambition of every community to become another New York.

truth and of the consequences to those who accepted the invitation is vividly brought out in Mari Sandoz's biography of her father, *Old Jules,* and in my mother's autobiography, *Days of My Life.* It was ironically and bitterly described by Charles Dickens in *Martin Chuzzlewit.* But those days are past.

One might think that this population fetish derived from agricultural ideals, if it were limited to agricultural people. On the farm, where there was plenty of room, the more pigs that were farrowed, the more calves that were dropped, the more eggs that were laid—the better. All these could be turned into money, and life was thus made easier for the human beings who sponsored these increases. The more of everything, the better. Formerly this was true of children, too; they, like the other livestock, were worth money, and so it was good economic gospel to encourage large families. But all this is no longer the case. On the farm today, even the children are an expense, and *not* necessarily an economic asset. Figures show that only about one-third of the children born on farms can be absorbed by agricultural labor requirements.

"Mankind is like a forest of trees too thickly planted," wrote George Drysdale in England in 1854,[7] and he went on:

All indeed suffer more or less, but the more robust struggle upward, and in so doing destroy their weaker neighbours. . . . This age, and all past ages in old countries, have been ages of mutual destruction. We eat the food of our fellow-beings, we breathe their air, we enjoy their loves, we suck their life's blood. . . . It is easy to bear the ills of others with Christian fortitude. Yes; although we, who look on, may reconcile ourselves to this horrible condition of the majority of our fellows, although we may seek to disguise it by vain boasts of the advance of civilization, the poor themselves can never be reconciled to poverty, their human flesh and blood cannot stand its insufferable miseries, and to them all big talk of the progress of mankind is a delusion and a lie.

The life of our working classes is worse than that of most of the beasts of burden. They toil unremittingly for ten or twelve hours a day at a laborious, monotonous, and in many cases a deadly occupation, without hope of advancement or personal interest in the success of the work they are engaged in. At night their jaded frames are too tired to permit their enjoyment of the few leisure hours, and the morn wakens them to the same dreary day of ceaseless toil. Even the seventh day, their only holiday, brings them in this country little gaiety, little recreation; a solemn sermon and two hours of sedentary constraint is all that is provided for them. The clergy and others, who are indignant that a poor working man does not go to church on his only holiday, should themselves try his life for six months and see then what appetite they will have for church, when their limbs are wasting with incessant toil, their nerves beginning to give way, and their hearts embittered by a life of constant drudgery and care.

Thus have the poor to toil on, as long as their strength permits. At last some organ gives way, the stomach, the eyes, or the brain; and the unfortunate sufferer is thrown out of work and sent to the hospital, while his wife and family are reduced to the brink of starvation. Often the man, rendered desperate by his hopeless position, plunges into drink and gives himself over to ruin. At other times the working classes in a frenzy of rage at their infernal circumstances determine that they will have higher wages or perish. Hence result the disastrous strikes and the terrible social revolutions that have in recent times so often convulsed society. But they are vain; they are but the blind effort of men to do something or die, the fruitless heavings of a man in a nightmare. The mountain of misery invariably falls back again upon their breasts with only increased pressure and forces them, worn out by impotent struggles, to bear it quietly for another little season.

Granted that there have been great changes in labor conditions since Drysdale wrote his brilliant, if somewhat emotional, book, much of what he says is just as true today as it was in 1854. Have we the right to expect that children brought into the world in such circumstances can be *taught* to love and not hate their fellowmen?

I am not suggesting that only those fortunate people who are able to afford children should be permitted to have them, or that the privilege of parenthood should be denied to the poor. But I am saying that it is illogical and suicidal to breed human beings who are condemned to a hopeless existence. It is unfair to them; it is dangerous to the rest of the world. If we were as concerned as we should be with the origins of hate, greed, oppression, crime, and war, we would begin with the unborn child. We would give him parents with the desire and ability to bear and rear him, and we would see that they received the co-operation from society which is necessary to carry through the task. And we would not force childbearing upon the unwilling, by direct or indirect means. That human beings should be miserable in order that the strength of armies or the census of church membership may be increased is totally incompatible with any conceivable decent moral order.

Many people who would concur in the belief that children should not be born into a home where there is not enough to eat would not agree that an aversion to parenthood on psychological grounds is an equally valid reason for not having children. The woman who prefers animal pets to a child of her own is often criticized contemptuously for her childless state. I think of this when my way into the elevator is blocked by one of the fifty or sixty dogs which inhabit the hotel where I stay when in New York. Leashes entangle my legs while the owners of the attached animals babble baby-talk, not addressed to me but intended to convey to me the impression that I am sharing the elevator with a darling, beloved, and innocent creature for whom I should spontaneously feel the same extravagant emotion which imbues my human fellow-traveler.

I can understand how one who sees this misdirection of human affection, who contrasts it with the realities of human life—the need of the little unwanted waifs who roam the streets, the starvation for human affection that he sees all about him—might experience strong emotions of righteous indignation, even to the point of feeling that such women should be forced into motherhood in order to make themselves of some account in the world. But this would be an absurd miscarriage of logic. Women who are capable of rearing children but who prefer to lavish their affection upon dogs, cats, and birds, who shudder fastidiously at the thought of pregnancy, are exhibiting an immaturity of psycho-

sexual development which indicates an unfitness for motherhood. A grown-up play-boy who prefers to walk around with a
big police dog instead of a son would never become an adequate
father, no matter how many impregnations he accomplished.
Please note that I said "instead of"; pets are certainly not evils
in themselves; in fact, they furnish important outlets for love.

In condemning the "parasitic" woman who could have children but does not, we should remember that we ourselves, as a
part of society, are not blameless in this state of affairs. The irritated feeling that there are too many people in the world smold-
ers everywhere. In urban apartment houses pets are tolerated
with far more grace than children by both landlords and other
tenants. Many friends with children have told me of their discouraging and fruitless search for living quarters where children
are "allowed." It is bad enough to imprison a dog in a city apartment; one would hesitate to cramp a child in the same unnatural
situation even if it were permitted. There is not enough room
for children today; not enough safe, open play spaces, too little
time for the cultivation of family relationships. Children need
to feel themselves necessary and valuable members of the community. Instead, they hear how much it costs to keep them in
shoes, how the cost of their summer camps or their education is
depriving their parents of sleep, how their presence is overtax-
ing and overcrowding homes, schools, parks, streets, and cities.

I think that this situation must be related to the uselessness of
the child in modern civilization; he realizes this, and grows to
feel himself an alien being, here on sufferance, who has no right
to rebel or protest until he becomes an independent adult. Parents are not to blame for reflecting the attitudes of a highly competitive society, hostile to all newcomers and potential rivals,
whether they be refugees from another country or children from
another world.

In the face of these unexpressed but poorly concealed hostilities, we often carelessly assume that women who satisfy their
frustrated maternity with pets could easily transfer their affec-

tion to a child. One error in this assumption is that pets are not always substitutes for children. They are often kept to increase the owner's prestige, to take prizes, or as ornaments to enhance their owner's beauty or aristocratic bearing. Or they may be used to increase their owner's sense of power; we often see the subtle sadism with which people treat their pets, inhibiting, training, and grooming them out of all resemblance to their fellow-creatures. One cannot misuse a child in this way with impunity.

Another false assumption is that affection can be freely mobilized or transferred from one object to another, when the latter is one's own child. I believe that this *can* happen spontaneously; I know that it often *appears* to happen, when in reality the initial hostility shown by the unwillingness to have the child is merely translated into more disguised forms of aversion to the child. The case of the woman I cited above, who rebelled violently against having a child and later exhibited an exaggerated but disastrous concern for it, is a very common one in the psychiatrist's experience.

It is only fair to admit that the feeling of being unwanted is not always discoverable in the psychology of children who nevertheless were very much unwanted at the time of their conception. Thoughtful religious objectors to birth control make two points here: First, they say that if parents are educated to believe that it is unrighteous and opposed to the will of God for them to entertain any resentment against pregnancy, such hostilities will not develop consciously in the mother, and hence the child will be spared them; secondly, they maintain that even parents who are unable to overcome their resentment during pregnancy forget it completely when the child is actually born or when he grows older, and hence the child never feels any such effects.

As to the first point, I agree that it is possible to make people believe it sinful for them not to have a child, even when having another child will make them and their other children more distressed and frantic. I agree this is possible, and I agree that it is being practised. But repressing or suppressing conscious resentment does not mean eliminating it. A deliberate program of enforced attitudes, backed up by pious references to the will of God, accomplishes its results only at the expense of inner conflict and real suffering.

The second objection, that parents often overcome their initial resentment against pregnancy and realize that they *do* want a child, and learn to love it, is a more weighty argument, I think. The conception and nurture of a child—or several, or (if possible) many children—is of paramount importance in mental health. The considerable renunciation of these satisfactions which civilization has made necessary is a menace to its very continuance.

"But if you admit this," continue the objectors, "you will also admit that some couples, who would be benefited by having children, reject or defer the idea and thus self-destructively deny themselves and the world what it would be better if they had no power to prevent. There will be vast numbers of people who will say, 'Yes, we want a baby, we want children, but not now. We are not quite ready; it isn't just the moment.' And for some the right moment never comes; they never become parents, and this is not good for them or for the world. Who would decide when the birth of a child might do more harm than good?"

I think this question has a very clear and direct answer: that the parents themselves can and must and will determine the solution best for them. It is well known that many intelligent people, including many Catholics, have known about and used contraceptive techniques for a long time and that this has not resulted in an increase of childless families, as has been shown by carefully collected statistics available to anyone. In Sweden, public enlightenment in regard to such techniques is said to have resulted in an *increase* in births in certain parts of the population. The wish for a child which so strongly dominates every woman will not allow specious arguments to deter her from obtaining this gratification if it be a reasonable possibility—and I refer not only to economic and physical possibilities but to psychological possibilities as well. The decision may be made unconsciously, but it will be made; and it can be safely left to those for whom during the subsequent years the child will be a primary responsibility. If it is not made, one may be assured that the resistances were so great as to act as danger signals so urgent that they could not be ignored. In fact, the opposite often happens: the impulse to have a child is so strong that parents often go beyond their emotional strength to have it, so that a "wanted" child may subsequently become unwanted.

If child-rearing were accorded its deserved importance in human life—if parents, and those who are to become parents, regarded their children as their highest achievement, giving them the best possible environment and training—then the failure to conceive among persons physiologically and economically capable of it would be regarded as evidence of a neurosis, an inhibition requiring treatment. Such a hypothesis would imply that parenthood, instead of being left to chance, ought to be a careful and deliberate choice dictated by intelligence, the same intelligence that must be used in the treatment of those neurotic failures who cannot bring themselves to enjoy children—who perhaps cannot enjoy anything.

3

Thus far we have been talking about children as the hope of the world on the assumption that it is only necessary for the parents to bear them and love them and support them for this hope to be realized. We have neglected that practical aspect of love which is represented by our efforts to pass on to the child such help as we can give him as a result of our experience. We call this education.

Education is a word so charged with optimism, so pregnant with the spirit of hope, that it is difficult to discuss it objectively. A thousand books have been written about education, and a hundred thousand have been written for education. It is through their education that we expect our children to redeem us and our world—throw off the shackles that we have placed upon them, avoid and correct our mistakes, explore the nature of the universe, suppress evil and promote good. Through education we expect children to learn to be citizens and even to achieve a democracy; and finally, we expect them through education to know how to educate the next generation.

For many people education is almost a religion. There is, especially in this country, a prevalent faith that schooling is a good thing for everyone, a good thing in almost any form, and so good that it cannot be overdone. One may criticize methods, scope, leadership, or personnel, but one must not question the axiom that formal education is something good and something essential to civilized life. Exceptions to the popular theory, like those of the comfortable, friendly Amish people of Pennsylvania, are regarded with a mixture of incredulity and disdain.

Just what is education? According to a recent authoritative report,[8] it "is the process of mastering the knowledge, the tools, the skills, and the institutions which mankind has slowly accumulated, of learning how to work with others, of understanding and making the most of oneself, and of forming ideals and habits. . . . We live in a constantly expanding world; the content of human knowledge is continually greater, the human institutions are increasingly complicated. Besides, there is an infinite variety in the nature, capacities, and character of individual human beings. Clearly, education cannot be standardized or static; it must grow with each advance of civilization, and it must, at the same time, fit those who are to be educated." *

---

* "Whom, then, do I call educated since I exclude the arts, sciences, and specialties? First, those who manage well the circumstances which they encounter day by day and who possess a judgment which is accurate in meeting occasions as they arise and rarely miss the expedient course of action; next, those who are decent and honorable in their intercourse with all men, bearing easily and good-naturedly what is unpleasant or offensive in others, and being themselves as agreeable and reasonable to their associates as it is humanly possible to be;

But let us risk it—*why* is education "a good thing"? This has been asked before and it has evoked an extraordinary variety of answers. Aristotle answered by saying that "education is good because it promotes happiness through promoting virtue," but since Aristotle no one (with the exception of James Mill) has been quite so frankly hedonistic. "Education prepares one for more effective service in the church and state," said Luther. "It enables men to obtain dominance over things," said Bacon. "It contributes to the development of a better state," said Kant. "It enables one to realize a holy life," said Froebel; "to realize the fullest satisfaction of human wants," wrote Thorndike and Gates; "to develop a deeper insight," said Gentile; "to develop social efficiency," said Dewey. One could extend this list almost indefinitely.

There can be no question that the functions of what we call education are multiple and variable. In both the good and the bad senses of the word, these functions have always been markedly opportunistic. The early Protestant sects believed it morally necessary that each person acquire salvation in a certain way, which involved the necessity of consulting the Bible—which made it necessary that one be able to read—which justified teaching. A little later, as Charles Beard has outlined in *The Unique Function of Education in American Democracy*,[9] education was seen as an aid in sustaining democratic government; the assimilation of aliens and the equalizing of economic opportunities began to have importance. It is scarcely necessary to define the ends to which

furthermore, those who hold their pleasures always under control and are not unduly overcome by their misfortunes, bearing up under them bravely and in a manner worthy of our common nature; finally, and most important of all, those who are not spoiled by their successes and who do not desert their true selves and become arrogant, but hold their ground steadfastly as wise and sober-minded men, rejoicing more in the good things which have come to them through chance rather than in those which through their own nature and intelligence are theirs from birth. Those who have a character which is in accord, not with one of these things, but with all of them—these I contend are wise and complete men, possessed of all the virtues of man." (Isocrates [436-338 B.C.] in *Panathenaicus*, sec. 31, 31, 32, translated by George Norlin, Loeb Edition, Putnam, 1929.)

the Roman Catholic parochial schools in this and other countries, and the public schools in Germany and Russia, are dedicated.

Forward-looking educators have always sought to find a more universal philosophy for education. What is education supposed to accomplish? What changes in human conduct do or should the schools effect? What are the real objectives of education? Many answers * have been proposed; I like those listed by William G. Carr and associates in *The Purpose of Education in American Democracy*.[10] (1) *Self-realization:* this includes intellectual curiosity, articulateness, literacy, ability to calculate, health knowledge and training, and recreational, esthetic, and intellectual cultivation. (2) *Human relations:* including respect for humanity, the cultivation of friendships, social co-operation, courtesy, home appreciation, and homemaking. (3) *Economic efficiency:* including workmanship, occupational selection, occupational efficiency, adjustment and appreciation, planned economics of personal life, consumer judgment, and consumer protection. (4) *Civic responsibility:* including sensitiveness to social disparities, corrective social activities, social judgment, critical judgment as regards propaganda, tolerance, conservational interest, world citizenship, law observance, political citizenship, and unswerving loyalty to democratic ideals.

I submit this competent and modern analysis of the functions of education, endorsed by the official body of American teachers, with the purpose of demonstrating that however blind and unthinking the American public may be as to the real purpose of their schools, some educational leaders have given it productive thought. But the fact remains that the present educational system is based largely on the assumption that it is intellectual activity which constitutes the basic material of education—not behavior, not emotional development, not even intellectual development, but intellectual exercise. The assumption is that mental develop-

* Carr points out that one author found 349 different areas of human activity to which education should contribute.

ment will follow. Knowledge is supplied on the principle that it will be dutifully lapped up like so much milk in a saucer by the hungry puppies brooded over by a fluttering foster mother, whose chief duty is the administration of the right quantity of milk and the right additions of more solid food at the proper moments. This foster mother has been to normal school and hence she knows that addition should be taught before subtraction, that one must learn to write before he can study geography, that class periods may be lengthened from thirty to forty minutes as the child grows older, and that reports must be in the hands of the principal at 3:50 P.M. on Fridays. With this type of technical training, the teacher is considered equipped to supply the pap which will nourish the intellects which will grow spontaneously to the point from which all the fine things conceived of in education by Aristotle, Plato, Comenius, Herbart, Huxley, Spencer, Dewey, and others will inevitably follow—and thus the hopes of the world be sustained.

I do not mean to be unjustly ironic. I am only trying to emphasize that there is an extraordinary gap between the pedagogical theory of education and the psychological philosophy of education —a gap admitted by many educators—and that the failure to bridge it has been due to persistent ignoring of the contributions of psychology to the understanding of the learning process. Twelve years ago I wrote in *The Human Mind* that, just as the professional peculiarity of doctors is that they will not take their own medicine, so the professional peculiarity of educators seems to be that they will not learn. This may be a little harsh, but I still think it is true.

These strictures are directed not at individual teachers, but at the predominating spirit of the educationalists in authority. I admit the many individual exceptions; I recognize the lag resulting from educational tradition; I know that many of the younger teachers are more receptive to these ideas. I am acquainted with the aims and techniques of "progressive" education, whose exponents believe themselves to be more psychologically minded. And yet, in spite of these concessions, I stand on the statement that, by and large, psychology is as neglected in education as it has been in medicine. I could go further and say that psychology is deliberately excluded. Year after year I have taken part in a summer school institute for giving teachers some grasp of the emotional problems of childhood; and each year on the final day the intense enthusiasm of the little group of teachers who have taken the course stands out in sharp contrast with the difficulties encountered by the Institute in obtaining a representative attendance, and the difficulties of the individual teachers in overcoming the opposition of their superintendents and principals to their attending it. I see a bitter warfare between the earnest, conscientious teacher whose daily experiences with children teach her the importance of their emotional life, and the psychologically blind and technically ignorant superintendent who treats the school system as if it were a factory and devotes his chief energies to putting on a good front before the taxpayers. Year after year I have seen the bitterness that this conflict arouses in the teachers, a bitterness that I know must be passed on to the children. It is my serious recommendation to any teacher who has political and economic ambitions that he lay aside this book, forget all he has learned from experience or study about the child's heart and mind, join the local Rotary Club, and talk there with a broad smile about "our little folks" and with sententious seriousness about the problem of taxation for rural schools. This will deeply impress the leading taxpayers, and they will come to consider him a great educator.

I consider it useless to write for superintendents and principals as a class. Of course there are many exceptions but most of them will change only when popular opinion forces them to change. As I have seen them, they are not interested in the psychological problems of the child. On the other hand, the average teacher is, and it is for her and for the general public that I am writing this.

It is trite to say that the development of the emotional life is

just as important as the development of the intellectual life, but
it is true. As a matter of fact, the development of the intelligence
is based on the gratification of certain emotional needs, and so long
as the teachers and the administrators steadily refuse to recognize
the function of the school system in fulfilling or frustrating or
distorting these needs, just so long is the school system going to
remain a clumsy, inefficient, disappointing institution, in spite of
all the time and money we continue to lavish upon it, and in spite
of the high hopes for it which we all continue to cherish.

Whether or not the school recognizes emotional needs, it inevitably furnishes some kind of emotional education. My quarrel with
"Education" is not so much that it *neglects* emotional factors, as
that it denies that it deals with the emotions, and that it fails to
require of its teachers any preparation for this most important
branch of learning. Discipline used to be an important item in
teacher education and was the subject of much discussion, on the
principle that the child must be emotionally checked in order to
allow his intellect to function untrammeled. This idea, while still
greatly in vogue with parents, is not so popular with educators.
But almost as fallacious is the educational theory that if the child
is interested, absorbed, and active in intellectual pursuits, his emotions will automatically be held in abeyance, or rather that intellectual activity will absorb them. Both theories may appear to
work, but they do not utilize what we know about the emotions
today, and they view the emotions as an interference with learning rather than as a co-operative force. It has been my observation
that even the most modern educators often prefer to believe that
if the teacher is very skilful the existence of emotions in the
schoolroom can be ignored.

When I say that education is a matter of supplying the child
with certain information and certain techniques, I do not overlook
the fact that there are various *methods* of offering this material:
there is the "stuffing" technique, which regards the child as an
empty vessel to be filled; there is the "entertaining and amusing"

technique, which is supposed to make the child like the school and hence the subject matter; there is the method of providing the child with materials and freedom to experiment so that he may learn the need of knowing facts, and allowing him to seek them out, with some leadership from the teacher. It is assuredly necessary that certain facts should be presented to children in certain stereotyped forms, and it might be well to indicate why this is necessary. The accumulated factual knowledge of the past few hundred generations of human beings is now too great to be experimentally acquired by any individual in a lifetime. Formal schooling consists in the imparting of what are regarded as fundamental techniques—a process which supposedly requires only a few years—and then in the progressive training in the use of these techniques in a superficial survey of the various specializations of man's knowledge. The child is, for example, taught to read, and then he is allowed to read enough geography to acquaint him with the fact that there is such a country as Argentina; he is taught to add and subtract, and then he is induced to calculate how many more people there are in Argentina than in Peru. But it would be manifestly impossible for him to learn *all* about Argentina, without neglecting what there is to learn about Russia, Australia, and the United States. Meantime, he must also learn something of how the people of Argentina and the people of Dayton, Ohio, earn a living, because in the final analysis he, too, must earn a living.

Hence, one task of education is to condense the elements of this knowledge and teach it to the child, or make it available to him so that he may have a background in common with his fellows and so that he may have a short-cut method of finding out which field he is going to settle down in for more intensive personal investigation and application.

Now this first function of formal instruction is combined with a second function, that of teaching the student how to use the knowledge he acquires, how to judge between opposing or divergent interpretations, etc. This part of education has occupied many thoughtful students, with widely variable results. All agree that the results have not been encouraging. Psychoanalysts call it reality testing. Educators call it critical judgment.* It is, to quote William G. Carr,[11] "an acquired ability which comes as the result of innumerable opportunities to make choices and to arrive at conclusions, under the guidance of an expert teacher. In other words, critical judgment is developed just as is the ability to play chess, or to read a book, or to solve problems in geometry; that is, by long and continuous practice under the criticism of someone qualified to evaluate the decisions. The child must learn the value of evidence. He must acquire a reverence for facts, must desire to find them, and must learn where they can most likely be secured. There are certain sources of facts, certain repositories of knowledge, that have been authenticated through the years. The student must learn what they are and acquire the technique of using them, and develop the habit of turning to them when called upon to solve problems. He must learn to defer judgment, to consider motives, to appraise evidence, to classify it, to array it on one side or the other of his question, and to use it in drawing conclusions.

* Recently in a talk with the head of a large advertising firm, I complained about a certain radio campaign carried on by the manufacturer of one brand of a widely used product. "Everyone knows," I said, "that the exaggerations, the enthusiasm, the peculiar qualities emphasized on that program are nonsense. The palpable dishonesty and the histrionic earnestness of that radio advertiser are so nauseous and repugnant that I wouldn't buy the commodity he mentions now under any circumstances. Why can't he say, 'Our brand of this product pleases many people; naturally, we think it is better than competitive brands and we would like to have you think so; consequently, we are trying to enlist your goodwill by financing the following program. The more packages of our product that we can sell you and your friends, the more programs like this you will get,—why can't he say that?'"

My advertising friend replied: "In the first place, if you are the Ford Motor Company, you can do that (although it doesn't). But if you are anything less powerful, you cannot. The public might be suspicious that you were giving them programs instead of quality in your product. But the most important reason is that every experiment in advertising copy shows that extravagant claims, boasting, promises held out, etc., produce better results than simple straightforward announcements. Wishful thinking and simple hopefulness influence the actions of human beings far more than rational intelligence. Effective advertising is therefore based upon emotions and not upon intelligence."

This is not the result of a special course of study, or of a particular part of the educative procedure; it results from every phase of learning and characterizes every step of thinking."

If we agree that education must provide knowledge and techniques for easier or happier or richer or more socialized living, which is essentially what all types of education prescribe, toward what specific object should such living and hence such training be directed? The answer will, of course, depend upon one's philosophy of life. If, as in the case of Sparta and Germany, the object of living is recognized to be warfare, then the answer to this question of education's purpose would be largely determined by that principle. If, on the other hand, life is seen as something religious ("The chief end of man is to glorify God"), then the methods of education practised by the Roman Catholic schools would seem wholly justifiable. If the object is to compete in the contemporary economic system, then the techniques of economic warfare should replace the emphasis upon the techniques of military warfare as practised under Lycurgus. At the present moment we do not seem to know whether the world we live in is dominated by religious warfare or by economic warfare or by military warfare, so it is no wonder that our objectives are a little confused.

But whether we like to admit it or not, the present educational system seems to exist for the purpose of training the youth in some kind of warfare, and psychologically this is sound. But warfare against what, and warfare of what kind?

I do not mean that education does not have the responsibility of teaching children to enjoy life and to learn how to live with one another. I only want to emphasize that living with one another involves overcoming certain aggressions which are instinctual, and that denying these aggressions is like denying the competitive element in business. It was popular a few years ago to glorify the slogan, "He profits most who serves best." Men known to be out to cut one another's throats in business would attend meetings and join in songs about service whose purport was that no one was out to make any money, but only to give service—the implication being that all the members would have to shut down their businesses at once were it not for the fine service they were rendering the community by selling coal at the highest price they could get or inducing people to be satisfied with second-rate beef because the first quality got shunted off to Chicago. If it had been true that service *was* their primary motive, I don't think they would have had the bad taste to sing about it; what led them to gather together to exalt disinterested sacrifice was the need to deny their actual aggressive competitiveness.

But it is still the fashion to sing about service in education to the complete neglect of psychological realities. If a child goes to school and believes all he is taught about the beauty and peace and goodness of the world, he discovers as soon as he emerges that he has been duped. The more seriously he took these teachings in his education, the more disastrously he is going to be defeated and crushed in the disillusionments of the real world. Fortunately, he has learned a great deal about real motives in extracurricular activities, on the playground, and at home, and has discovered quite early in life that education is quite remote from life as he knows it. If he is a discriminating child, he may even have learned that his teachers can be trusted on some points (arithmetical equations, chemical formulas, etc.) but are entirely hypocritical about other phases of living. But to learn such a lesson he has already suffered a disillusionment which has led him to discard much that could be worth while.

By shutting its eyes to the emotional nature of human beings, the educational system remains confused in its aims, purposes, and methods, and succeeds only in falsifying the world and misleading children. The world *is* full of sweetness and light, but it is *also* full of darkness and bitterness. The human personality has loving, constructive tendencies, but it also has destructive tendencies, and there is no use playing the ostrich in such matters.

To the psychiatrist it seems more scientific, more truthful, and more realistic to deal frankly with this element of warfare. If we look at a group of children in a schoolroom we realize that these children have to be trained to live together, to co-operate, to love one another. But we realize, at the same time, that they have to be taught to love one another just because instinctually there is a tendency to hate one another, which has to be overcome by the encouragement of the opposite tendency. One must admit, if one is honest, that when these children grow up they will be spending a large part of their energies in trying to outsmart one another, outdo one another, grab from one another, and so on—to say nothing of the energies spent in quarreling, snubbing, insulting, placating, and avoiding one another. Of course, if the schoolroom is small enough, this statement would have to be modified to say that it is not with one another that the children will ultimately compete, but with the children in another schoolroom, perhaps five miles or one hundred miles or three thousand miles away. We know they are going to be doing their best to persuade other people that *their* brand of cigarettes, or *their* set of ideas, or *their* variety of religion is better than that promoted by the man who was once the little boy who sat across the aisle. If some of them have enough money, or if their parents have enough money, they will go as far as possible in learning all the techniques likely to assist them in being the most successful contenders in the battle of life. Not the battle against nature, not the battle against intolerance, not the battle against hate—but the battle against one another. They will spend years going to the best training schools, the best academies, the best law schools, medical schools, business schools, and engineering schools. This takes brains, but it also takes money, and if one's father has been a little more successful in beating down his competitors and has thereby acquired a little financial reserve, this enables the son to start with a little more leverage in his campaign for pushing himself above the level of his fellowmen at their expense.

I am fully aware of the angry challenge that these remarks will

arouse in some readers. I have set them down at the deliberate
risk of being called anything from a misanthrope to a communist,
although I believe I am far from being either one. But I don't
know how better to puncture the hypocritical sanctification of the
educational theory which prevails in the popular mind, and even
in the writings of many educators. Only by puncturing it, however, can we develop the possibility of seeing education in such a
light as to make it more effective. When I read that education
exists "to enable us to live and live more abundantly," I think of
some of my illiterate friends on western farms or in the northern
wildernesses, and compare the richness and fullness of their lives
with the sterility, emptiness, and frustration of the lives of many
so-called "educated" people. It almost seems to me sometimes
that education is something we force children to undergo in order
to prevent them from enjoying life. I am sure many a child has
the same sentiments.

The reader may well ask, at this point, "What would you have
the teacher do about all this? Do you expect her to change human
nature? How can she—how can education—do anything about the
economic system or the acquisitive tendencies or the aggressive instincts? Should the school attempt to prepare the child for life
by teaching him how bad the world is? Is it not enough to give
him intellectual standards and to supply him with facts and knowledge which will arm him for competitive living later on?"

No, I don't expect the teacher to change human nature, but I
do expect her to know more about human nature than she does
and to take account of what she knows, not only in what she
teaches but in how she teaches. Only in this way will the child
ever succeed either in adjusting himself to the present systems or
in contributing to their improvement. Attitudes are more important than facts; and the attitude of the average teacher is colored
by hypocrisy (which is enforced upon her) and ignorance (for
which she gets little real help from teachers' colleges). Of the
attitudes I shall say more presently; of the hypocrisy I have al-

ready spoken; of the ignorance, nothing is more illustrative than the fact that we know so little about the fundamental nature of the learning process.

Professor Lashley of Harvard recently wrote, "It is doubtful that we know anything more about the mechanism of learning than did Descartes when he described the opening of the pores in the nerves by the passage of animal spirits." [12] And, "It is amazing," wrote Professor Daniel A. Prescott, "that school people so seldom ask themselves the questions: Have children any real reason for learning this material which we are offering them? Is there any real reason which we can demonstrate to them for learning this material?" [13]

There have been numerous experiments in regard to such things as the effect on learning of praise, reproof, reward, punishment, and ignoring. In general, praise and reward have been shown experimentally to accomplish more than reproof and punishment; ignoring a student accomplishes least of all. This gives a clue to something which we shall later expand; namely, the influence of the personal interest of the teacher. Experiments have been made by numerous physiologists and psychologists on the motives for learning in animals. Simmons found that the most effective motive for learning in rats was the detection (by smell) of the proximity of sexual gratification; the next most, food plus return to the home cage; the next most, the finding by a female of her litter at the end of the maze; the next most, food alone. [14] Simmons also found that providing a greater incentive led to a great increase in speed of learning. So far as I know, neither sexual stimulation nor food nor the desire for motherhood is included in the vocabulary, techniques, and philosophies of any educators. According to them, the wish to learn is just "a natural process" inborn in every right-minded child. A more fatuous piece of unrealistic thinking and lack of scientific curiosity can scarcely be imagined.

The experiments cited are interesting, but they are insufficient to supply us with any broad conclusions by the inductive method. Supported by them, however, we might offer a deductive theory in line with clinical experience and with psychiatric theory. This would be that the child's motive in learning is based upon certain instinctual needs (though certainly *not* upon a hypothetical need for knowledge). We already know what these are—or at least the reader knows what the author thinks they are. They are the need for exchanging love with other human beings and the need for expressing in socially approved ways the aggressive tendencies.

At the time he comes to school the child is still largely under the dominance of the infantile type of thinking, of thinking according to the pleasure principle. He has had some experience, however, in the necessity of modifying this method of thought by reality testing. He has begun to suspect that there is no such thing as Santa Claus, no such thing as fairies, no such thing as Aladdin's Lamp, no such thing as living happily ever afterwards. I say he has begun to *suspect* this, but he does not know it "for sure." He still has some hope of being supported in the type of thinking that has dominated his infancy; consequently, this quest for the substantiation of fantasy is fused with the practical impulses to test reality by experience.

In this experience, he is constantly urged and expected to make more and more renunciations of fantasy in favor of a postponed gratification held out by the alleged power of increased knowledge. In other words, he learns that some of the pleasures he had hoped to attain can never be his. But he also discovers that there are other pleasures in the world which, while not so satisfying as those of his babyhood, have something to commend them. He learns that he may erase the blackboards and may even become President of the United States. In his heart he would still rather be the favorite child on his mother's bosom, but since this proves to be no longer practicable, and since other pleasures are held out as desirable if and when they are attained, he is willing to make some of the efforts required, just as the rats in the experimental maze will, if necessary, learn the tedious tricks of getting past the barriers in the hope of the food or sexual gratification which their previous experience, sometimes aided by their sense of smell, leads them to believe awaits them.

But this is only one aspect of the motivation of learning. It is, on the whole, a somewhat rationalized aspect and certainly not the deepest motivation. For why should anyone surrender a bird in the hand for two in the bush? Why should anyone repudiate pleasure thinking for reality thinking?

One may reply that one does so because he has to, but this is a great error in thinking. The child does not have to do these things. No legal powers, parental powers, or any other powers can make him. And, as a matter of fact, a good many children *never do* learn very well in spite of all these pressures. Nobody can *make* anyone want to learn.

Why then *do* we learn? Why are children willing to make the renunciation of infantile satisfactions and struggle in the direction of emotional and intellectual maturity? For one primary reason: because they need the love which they fear they will lose by not learning and which they believe they can retain by making the renunciations necessary to accepting pieces of reality. In other words, children learn chiefly in order to please the teacher and the parents for whom she stands. The particular pattern of learning is, of course, acquired long before they ever see a teacher, but it is strengthened, developed, distorted, or ruined by subsequent teachers according to the personalities of those teachers.

I have said that this is the primary motive, but some important secondary motives should be mentioned. I call these "secondary motives" because they are less powerful than the primary and because they derive, indirectly, from the more directly instinctual motive of wishing to express and win love. One of these is the child's expectation of obtaining answers to questions stimulated by his great curiosity about incompletely understood physical phenomena. These questions relate chiefly to his own body and its sensations, and by extension to the bodies of his parents, brothers, and sisters. They involve the great mysteries of sex, and where babies come from, how, and why. He always expects to arrive some time, somewhere, at fuller information on these tabooed subjects. Another secondary motive is the wish to gain increased power or authority by techniques which appear to be the common property of his superiors. And finally, he is undoubtedly stimulated to attempt the use of his expanding powers for mastering new situations, such an impulse as we see repeated in a minor form in adults who enjoy working puzzles. This reaching out for new experience and finding satisfaction in the joy of successfully accomplishing or achieving is a precious and easily injured motive which the proper techniques of teaching can do much to develop or extinguish.

Here we come back to the question of teachers' attitudes. Let me illustrate what I mean by describing the imaginary thoughts of two teachers:

One teacher faces her schoolroom in the morning with some such attitude as this: "Here are twenty students, the offspring of twenty taxpayers who have hired me to tell these children that $6 \times 6 = 36$. They could find it out for themselves in time, but they will never get to long division and the computation of interest rates if I do not hurry them up and make them take this for a guaranteed fact right now and remember it forever. They may not see why $6 \times 6 = 36$, and I don't know why it is myself; they may not see why they have to learn it and I can't make it seem very reasonable to them, so I will just tell them they *have* to learn it. They haven't anything else to do; they won't have the courage to defy me and refuse to believe it; I am bigger than they are, and I am the teacher, and so I can make them say it and if I make them say it often enough it will stick. Later they will be grateful to me. Maybe, in the meantime, their parents will consider me a good teacher and not complain to the principal."

In addition, of course, this same teacher may be chafing at the necessity of teaching the third grade when she would like to teach the eighth grade, resenting the obstreperousness of certain of the children, brooding over the principal's reproaches of yesterday, worrying over the impossibility of doing justice to so large a class as she has been given, etc. But these things I ignore for the moment, because I want to concentrate on the teaching philosophy.

Another teacher might face her class with some such attitude as this: "These children love me. They think I know lots more than I do. I tell them that 6×6 is the same as 3 tens plus a 6, called "thirty-six" by agreement, and I must tell them that this is one of those conveniences that people have agreed upon in order to save time. I will show them that they could count this up for themselves every time if they liked, and I will do it for them once, to show them how one *does* save time by remembering it instead of having to count it up. I will show them how much fun multiplication is, and I can tell them how 6 is one of the numbers that always show themselves again when they are multiplied by themselves. I will tell them how the numeral came to assume its present form. I will show them how much easier it is to multiply with an Arabic 6 than with a Roman VI. I will make 6 have a personality for them different from the personality of 7 or 3. I realize that the personality of 6, 7, 3, and all other numbers I tell them about will be reflections of my own personality. And because they love me and because they want so much to please me, they will be interested in my numbers, and in all that I tell them, and they won't have to *try* to remember anything. They will remember it automatically, just as they will remember me. Then, later, when someone tells them that $6 \times 6 = 40$ or that one can spend money and still have it, they will not be impressed or misled. They will remember, not that Miss Jones made them learn the multiplication table, but that there was a Miss Jones once who knew them and loved them, and knew the world too and loved it—and showed them the 6's in the world and what the 6's do to one another."

Some will insist that this is merely a difference in skill or intuition in teaching. And with this I should not quarrel, because intuitive skill in teaching depends upon the intuitive recognition of the child's need for love, and I am sure some teachers have it in spite of their training and in spite of oppressive systems.

It may also be objected that this example had nothing to say about aggressions. I did not mean it to have. I do not expect any teacher to say: "You must look out, children. People will try to cheat you; they will tell you $6 \times 6 = 40$. You must fight fiercely against such cheaters. We learn multiplication so that other people won't cheat us." Children know that without being taught it. Children don't need to be taught that they are aggressive or that other people are aggressive; they need to be taught the techniques whereby these aggressions can be disposed of. The very process of multiplication, of any calculation, involves the investment of a certain amount of aggressive energy cast in a constructive mold. Under the benevolent influence of a teacher whose fairness and friendliness and affection for her children are unclouded by confusion or resentment of her role, the child has not only a model but a technique for mastering aggressions or directing them fruitfully.

I think that with such a conception the content of the curriculum could be definitely directed toward the two sublimative outlets discussed in previous chapters: work and play. This would end once and for all such academic questions as whether or not Latin should be required of all students. If it contributes to a prospective type of work or to an enjoyed type of play, it is necessary; if it does not, it is worse than unnecessary. Similarly, the question of athletics can easily be settled: if it is play or preparation for work, it is necessary; but if it is work instead of preparation for work, it is harmful, because the work of the school period is by definition the work of learning and not the work of doing. Education is itself a kind of work in preparation for more mature work, and also in preparation for play.*

Such a conception of education would not eliminate all of the present difficulties. It would not alter the operation of inflexible time schedules, the problem of handling large numbers of children in an orderly way without regimentation, the disciplinary considerations which would be present in spite of the most ideal situation, the overloading of teachers, or the problems of truancy, mental retardation and childhood neuroses.

But it certainly would tend to correct many other difficulties which seem to me to be more important. The frustration of the spontaneous curiosity of young children seems to me to be one of the most discouraging aspects of the present method. For twenty

---

* This conception of education has been put in more conventional terms by Professor Prescott in an epoch-making report on behalf of the Committee on Relations of the Emotions to the Educative Processes to the American Council of Education. (Daniel A. Prescott, *op. cit.*, p. 108.) In this book the role of education in influencing the development of the emotions is carefully examined. Leaving aside questions of communicating facts, this committee declares the role of education to be as follows:

"*a.* To identify in individual children those patterns of emotional behavior which do not fall within the accepted range and to undertake re-education;

"*b.* To provide all children with experiences that will stimulate the progressive development of patterns of emotional behavior recognized as mature in the light of the basic needs of the individual and in the light of the cultural pattern in which these needs must be met;

"*c.* To provide children with æsthetic experiences and training in æsthetic expression that will develop patterns useful to them for maintaining morale, for relieving tensions, for identifying themselves with a cultural group and, in general, for sensitizing them to beauty;

"*d.* To provide children with experiences that offer them the chance for the development of a 'mature' value sense and of loyalties so genuinely associated with value for them as to be characterized accurately as affective loyalties;

"*e.* To provide children with enough opportunity for the *active practice* of behavior growing out of these value concepts to establish in them a technique or habit of more or less continuously re-evaluating their loyalties in the light of experience."

It will be seen upon inspection these are carefully worded descriptions of what I have tried to say above in more general terms. Maintaining morale, relieving tensions, identifying themselves with the cultural group, sensitizing them to beauty, developing in them a sense of loyalties—what do these mean but to provide children with devices for mitigating the strength of the self-destructive tendencies, or, shall we say, for deflecting the aggressive tendencies from undesirable goals by means of sublimation?

years I have taught a few classes in a college every winter—Harvard, Washburn, Kansas, Columbia—and year after year I re-experience the same shock of disappointment in discovering the passivity, the indifference, the uncurious, unchallenging attitude of the students—the result of a method of "education" which has ignored its true function.* Recently I saw a patient's record which indicated that at the age of three he had been taken to a psychiatric clinic for the sole and unelaborated complaint, made by his parents, of "curiosity."

The special applications of psychiatric educational techniques to the problem child are beyond the scope of the present chapter. One point I should like to make regarding them is this: the extraordinary and particular efforts necessary to understand and redirect the personalities of the problem child, the inhibited child, the aggressive child, the neurotic child, are the source of our assurances regarding the psychology of learning. From their tribulations has come knowledge that will advance the education and happiness of the unafflicted.

The greatest difficulty hampering the successful application of the psychiatric concept of education is the problem of personnel. It has been pointed out many times of late that a significant proportion of teachers are either mentally ill or suffering from serious emotional maladjustments. How can such a teacher inspire or bestow love? Many others have so meager a background of experience in life that they lack adequate grasp of reality or any possibilities for either insight or genuine affection. To the extent that they attain any influence with their students, they often foster prejudice, superstition, emotionalized attitudes, and, worst of all, fears and withdrawal. The drab, colorless, empty lives of many

* "Let any adult who has just completed the reading of an absorbing book imagine what it would have done to his interest to read it at the rate of five or ten pages a day over a period of one or two months, meantime making analyses of plot, language structure, use of words, and the like. We do not contend that there is no place for this latter type of work, but there is certainly also a place for a more spontaneous enjoyment of literature, music, art, and discussion. . . ." Prescott, op. cit., p. 237.

teachers, lacking in esthetic sensitivity or cultural background, not only fail to stimulate latent capacities in students, but indeed discourage the expression of those capacities in students who show them spontaneously. Other teachers reveal their emotional pathology in the form of moodiness, sulkiness, sarcasm, hypercriticalness, bullying, and domination. Many teachers are best remembered by their children for the hate-charged atmosphere of their schoolrooms.

Still other teachers suffer from pronounced neurotic conflicts—inferiority feelings, racial prejudices, hypochondriasis, depression, feelings of being discriminated against. Such afflictions make them sources of psychic contagion and induce them to use the teaching situation as a means of obtaining relief. The effect of such teachers upon children is incalculable.* And yet all these things are deemed of no consequence if only the intellectual qualifications of the teacher are to be considered important in education. It is only if one accepts the thesis that the process of learning depends upon the stimulation of love by the teacher that the full importance of a normal personality appears. One might almost say that a teacher, by very virtue of her role of teacher, must be not only a normal but a supernormal person. She must be able to give large quantities of love, regardless of the preliminary attitudes or the direct personal responses of the children. *That her pupils will love her in return is secondary; if it becomes primary, her usefulness as a teacher is handicapped.* For this reason we must add to the categories of unsuitable teachers three more:

1. The teacher whose personal need for love is so great or is to such a degree unsatisfied that she seeks it in a direct expression of the children's love. This attitude encourages love situations rather than sublimations. For the teacher must constantly live as if to say "I love you; I will show you this by my genuine attitude and by the patience and honesty and vividness with which I

* Some of the phrases in the above passages are taken from Prescott, *op. cit.,* pp. 265-266.

communicate to you the information you are scheduled to receive. That you love me in return I will infer from the extent to which you accept my teaching." It is the art of teaching to obtain love in this sublimated form instead of through a direct expression.

2. Teachers who have a conscious or unconscious resentment toward children in general, or toward certain children in particular, or toward their administrative officers, or toward the need of having to earn a living at all—such teachers by inflicting their hostilities upon the children will not only retard their pupils' acquisition of knowledge, but will arouse in them patterns of retaliatory hostility which will subsequently be inflicted upon other people.

3. The teacher whose neurotic guilt feelings are so dominant that teaching for her is a kind of penance, an absolution from guilt. The result of such teaching is the infusion of compulsive attitudes toward the subject matter in the child, and even a turning from it.

To summarize all we have said about personnel in education: *What the teacher is, is more important than what she teaches.* As to what it is ideal for the teacher to be, we can say, negatively, that she should not be one who stimulates hate or discouragement or fear in her children, and, positively, that she should be one whose emotional maturity is such that she can give love without the expectation of its direct return, but with a deep satisfaction in the direct reward of having her own patterns of sublimation reproduced.

This might lead us to a consideration of just what emotional patterns lead to the selection of teaching as a vocation. In the chapter on work sublimation I suggested that probably all professional work is to be looked upon as a sublimation of aggressions according to some particular mold. It is the breakdown in those sublimations that results in the undesirable neurotic teacher already discussed. What, we might ask, are the unconscious emotional needs in the teacher which are gratified by teaching? What is the peculiar influence upon the aggressions which converts them into teaching?

Professor Symonds of Teachers College (Columbia) studied this problem in a stimulating article,[15] discarding such motives as that of earning a living or following the family tradition as being insufficiently specific. A study of the autobiographies of fifty women teachers seemed to him to reveal motives which correspond to my own less systematic observations in clinical cases. Identification with children in an effort to relive an unsatisfactory childhood and gain the approval and affection of the elders is a very prevalent theme. The need to exert authority and domination to overcome feelings of inferiority is also common. There is frequently a discoverable tendency toward self-punitive and atonement mechanisms—asceticism, self-denial, social martyrdom, self-sacrifice, long-suffering patience, self-pity, and projected self-pity. Symonds raises the question whether women should be selected as teachers who seem obviously to be satisfying such unconscious needs by choosing this vocation, or whether candidates should be sought who seem less impelled to solve their unconscious needs through pedagogical work. He arrives at the cogent conclusion that teachers should be selected from young women who have exactly such needs, and that a teacher becomes undesirable only when her needs are so intense, so extreme, as to be ungratifiable by the vocation. In the latter case her aggressions are revived by the frustration instead of being comfortably sublimated, and the schoolchildren become the victims.

Naturally, this gives rise to the question of the extent to which teachers are able to attain such a level or to stay at that level, and how much of such teaching a human being can do without emotional exhaustion (as well as physical fatigue). One wonders whether the life that the average community permits its teachers is such as to provide sufficient opportunities for recreation, esthetic development, cultural stimulation, and emotional gratification. I have frequently asked educational administrators why they do not have better teachers, and they always reply that the financial rewards are too little and the social restrictions too great. The public has the impression that teachers are well paid; they *are* well paid if teaching is to be regarded as an unimportant clerical task for which anyone who has fulfilled certain curricular requirements is eligible. Even as it is, the teachers frequently constitute one of the most intelligent and cultured elements in society and often do more for their community in proportion to their numbers and resources than any other members. But the fact is that the hostility toward children which I pointed out in the early chapters of this book expresses itself nowhere more glaringly than in the low estate to which our financial niggardliness has reduced the teaching profession. I have often said that teachers and policemen ought to be the highest paid and most carefully selected officials in the community, because they have the most important responsibilities. And of these, I hope it is unnecessary for me to add, I think the responsibility of the teacher is the greater, especially the teachers of the kindergartens and the first six grades, who are, at present, the worst paid. If we took our educational system seriously, elevated our standards for teachers in terms of personality equipment, required of them a basic understanding of child psychology, and paid them each a minimum monthly salary of $300, we might have less money with which to pave streets, maintain state universities, and build state hospitals, but we would have a far different type of teacher for the critical years of child training, and the results of our work would be apparent within a generation.

Nevertheless, we must conclude that even in its present imperfect state, education clearly serves the purpose of harnessing and mitigating the aggressive tendencies. It does so by providing the individual with new tools, new techniques, new direction, and new opportunities for investing his life, and hence his love and hate. It strengthens the processes of suppressing and repressing inadmissible primitive impulses through discipline, through example, through enlightenment, and through affection. By means of its emphasis upon the social responsibilities of each individual, education tends to improve the environment, to alter its structure in the direction of greater opportunity and less frustration, which in turn diminishes the occasions of stimulated aggressions. Finally, it provides a profession in which the aggressive and erotic energies of certain older persons may be sublimated in the task of ministering to the personality needs of younger ones, a position of limited foster-parenthood.

To conceive of the function of education as learning to live with one's instincts, and hence learning to love and hate wisely is a somewhat different view from even that of the "New Education." A recent book by John Dewey and others [16] reviews the achievements of educational reform in the past fifteen years; sadly enough, the consensus is that these achievements are not so great as we had hoped. The slogan of the "New Education" was that children should be educated for a changing world, that the only thing constant about education should be the development of the capacity for change. But I believe these leaders have come to realize now that if the change in the changing world is progressively for the worse all the time, one can scarcely educate children to adapt to it nimbly or profitably. I should be inclined to aim in a different, more positive direction. I would see education beginning at the cradle with the encouragement in the child of more freedom for aggressiveness, destructiveness, and cruelty, and with the giving of more affection, interest, and attention by his elders. Childhood is the time for the children to be bad and the parents (and teachers) to be good, instead of vice versa.

In this digression about education, I have not forgotten—and I hope the reader has not forgotten—that our main topic is hope. If the child is the hope of the world, his education is of paramount importance, and I thus justify the space given to discussing it.

But hope finds expression in other ways, and as a physician I think most often of the hope implied by the existence and function of my profession. The very fact that we believe we can ameliorate a condition, that we can heal an illness, is a confidence born essentially of hope. Our hope has in many instances been empirically supported, it is true, but treatment implies that change can be effected, that a victim may be extricated from a predicament and saved from the consequences of his own mistakes or the mistakes of others which are now causing him pain, and this expectation of an effected change springs from hope. As I have said elsewhere,[17] the physician brings to his task an optimistic hopefulness which he shares with innumerable workers in science who, though they be daily reminded by the very content and discoveries of their own researches that all of our petty human activity and knowledge amounts to but little in the immensity of the universe, nevertheless plod steadfastly and hopefully forward in the direction of increasing our defenses against death.

Medical treatment, in the ordinary sense, puts its chief reliance upon physical and chemical changes, while psychiatry places its chief reliance upon psychological changes, and these changes it brings about through what, in its essence, is simply education. Sometimes we specify that it is education of the emotions rather than of the intellect; sometimes we refer to it as re-education to indicate that the patient must unlearn some things before he can learn new things. Freud said that the voice of the intelligence is weak but added that it is persistent and, hence, may be expected to assume a larger control over the instincts if it be granted time, encouragement, and assistance.

The whole theme of this book has been that recognition of the forces within us constitutes the first step in their control; and that our intelligence should be applied to forestalling or repairing damage rather than to devising more ingenious forms of retaliatory destructiveness. Applied to the suffering individual, this is the principle of psychiatric therapy; applied to the difficulties of the world, it is a rational educational philosophy. In either case it is based on hope.

Chapter 10. Love

THROUGHOUT this book we have tried to keep in the fore-front the power of love in the war of the instincts. Love transforms the impulse to fight into the impulse to work or play. Love is implicit in our hoping and in our believing. Love can be frustrated but it can also be encouraged, and in this final chapter we shall consider practical ways in which the latter can be done. To attempt more would be vain, since "to enlarge [upon] or illustrate the power and effect of love is to set a candle in the sun." [1]

When the scientist begins to talk about love, he is between Scylla and Charybdis. If he adheres rigidly to the conventional language and formulae of science, he will end in that same sterile futility that has long characterized science in its application to human social life. If, on the other hand, he abandons his scientific habits for a greater reliance upon intuitive truth, he risks verging upon the sentimental and the poetic. Sentiment and poetry are not necessarily antithetical to truth, but the scientist who uses poetic terms is likely to be as discredited as a poet who uses scientific ones.

This dilemma gives rise to the illusion that love is something about which we have no scientific knowledge. Everyone except the scientist is supposed to know something about love. Love sickness is the one sickness for which people do not consult a physician, or for which—if they do consult him—they get little help,* although

* In the Middle Ages this was not true. Many readers are probably familiar with the pictures of Ter Borch, Van Ostade, Dou, and others among the Dutch and Flemish painters especially, in which a long-robed physician is peering solemnly at a flask of urine to determine whether or not a woman patient is in love, or is pregnant. One of the more famous of these pictures is labeled *Das Liebenkrank.*

we speak of "falling in love" as if strong consciousness of affection were an abnormality, a descent into a temporary pathological state.

But when Freud investigated, systematically and scientifically, the development of the sexual life of the human being he put the whole subject of love upon a basis such that it can no longer be considered the exclusive realm of the poet, the novelist, and the philosopher. In this he was helped by the collateral researches of Havelock Ellis, Krafft-Ebing, and others who explored some of the pathological distortions of love which threw light on its normal evolution. What Freud really showed was that one does not "fall" in love: one *grows* into love and love grows in him; and this starts not in adolescence nor in maturity but in infancy. By now it is fairly well accepted by everyone who reads and thinks and lives his life with his eyes open that the child begins to express its love life in the first days of its existence. Using all the organs of his body, he attaches himself with pleasure to a succession of love objects in response to the satisfactions they offer and afford him. His mother, his father, later his brothers and sisters, still later his playmates and teachers, and finally his adult companions, become successive foci of the direction of his love. Conflicts and rivalries develop. Certain patterns of solution are arrived at, based on his earliest experiences, which usually, of course, involve his mother and father. We have already discussed some of the complications introduced by the interference of hate.

All this is well known and I refer to it again here only to substantiate my statement that there does exist a scientific knowledge of love, although few have it or make use of it. People go about in pursuance of their troubled love affairs in as bland an ignorance as that of the West Indian natives infected with malaria and yaws before the introduction of scientific medicine. The idea of going to a scientist for advice about love problems would still never occur to the vast majority of American citizens.

The "libido theory" has been a part of the body of scientific knowledge for nearly fifty years. It was first introduced to science in Freud's celebrated *Three Contributions to the Theory of Sex*. It is elaborated in many volumes of psychoanalytic and psychiatric literature. In its original form this libido theory traced the natural history of the evolution of the erotic instinct as observed and interpreted before the aggressive instinct was recognized. Numerous phenomena convinced Freud that a monistic interpretation of human motivation is insufficient to explain the observed facts. Consequently, the libido theory was supplemented by a "thanatos theory," just as in physical science it was discovered that the electron theory in its original form required the postulation of neutrons and protons to supplement it. Even now, in some psychiatric literature, authors continue to speak as if the antiquated libido theory had never been modified by Freud or anyone else.*

Thus the scientific theory of love has become the theory of the interaction and fusion of the erotic and destructive † instincts, a theme that we have been developing throughout this book. It is

---

* Take, for example, the condition known as paranoia. This is a definitely abnormal psychological state in which an individual feels that others are persecuting him. According to the old libido theory, this was explained by a very ingenious shuffling of the cards to the effect that the person who felt himself persecuted was actually attracted homosexually to the alleged persecutor and was defending himself against this by a delusion that effectually made such a seduction impossible. The layman reading these words may not realize how profound this interpretation was in influencing the thinking of medical science; it has been accepted by psychiatrists pretty generally all over the world, in spite of obvious logical fallacies. These fallacies were rectified, however, by the subsequent recognition of the destructive tendencies and the impulses of hate. The man who feels himself persecuted is obviously defending himself not against his love of someone so much as against his hate for someone, someone whom the persecutor represents. He defends himself by saying, "It is not I who hate him, but he who hates me." That this is mingled with homosexual attraction is undoubtedly true, but that it is primarily determined by erotic attraction is a misrepresentation of the very nature of love. The original interpretation of paranoid symptoms occurs in Freud's "Psychoanalytic Notes Upon an Account of Paranoia" (*Collected Papers*, 3:390-470, London, Hogarth Press, 1925, originally published in 1911). For a revision of the theory in the light of Freud's subsequent changes in the instinct theory, see R. P. Knight, "The Relationship of Latent Homosexuality to the Mechanism of Paranoid Delusions" (*Bull. Menninger Clinic*, 4:149-159, 1940).

† For a further discussion of the theory of the instinct, see note 1, for Chapter 1, in the Source Notes.

necessary for the ego to make compromises between what our instincts demand and what our intelligence and sense of social reality permit us. Primitive man could kill what he liked and could gratify his love instinct without reference to any restrictions. Contemporary man can do neither.

It is this idea of fusion that must be emphasized. Love, as we have seen in the latter part of this book, is capable of modifying the hate impulses and bringing them within the range of social acceptability and usefulness. But, on the other hand, the love instinct itself has to be modified and altered. "All the instinctual impulses that we can study are made up of such fusions or alloys of the two kinds of instincts. Naturally, they are to be found mixed in the greatest variety of proportions." [2] There is, therefore, no such thing as pure love (or pure hate).

The expression of the life instinct, then, is to be seen in love, and love in three forms. First of all, it is absorbed in the partial or complete neutralization of the destruction instinct—in other words, in the accomplishment of sublimation. Secondly, it is expressed in diffuse extensions of love to nonsexual objects, or to objects that are not sexual in the ordinary sense of the word. I refer here to the love we have for nature, inanimate objects, pets, social friends, and society at large. The energy for such attachments comes from the erotic instinct, but the object selected and the feelings experienced for it are not consciously recognized as pertaining to sexuality. Finally, the love is expended directly upon objects which must be called "sexual" in any meaning of the word.

Since the last few chapters have been devoted to the way in which love carries out the first-named function, that of fusion with the hate impulses to accomplish sublimations, we shall devote this chapter to a consideration of the direct expressions of love and the possible means of encouraging these. To begin with the more attenuated expressions of love, we might speak first of those investments which become deflected from human beings to inanimate objects. One frequently sees a concentration of affection upon auto-

mobiles, watches, garments, books, and many of the other tools of
living. These objects become almost a part of the self but are
praised, adored, and tenderly cared for with a highly sentimental-
ized affection. It might be assumed that such affection is entirely
denatured of any conscious sexual element, but sometimes this is
obviously not the case. Of Napoleon's cannoneers, who dragged
their dismembered guns over the Alps, Abbott wrote:

> It was now the great glory of these men to take care of their guns.
> They loved tenderly the merciless monsters. They lavished caresses and
> terms of endearment upon the glittering, polished, death-dealing brass.
> The heart of man is a strange enigma. Even when most degraded it
> needs something to love. These blood-stained soldiers, brutalized by
> vice, amid all the horrors of battle, lovingly fondled the murderous
> machines of war. . . . The unrelenting gun was the stern cannoneer's
> lady-love. He kissed it with unwashed, mustached lips. . . . Affec-
> tionately he named it Mary, Emma, Lizzie.

It is only a step from the love of inanimate objects to the love
of animate but nonhuman objects, such as flowers, trees, birds, and
especially domesticated animals and pets.[3] The personification of
inanimate and nonhuman objects and the bestowal of love upon
them is a familiar phenomenon of childhood; dolls, rabbits, dogs,
toys of all kinds take on human qualities and are beloved, sometimes even beyond any human beings. A passage in my mother's
autobiography [4] describes this quite vividly, I think:

> . . . Many of my thoughts were associated with those lovely hills and
> they were very dear to me. It was harder for me to say good-bye to the
> hills than to any of my living friends, and today their memory is the
> brightest thing I hold from the Pennsylvania years. I well remember
> how, on the last afternoon in the old home, I went out back of the
> bake oven and sat under a big old apple tree that commanded a view
> of the hills, and to each I said good-bye out loud. Then I cried awhile
> to myself and said, "I want God to bless all of you because I love you.
> I know I shall miss you terribly; I hate so much to leave you and
> maybe I will never see you again." It took only a few short weeks
> for me to learn how truly I *did* miss them, and many a time I have
> been very homesick to see my hills again. But I never have.

Some of the meanings of these personifications are indicated by another passage in my mother's book which will undoubtedly revive memories in the minds of many readers:

. . . In the meadow near the house was a big shellbark hickory tree, which yielded bushels annually. I did not know much about fairy stories, but I peopled the branches of this old tree, or the spot beneath them, from all the stories that I knew. I named the tree Goliath and when my father asked me one evening why I had done so, I said, "Because he takes care of us all the week while you are away." He said, "God takes care of you—not Goliath." I answered him by saying, "God is watching Goliath, and if he does not do the right thing, God will send a stone of fire right out of David's sling, that he has saved up in heaven, and he will kill Goliath." Father said, "That is a funny story for a little girl to think about a tree." But I believed it.

The extent to which these attachments to nonhuman love objects continue in adult life * with a repression of the personification would probably amaze anyone who has never been introspective about it—the loving treatment accorded his flowers by the gardener, the affection for "mother earth" of even such characters as Jeeter Lester, to say nothing of many more sophisticated ones, the passionate attachment to dogs and cats and canaries and even pieces of furniture, the treasuring of collections by the hobbyist, or of his knife and top by the small boy. These are useful forms of loving that should be cultivated and encouraged. This has been recognized by some authorities on civilian morale who have urged that in wartime the public continue and even increase its indulgence in hobbies, but it seems a pity that there must be a war in order for us to recognize and take advantage of the opportunities available for increasing the range of our loving.

The concentration of affection upon nonhuman objects is some-times described in technical literature as infantile, fetichistic, or

* In our culture, especially. "So far from being possessed by their things and feeling their possessions a burden the Eskimos are careless of them to the point of contempt . . . material possessions hardly enter their scale of values and the giving of presents is regarded as a perversion." (G. de Poncins, *Kablaona*, Reynal & Hitchcock, 1941.)

totemistic. The psychological process of substituting a part for the whole and identifying nonhuman objects with human beings, particularly the parents, and loving them instead may, it is true, be carried to an extreme. They may absorb so much love and become so exaggerated in their relative importance that the expression of love for human objects is seriously impaired. One sees this in misers, and in persons who are very kind to animals but very unkind to their human associates. But kept within proper proportions the investment of love in nonhuman objects is not a symptom but a form or variety of love. It is a particularly necessary form for those people for whom human objects have been found unsatisfactory or insufficient, especially in childhood. To some extent this is always true; this is why little girls turn to dolls and little boys to trains. Sometimes it is more extreme; in my mother's book, from which I have just quoted, she makes it very clear that as a little girl she felt that her parents were too much involved in the care of the other children, farm work, and schoolteaching to be sufficiently concerned with her, and so she turned to "Goliath."

In this connection we ought to mention the fact that one frequently sees the totemistic object treated ambivalently; I mean that hate as well as love can be directed toward these nonhuman parental substitutes. A patient of mine who was an ardent and proficient duck-hunter did not recognize until far advanced in psychoanalytic treatment, which he undertook for quite a different reason, that as a child he had thought of his mother as a duck, because of a peculiar waddling gait caused by a bone disease which had led his uncle to refer to her as "an old duck." Unconsciously he had identified his mother with ducks long before he became adept at killing them.

2

Leaving now the nonhuman object investment of love, ambivalently tinged with little or much hate, we shall turn our attention to the many ways in which human beings attach themselves to one another in groups, in a supposedly nonsexual way. This has been called gregariousness and described by some, more eloquently than accurately, as due to a "herd instinct" [5] similar to that which impels the flocking of certain birds and beasts into large assemblies. But there is no need to postulate any such special instinct. Men gather together at times for the simple reasons of greater economy or greater safety or greater power. But there are other gatherings that occur daily, in villages and by roadsides and hearthsides, in which the affection of people for each other is the moving spirit. In the custom to which our own country is so particularly given, of organizing clubs, societies, associations, unions, and the like, one can see a spontaneous tendency toward increasing the opportunities for loving and understanding one another. The words ascribed to Jesus, "where two or three are gathered together in my name, there will I be also," are usually interpreted by the Church to refer to the circumstances under which religious services may be considered to have a quorum. But these words have a far more profound meaning. Where two or three people are gathered together, there is bound to be an exchange of feelings and the mutual stimulation of affection. It is an unusual individual who does not to some extent enjoy meetings and gatherings, and we are all better for them.

Freud [6] ascribed the cohesiveness of the group to a common devotion to a leader, a devotion in which the hostile elements are kept in abeyance through a kind of tacit recognition that ultimately he—the leader—will be replaced by one of the followers, who meanwhile suspend all mutual hostilities. Each follower thus identifies himself with the leader, and hence to some extent with all the other followers. The successful leader must manage to keep the constantly accumulating aggressions of the group discharged by directing them to this or that *external* danger or project. Such a reinforcement and concentration of emotion is like a Leyden jar: it has an enormous potential and can be exploited by psychopathic leaders to accomplish great harm. Examples of this are to be seen

in Adolf Hitler's career, in the lynching bee and other mobs, and
even in some "good" organizations which suffer for a time under
"bad" leaders.

But honest leaders, who will not distort reality to manufacture
"enemies" in order to increase internal solidarity, are far more
numerous than dishonest and psychopathic leaders; the latter are
only more conspicuous. And in organization and group association,
formal and informal, there is an investment of love which is mutually reinforcing, and, hence, highly desirable.

Fortunately, almost everyone can belong to some organization.
I said "can"; let me say also "should." The value of service clubs,
women's clubs, literary clubs, medical societies, labor unions, even
political organizations and rallies, lies not so much in the practical
things these organizations achieve as in the service they perform
in uniting their members in a friendlier spirit. Along with many
others, I have at various times made fun of the somewhat juvenile
sentimentalism of some of these organizations, but I think I have
been wrong in doing so. To the outsider it may seem a bit ridicu-
lous for a bunch of grown men to give a part of their working
hours to the joint singing of "For He's a Jolly Good Fellow." But
the words of the song and even the singing of it have a deeper
meaning than appears.

Hayakawa [7] gives an illustration which I shall paraphrase. It
is a hot, dusty day and you are in a hurry to reach some destina-
tion, when you hear the ominous and sinister sounds of a flat tire.
In anger and frustration you pull the car to the side of the road,
clamber out preparatory to soiling your hands, your clothes, and
your disposition by replacing it. At this moment a farmer strolls
up and asks the apparently casual question, "Gotta flat tire?"

If one takes these words literally, one must conclude that the
farmer is a fool or a blind man. But the psychological meaning
of such an inquiry is quite different—it is an awkward but somewhat conventionalized way of saying something like the following: "Hello—I see you are in trouble. I'm a stranger to you but I

might be your friend now that I have a chance to be if I had any assurance that my friendship would be welcomed. Are you approachable? Are you a decent fellow? Would you appreciate it if I helped you? I would like to do so but I don't want to be rebuffed. This is what my voice sounds like. What does your voice sound like?"

Of course this could be done in a more direct and businesslike way; the farmer could say, "I would be glad to help you, stranger." But people are too timid and mutually distrustful to be so direct. They want to hear one another's voices. People need reassurance that others are just like themselves.

Mr. Jones is a good lawyer who does not have much occasion to call upon Mr. Brown, president of the bank, and has a suspicion that Mr. Brown is a very crusty person who had best be let alone. He has no idea that Mr. Brown likes to sing "Sweet Adeline." Mr. Brown, on the other hand, who frequently practises "Sweet Adeline" in the bathtub before parading to his very impressive bank, has secret ideas that Mr. Jones, the attorney, is a very intelligent, shrewd, and sophisticated fellow who would be disgusted to learn that the president of the bank sang in the bathtub or anywhere else. Therefore, when Mr. White, president of the Kiwanis Club, calls for a verse of "I Want a Girl Just Like the Girl That Married Dear Old Dad," what Mr. Brown and Mr. Jones learn about each other is not the fact that they were familiar with the same tune, but something a great deal more important.

Imperfect as clubs and organizations are in relieving individual loneliness, they do give practice in the techniques of social intercourse, and they do furnish fellows who by joining the organization have indicated their accessibility to the other members. They offer a kind of reassurance against the fear of not belonging. The inherent danger in the group, the club, the society, the organization, however, seems to be the tendency to become static. The promise of a growth in friendship is often unfulfilled. There is rarely a sufficiently strong central interest or unity of purpose to

keep the group welded together in a common goal; internal dis-
sension, distrust, jealousy, undue ambitiousness, and envy overwhelm the erotic bond. Afraid of their own hostilities, the members
shrink into smaller and smaller units or cliques or compensate for
their own hollowness by an overemphasis on the snobbishness and
exclusiveness of the group. A typical example is the petty gossiping
and mutual hostility of the members of the proverbial small-town
sewing circle.

Naturally, the more homogeneous the club, the greater the peril
in this quarter. The tendency of all groups to select members who
in some way resemble each other leads to rivalry on the one hand
and to staleness on the other. One prophylactic measure against this
danger is the periodic infusion of new blood, the addition of new
members. This requires a readjustment of the emotional linkages
of all members and affords intellectual stimulation as well. If the
differences between the new members are as great as their resemblances, the club is strengthened to the extent that it can absorb the new and continue in a more cosmopolitan unity.

The person who can find resemblances in himself to many
widely divergent groups has the chance to seek companionship
in many places, and this is often the chief motivation in the person
who is continually joining and organizing societies. What we see
as a variety of interests in games, sports, hobbies, and study in one
individual may actually be an unusually strong desire to know
people and to be loved by them, which leads to an assiduousness
in learning and doing what others are doing in order to be accepted
in their circles.

I am aware that some readers unfamiliar with psychological
science will find it difficult to believe that the feelings of positive
attraction that bind the members of groups and that bind doctor
and patient are identical in nature with those bonds which exist
between a lover and his sweetheart, or a man and his wife. They
will fall back upon the conventional distinctions between liking and
loving. But there is no scientific justification for this distinction;

liking and loving differ only in intensity. If we leave aside large
groups of people and think for a moment of those intimacies which
spring up between friends, let us say between two friends, there
will be less difficulty in accepting the thesis. Whether it is between
father and son, or father and daughter, or the fathers of two sons,
the essential nature of the positive attraction and feeling is the
same. It is true that it will be differently expressed, and this we
shall presently discuss further.

The cultivation of friends and of friendships is certainly of
more importance than is generally recognized. If friends are
merely recreational resources or convenient distractions from the
routine of life, the relationship with them is of minimum value
psychologically; it can scarcely be called friendship. The man with
no friends has already abandoned himself to the fate of his own
self-destructiveness. Psychiatrists realize from clinical experience
what poets have proclaimed in inspired verse, that to retreat permanently into the loneliness of one's own soul is to surrender one's
claim upon life.

But at best it is hard for human beings to really get together;
it is hard for even the best of friends to understand and to feel
with one another sufficiently to promote a continuous, peaceful
affection. This gives rise to that vague feeling with which we are
all familiar of having parted from even our best friend without
having fully expressed the affection we feel or fully realized the
affection we hope he feels for us.

Observing the timid and conventional approaches which people
make toward one another, the forced cordiality, the jovial and
often crude "razzing" which they inflict on each other, the necessity many people feel to have a few drinks in order to "break the
ice" and to feel closer to one another, the fatigue that sets in so
quickly after a social round, one cannot help sensing the tremendous striving for love, appreciation and companionship that all
people have, and also the barriers that prevent their receiving
these gifts in full measure. Ferenczi said, "They want to love

one another but they don't know how." Frustrated and hungry for a word, a touch, a smile, a shared experience that would satisfy this universal hunger, many people try feverishly to fill the void with semblances of love: activity, popularity, philanthropy, prestige— there are thousands of ways of extracting recognition in lieu of love, none of them satisfactory.

Love is impaired less by the feeling that we are not appreciated than by a dread, more or less dimly felt by everyone, lest others see through our masks, the masks of repression that have been forced upon us by convention and culture. It is this that leads us to shun intimacy, to maintain friendships on a superficial level, to underestimate and fail to appreciate others lest they come to appreciate us only too well.

Hence, in an initial contact between two persons, each tries to impress the other with a certain presentable front, a mixture of conventional and personal ideals. From this inevitably emerges, however, an expression of needs which either clash or reciprocate. In the latter case a friendship is begun through mutual satisfactions offered and received, with many reservations and concealments in the background. As time goes on and friendship "develops," more and more of this background material is revealed and friends become better "acquainted." Before complete identification in friendship or love can occur there must be some mutual understanding, and for the accomplishment of this we must study one another as well as ourselves. It is amazing how many friends, even marital partners, live out their lives in complete ignorance of one another's natures—beyond certain mechanical externals.

Love is experienced as a pleasure in proximity, a desire for fuller knowledge of one another, a yearning for mutual identification and personality fusion. This we show to one another by our efforts to be understood, and by indulging the less imperious longing to understand. To be understood means, of course, that some of our *worst* impulses as well as our best ones are recognized by our friend, who knows all about us and likes us, anyway.

Once this mutual understanding and identification are established, friendship merges into love. And how is it shown? "They do not love that do not show their love." In the vast majority of instances our love for one another is expressed in nonphysical ways, in the interchange of ideas or the common enjoyment of some pleasure. One of the time-honored forms is the ritual of eating (or drinking) together. Being given food is the first expression of love which the child understands; it is his introduction to love. Hence the symbolic value of being fed remains high throughout life. In the unconscious Food = Love. It is understandable, therefore, why the dinner party or the social luncheon, for all its banality, is a perpetual medium of friendship. One of the first impulses of two people attracted to each other is to eat together, and while these occasions are generally thought of as mere expedients—opportunities for conversation or a setting for courtship—the symbolic meaning of the eating * is deeper than the conscious meaning of the words exchanged. The Christian religion recognizes this in the institution of a service in which an act of eating is actually designated "communion."

The sharing of food as an expression of love, going back as it does to the maternal function of nursing, leads directly to the allied form of expressing love—the giving of gifts. The child has little to give in return for the food given him, but that little he tries to give. As he grows older his gifts become more substantial, and represent—increasingly—a sacrifice of something prized by him. The gift expresses love because it symbolizes the giver himself or an important part of himself; it may even be his life— "greater love hath no man than this."

Thus the gift is more than a bribe, a purchase price offered for love; we rebel in our minds against the thought that love is

* It is also true, of course, that eating has an unconscious aggressive meaning which extends back to the primitive customs of devouring one's enemies. (See *Man Against Himself*, pages 40-46 and 122-123.) In the normal individual this meaning is deeply buried, while the erotic meaning is very near the surface of consciousness.

"bought" or "earned" or "repaid"; nevertheless, it is a fact that a certain exchange is made and a certain balance is inevitably established. We do measure love and weigh it, even if not accurately. We are most inaccurate when we assume that the balance is in the favor of the recipient rather than the giver. That it is more blessed to give than to receive is psychologically true because giving stimulates love while expressing it. "The mother gives [milk] to the child. By her giving she creates her love. To create love we must begin by sacrifice. Afterwards it is love that makes the sacrifices. But it is we who must take the first step." [8] Here then is a practical suggestion for the fostering of love.

Another way in which love can be fostered is by talking together. It has been said, in various forms and by several writers, that speech was given us for the purpose of disguising our thoughts. We do use it so, no doubt; and yet understanding does come through words finally, through many words—and through more than words, for actions speak louder. Especially differences, disagreements, and dissatisfactions should be talked out by friends —or lovers. The reason that the course of true love never does run smoothly is the fact that true love can endure only if the provocations of anger and resentment which inevitably develop are freely expressed and discussed and readjusted to. I certainly do not mean wrangling; both parties must make some conscientious effort to achieve objectivity and not simply indulge in temper tantrums. "A soft answer turneth away wrath but grievous words stir up [more] anger." It always seemed to me significant that among the Jews, where there is such a noticeable tendency to express aggressions in argument and verbal combat, there are so few divorces and so little physical violence. It is my idea that, even if the Roman Catholic church did not forbid it, divorce would still be infrequent among the Irish and Italians, because of their relatively great facility in expressing their emotions. It is often assumed by the silent, dignified, sulky Anglo-Saxon that the avoidance of verbal or even physical conflict between husband and wife promotes peace and happiness. The story of the European peasant woman who wept because her husband had not beaten her for a month seems grotesquely and pathetically amusing, but it is psychologically true. If a woman has to choose between being ignored and being beaten she will certainly choose the latter. Although this might be construed as a recommendation of wife-beating, that is certainly not what I mean; I do mean that if hostilities cannot be repressed or diverted, it is better to have them *out* than to have them *in*.

Women, as a rule, have a greater fondness than men for "talking things over." They have some compulsion to discuss all the aspects of an interpersonal problem which men often shun, sometimes with justification. To such questions as, "Why didn't you remember our anniversary?" or "Why don't you love me more?" the real answer is unknown; the reasons are unconscious, and the man realizes this even if he knows nothing about psychoanalysis; he knows that anything he says is "wrong." His refusal to say anything, however, is frustrating to the woman. If we were to draw practical conclusions, we might say that such problems ought to be talked out more than they generally are and less than some women want them to be.

Perhaps more important than talking is just listening. I believe listening to be one of the most powerful and influential techniques of human intercourse. The principal element in the technique of psychoanalysis is listening—uncritical but attentive listening. A good many hundreds of pages have been written about this in the technical literature, but I do not recall anything else so eloquent and, at the same time, so sound as an article by Brenda Ueland, published not in the *Psychoanalytic Review*, not in the *American Journal of Psychiatry*, not in the *Journal of the American Medical Association* (where perhaps it should have been), but in *The Ladies' Home Journal!* In the issue for November 1941 Miss Ueland writes:

Listening is a magnetic and strange thing, a creative force. . . . The friends that listen to us are the ones we move toward, and we want to

sit in their radius as though it did us good, like ultraviolet rays. . . .
When we are listened to, it creates us, makes us unfold and expand.
Ideas actually begin to grow within us and come to life. . . . It makes
people happy and free when they are listened to. . . . When we listen
to people there is an alternating current, and this recharges us so that
we never get tired of each other. We are constantly being re-created.

Now there are brilliant people who cannot listen much. They have
no ingoing wires on their apparatus. They are entertaining but exhaust-
ing too. I think it is because these lecturers, these brilliant performers,
by not giving us a chance to talk, do not let us express our thoughts and
expand; and it is this expressing and expanding that makes the little
creative fountain inside us begin to spring and cast up new thoughts
and unexpected laughter and wisdom.

I discovered all this about three years ago, and truly it made a revolutionary change in my life. Before that, when I went to a party I
would think anxiously: "Now try hard. Be lively. Say bright things.
Talk. Don't let down." And when tired, I would have to drink a lot
of coffee to keep this up. But now before going to a party, I just tell
myself to listen with affection to anyone who talks to me, *to be in their
shoes when they talk;* to try to know them without my mind pressing
against theirs, or arguing, or changing the subject. No. My attitude is:
"Tell me more. This person is showing me his soul. It is a little dry
and meager and full of grinding talk just now, but presently he will begin to think, not just automatically to talk. He will show his true self.
Then he will be wonderfully alive." . . .

I have quoted Miss Ueland's article because it is said more
effectively, more feelingly than I could say it. The technique of
listening was not invented by the psychoanalysts; it was only developed by them, and it is clear that Miss Ueland knows about it
intuitively. She is discerning enough to recognize that the power
of listening derives from the affection that it represents and the
affection that springs from putting oneself in the other person's
place. This capacity for identification is not given to all people. I
confess I cannot decide in my own mind whether love is determined by identification or identification by love. All that I am sure
of is that they go together. This does not contradict what I have
previously said, that some identifications are unconsciously hostile

in intent; I am not speaking now of unconscious identification, the psychological process—I am speaking of conscious identification, the conscious attempt to imagine or to perceive how the other fellow feels. This is an art; perhaps it is the basic art of love. At any rate, it is difficult for love to flourish without it.

Identification leads by extension to a wish for fusion. This fusion may be idealistic, it may be intellectual, it may be social, it may be physical. In a general way, these are the steps in the program of love. In his *Symposium*, Plato put into the mouth of Aristophanes the following legendary explanation of this striving for fusion:

> Human nature was once quite other than now. Originally, there were three sexes, three and not as today two; besides the male and the female there existed a third sex which had an equal share in the first two. . . . In these beings everything was double; thus they had four hands and four feet, two faces, two genital parts, and so on. Then Zeus allowed himself to be persuaded to cut these beings in two, as one divides pears to stew them. . . . When all nature was divided in this way, to each human being came the longing for his own other half, and the two halves embraced and entwined their bodies *and desired to grow together again.*

To accomplish this fusion is the object of the love impulse. To promote it in every known way is the prescription for happier living. We have spoken of the function of eating together, exchanging gifts, talking and listening to one another for the furtherance of this mutual identification. Two more practical devices which can be used in the furtherance of the process are work and play.

Working together has been made difficult for husbands and wives by the advance of civilization. On the contrary, the increasing subdivision of labor and the development of co-operative enterprise whereby many people work together on a project has developed other outlets for love, especially for men, which wives frequently feel to be a threat to marital love or a distraction from it. There is no question but that people who work together grow to love one another. But it is a mistake to assume that love is a limited quantity which if expressed in one direction and toward one object is thereby subtracted from another. The capacity for love normally increases with the opportunities and occasions given it for development; the man who is loved and beloved by his fellow workmen is usually the man who loves and is loved by his wife. The real danger in working apart from each other is the separation of interests and the consequent loss of opportunity for sharing experiences—the opportunity that provides further identification.

Many husbands and wives find that they can work together fruitfully. But many others feel the necessity of defending themselves against too complete an identification with each other, and these keep their work as a kind of island of separateness, a domain of their own. This is particularly true of the man who feels that his masculine independence is threatened by feminine help, or of the woman who fears that her personality will be submerged in a man's ambitions. And, of course, real obstacles—children and a lack of similar educational preparation—make it impossible for most couples to work at the same occupation, even if they wish to do so.

Nevertheless, the more people work together the more tolerance, understanding, and love they tend to have for each other; and wise husbands and wives will find ways to utilize this fact in such projects as making furniture for their own home, planting its grounds, keeping accounts, and sharing the care of their children.

But if working together has been made harder for husbands and wives, playing together has been made easier. The increasing participation of women in sports is one evidence of this, and a salutary sign. The great numbers of people who swim together, hike together, play together, attend football games together, speak for the intuitive recognition of the generation of love by the joint experience of the pleasure of recreation. All this proves that in addition to the harmless discharge of aggressions described in the chapter on Play there is a fostering and reinforcing of love by the

simultaneous enjoyment of play. The more people play together
the better they like one another. Family outings and vacation trips
certainly do far more to promote morality and prevent divorce
than the League of Decency.

3

There remains to be discussed finally the function of physical
union in the expression and cultivation of love. Logical and obvious though this may be, it is a curious fact that until relatively
recent times love was not considered an aspect of the sexual life.
In discussing this, Havelock Ellis said [9] that while our concept
of love is found, it is true, among some lower races, its development in Occidental civilization was slow.

The Greek poets, except the latest, showed little recognition of love
as an element of marriage. Theognis compared marriage with cattle-
breeding. The Romans of the Republic took much the same view.
Greeks and Romans alike regarded breeding as the one recognizable
object of marriage; any other object was mere wantonness and had
better, they thought, be carried on outside marriage. Religion, which
preserves so many ancient and primitive conceptions of life, has conse-
crated this conception also, and Christianity . . . at the outset offered
only the choice between celibacy on the one hand and, on the other,
marriage for the production of offspring.

Yet, from an early period in human history, a secondary function
of sexual intercourse had been slowly growing up to become one of the
great objects of marriage. Among animals, it may be said, and even
sometimes in man, the sexual impulse, when once aroused, makes but
a short and swift circuit through the brain to reach its consummation.
But as the brain and its faculties develop, powerfully aided indeed by
the very difficulties of the sexual life, the impulse for sexual union has
to traverse ever longer, slower, more painful paths before it reaches—
and sometimes it never reaches—its ultimate object. This means that
sex gradually becomes intertwined with all the highest and subtlest
human emotions and activities, with the refinements of social intercourse,
with high adventure in every sphere, with art, with religion. The primitive animal instinct, having the sole end of procreation, becomes on its

way to that end the inspiring stimulus to all those psychic energies which in civilization we count most precious. This function is thus, we see, a by-product. But, as we know, even in our human factories, the by-product is sometimes more valuable than the product.

It is surely no secret that, despite all that has been said and done scientifically, the popular attitude towards sexual pleasure is still largely a mixture of salaciousness and shame. Such pleasure is still regarded officially as something incidental to the serious business of procreation, and—apart from that—sinful, bestial, and unmentionable. How can one otherwise interpret the fact that so serious a condition as the absence of conscious sexual pleasure, a condition for which thousands of physicians are consulted daily by a small fraction of the total number of persons who are distressed about it, should receive almost no mention or discussion in the standard medical works of the day? How else could one explain the fact that the theater, the cinema, the night clubs, the newspapers, the popular novels, in fact all official public representations of contemporary life, are permitted by public consent to make obscene allusions, sneers, jests, and hints, but are forbidden any honest or frank or truthful representation of either the normal or the frustrated phenomena of sexuality? How else could one explain the fact that although physicians, lawyers, and judges intimately acquainted with the facts state that the overwhelming majority of divorces spring from inadequate sexual satisfaction, this is legal ground for divorce in only two or three states of the Union and is almost never cited in court? That sexual temptation and the necessity for a healthful solution of the sexual life are important features in a college career is not officially recognized, so far as I know, in any institution in this country. A few forward-looking individuals—physicians, clergymen, student counselors, and others—are not themselves blind to this fact, but work without popular support or assistance and without much scientific understanding or help.

One of the best definitions of love, and a very scientific one, was written by the poet Shelley: "That profound and complicated sentiment which we call love is the universal thirst for a communion not merely of the senses, but of our whole nature, intellectual, imaginative and sensitive. . . . The sexual impulse, which is only one, and often a small part of those claims, serves, from its obvious and external nature, as a kind of type of expression of the rest, a common basis, an acknowledged and visible link."

It might seem, logically, that the inhibition of our aggressiveness which civilization demands would bring about the encouragement rather than the denial of the erotic life as seems to be the case. But for a long time it has been recognized that—as Freud beautifully records in his *Civilization and Its Discontents*—the progress of civilization has been made at the cost of the erotic life of mankind. Freud is not the only observer who recognized this apparent opposition of civilization to sexuality. Havelock Ellis, Karl Pearson (in *The Ethics of Free Thought*), Friedrich Engels, and others have explained that society exercises control over the erotic life of mankind because sexuality is linked with procreation and procreation involves expense and increased competition.* If one thinks only in terms of economics, as so many people do, it is very easy to draw the conclusion that sexual restraint and subsequent sexual repression arose on that basis. But if one is equally attentive to religious and theological history, it is equally easy to believe that the economic explanations are only rationalizations for attitudes based primarily upon moral concepts. It is often stated that the introduction of Christianity served to crystallize the ascetic suppression of sexuality as if it, rather than destructive aggression, were the source of man's unhappiness.

* Thus, in an article in the *Atlantic Monthly* for October 1939, a priest takes the position: Those whose economic circumstances are such that they cannot support an additional child are deserving of sympathy but must practise noble self-restraint. Anything else is to "pervert their conjugal relations through mere selfishness," and "their conduct is . . . gravely sinful." He quotes Pope Pius XI as saying that poor married couples "should take care lest the calamitous state of their material affairs should be an occasion for a much more calamitous error. . . . [They should] preserve in wedlock their chastity unspotted." In other words, those who do not have money should not have sexual intercourse.

"There can be no doubt that the early Christian fathers desired to abolish sex completely. There were to be no exceptions, even matrimony being regarded as unholy. . . . It was some time before the Roman church came to compromise with sin and to enshrine it in Holy Matrimony." [10]

This concept of Christianity is dramatically illustrated in Leo Tolstoy's *The Kreutzer Sonata,* and in his less well-known autobiographical fragment *The Devil.* But the accusation should not be leveled exclusively against Christianity; it can be made with equal justice against many institutions, religious and secular. Sexual taboos exist in all primitive cultures, and they originate from internal repressions which are later ascribed to external teachings and fiats. In contemporary civilization, as in primitive civilization, the inhibitions in the erotic life of most men and women arise within and are related to religion only formally and nominally. This applies to people who do not have any conscious interest in religion, as well as to those who do. The primitive taboos have been incorporated into all religious faiths as well as into social customs. The reason that we blame Christianity more than others is because Americans and Europeans are more familiar with it and more influenced by it. It is true that some zealous early Christians castrated themselves, but so did many ardent Roman and Greek Cybelians and so do quite a number of neurotic and psychotic fanatics of the present day.*

To blame sexual inhibitions on institutions is thus to put the cart before the horse. It is absurd to deny that there are social pressures, but social pressures result from the accumulation and organization of the child's individual experiences with his parents.

Psychology is more fundamental than economics or religion; there are inherent emotional needs and conflicts, not entirely independent of but certainly not determined by economic and religious factors, that determine our way of life. In order to achieve what we hope to be the greater ultimate satisfactions of civilization,

* See *Man Against Himself,* Part IV; Focal Suicide.

we have increasingly held back the immediate gratification of some of our instinctual needs, with the result that the civilization we achieved has kept making greater and greater demands for renunciation until it has reached a point that we can now scarcely afford. It is as if an indigent couple should borrow money from a loan shark in order to buy a washing machine and thus save some manual labor for the wife, only to find that in the end both have to do ten times as much manual labor as before in order to pay the accumulating and increasing burdens of the loan for the "labor-saving" machine.

Thus, although they may differ in their explanations of the reason for it, the economist, the sociologist, the religionist, and the psychologist agree on the fact that civilization wars against sexuality. They word it somewhat differently—the economist stressing the falling birthrate, the sociologist deploring the lessened importance of the home, and the theologian pointing to the extent of immorality, divorce, marital unhappiness, childlessness, and celibacy. The psychiatrist, both from his psychological bias and from his medical experience, is impressed with the prevalence of overt sexual maladjustment and frustration; and the energetic absorption in business affairs, competition, production, and commerce which the economist is likely to view with satisfaction strikes the psychologist (the psychiatrist) with dismay. The man of religion says that these things are too worldly and indicate a neglect of the real purpose of living, that the means has become more important than the end. With this the psychiatrist would agree, but he would put it somewhat more empirically. He would say that men are more interested in their competition with one another than in their devotion to their wives and children, that they invest more energy in work and fighting than in the constructive problems of love.

The horror with which some parents learn of their children's interest in various forms of experimental sexual play is a reflection of the ambivalence in adults' attitude toward sexuality, especially to their own children's sexuality. Freud pointed out that parents are actually jealous of their own children, that they try as long as possible to prevent them from any theoretical or practical acquaintanceship with sexuality, punishing them for premature excursions into this forbidden field. It is an interesting corollary to this observation that the sexual approach of adults to children is associated with the most intense feelings of social disapproval; such episodes have not infrequently served as the basis for mob violence against the offender. The assumption is, of course, that children are irreparably ruined by such experiences. Without intending in the least to justify or excuse such criminal behavior, I may nevertheless point out that in the cold light of scientific investigation no such devastating effects usually follow (a fact which I hope will be of some comfort to certain anguished parents). Two psychiatrists (Lauretta Bender and Abram Blau) recently made a careful follow-up study of such cases and concluded that children exposed to premature sexual experiences with adults frequently turn out to be "distinguished and unusually charming and attractive in their outward personalities." [11]

The conclusions to be drawn from such observations need not be shocking; they simply bear out our contention that sexuality is not the evil and horrible thing it is generally conceived to be. Such experiences are traumatic to the child only when connected with deep hostilities; the furtive and desperate nature of such attacks, combined with the attitude of society toward them, tends entirely in the direction of unbearably stimulating the child's hostilities so that he conceives of sex as brutality. But when the experience actually stimulates the child erotically, it would appear from the observations of the authors cited just above that it may favor rather than inhibit the development of social capabilities and mental health in the so-called victims.

Of course, most children do not encounter such incidents, but all children meet with a conspiracy of silence and implied disapproval with respect to sexuality which effects deep, often insuperable, blockades of normal expression in later life. For many people it seems irreverent, indecent, and immoral to place any esteem upon the pleasurable satisfactions of sexual intercourse. They regard it as the transitory, inconsequential bait which nature uses as a stimulus to the perpetuation of the race, an insidious and rather shameful pleasure which impels a couple to do their duty by the world. For those who esteem it for its own sake without the wish for or expectation of a child, the occurrence of pregnancy is regarded as a punishment. In my professional practice I have often seen families in which the birth of a child is clearly looked upon as the inevitable sentence pronounced by nature for indulgence in "sins of the flesh."

Another obstacle to the direct gratification of the sexual instinct is ignorance of the technique of love-making, sexual play, and sexual intercourse. Ninon de l'Enclos is said to have declared that "it requires far more genius to make love than to command armies." The reasons for failure from ignorance and clumsiness probably include unconscious factors of the familiar sort, but as a practical matter it is an obstacle that can be overcome, granted the conscious wish to do so. Many doctors, by instructing their patients, greatly improve their sexual adjustments. But the trouble is or has been that the general taboo on sex extended even to the doctors, so that there was an actual lack of information on the part of many of them and a reluctance on the part of many others to discuss the subject. Thirty-odd years ago an intrepid physician (Robie), impressed by the astonishing ignorance of many of his patients in regard to elementary principles of sexual behavior, began a collection of case histories, recording in a very earnest, if at times somewhat naive, manner precisely what the experiences of a considerable number of his patients had been in this respect. These books were privately published and of course immediately banned, but they were followed by others, until gradually the investigation of the actual sexual behavior of twentieth-century human beings has become recognized as a proper subject for scientific study. Statistical investigations, more elaborate and careful histories, systematic treatises, and books of practical counsel have by now been published in considerable numbers; but even today a vast ignorance prevails concerning the actual sexual experiences of "normal" civilized human beings. At the present time, with the assistance of the National Research Council, a number of psychologists are attempting to collect statistical information in this field on a rather large scale. Although such data are likely to confuse the conscious interferences with the sexual life due to ignorance with those due to unconscious repressions, this is a step in the right direction.

Thus an enormous change has taken place in popular thinking within the past two or three decades. We can all remember when the only books pertaining to the sexual life were either medical treatises on perversions or solemn warnings to the young about the dangers of masturbation. Both types of books have mercifully disappeared. But even today there are few authors brave enough and honest enough to make the flat statements that masturbation never harms a child and that the child whose sexual life evolves without a period of masturbation is an exceptional and, one may say, an abnormal child. The pain and anguish which many parents experience even today for what they regard as the pathological sexual manifestations of their children are exceeded only by the suffering inflicted upon these children with the ostensible purpose of deterring them from wrecking their lives by a completely normal, utterly innocuous childhood activity.

While it is true that the former conspiracy of silence about pleasure in the marital relationship has been to some extent broken down, so that a considerable number of intelligently written books are now on the market, it should be remembered that this has been bought at a price—the violent denunciation, the humiliation, persecution, and imprisonment of the writers who first ventured to state publicly what every mature person must have recognized as truth. Furthermore, the very fact that such books have to be

written, that young men and women need to be told and encouraged to believe that they have a right to enjoy one another, is in
itself an amazing condemnation of the so-called moral attitude of
civilization—an attitude which can only be described as immoral,
obscene, and essentially destructive.*

It is from this curiously abnormal attitude toward joy in interpersonal relations that we endure so much self-imposed oppression. "We human beings," writes Rebecca West,[12] "plant in ourselves the perennial blossom of cruelty—the conviction that if we
hurt other people we are doing good to ourselves and to life in
general. To destroy this cancer of our spirit is our real problem."
The aggressive instincts, the impulses to self-destruction and the
destruction of others, are quick to seize every opportunity to
make men miserable. It is not only a philosophical desideratum
that we should seek and find pleasures—it is a psychological necessity for the realization and the preservation of life. And where
can we expect to find more pleasure than in love? As Havelock
Ellis exhorted: [13]

It is passion, more passion and fuller, that we need. The moralist
who bans passion is not of our time; his place these many years is with

---

* See the bold proposals of Réné Guyon in *Sexual Freedom* (translated from
the French by Eden and Cedar Paul, published by John Lane, London, 1939).
On this book the *International Journal of Psycho-Analysis* (January 1940)
commented: "M. Guyon is an able exponent of the extreme left wing of sexual
reform. He approaches the problems of sex from the point of view of 'integral
rationalism,' according to which sexual pleasure is healthy and desirable and therefore legitimately obtainable in any and every form, provided there is no interference with the rights of others; any attempt to curtail the opportunities for
such pleasure, whether on religious, moral or legal grounds, being an unwar-
rantable interference with the liberty of the individual, which should be resisted
by all who realize the immense importance of adequate sexual satisfaction for
physical and mental well-being. . . . A reading of M. Guyon's book provides
us with a salutary stimulus, inasmuch as it is calculated to make us realize very
forcibly the tremendous gulf that exists between our actual attitude to sex, determined as this is by centuries of superstition and taboo, and the attitude that might
ensue from a rational hedonism—an attitude such as might consistently have
been adopted by some of the Nineteenth-Century hedonists, but which they certainly have lacked the courage to advocate. . . . The purely rationalistic approach requires, however, to be supplemented by the psychological one, and it is
here that M. Guyon's treatment, for all its brave discarding of the lumber of
tradition, is apt to appear a little naive."

the dead. For we know what happens in a world when those who ban passion have triumphed. When Love is suppressed Hate takes its place. The least regulated orgies of Love grow innocent beside the orgies of Hate. . . . It is more passion and ever more that we need if we are to undo the work of Hate, if we are to add to the gaiety and splendour of life, to the sum of human achievement, to the aspiration of human ecstasy. The things that fill men and women with beauty and exhilaration, and spur them to actions beyond themselves, are the things that are now needed.

An excellent bit of psychology was revealed in James Hilton's novel, *Goodbye, Mr. Chips.* Mr. Chips was shy, inept, and provocative in his relations with fellow-teachers and students. Then he met a woman who loved him and whom he loved and married. He became more gracious, kind, and friendly with everyone—so much so that he grew to be the most beloved man in the school, and perhaps the happiest one. Thereafter, even tremendous disappointments did not unbalance him. It would sound romantic but it would be entirely correct to say that this was the effect of the love of a woman; it would be prudish to ignore the implication that love of this woman made possible for the first time in Mr. Chips's life a normal sexual relationship.

I am not unaware that many readers of these lines will be thinking of the frustrated sexuality of their own lives, or those of spinsters, bachelors, and widows of their acquaintance. They will doubtless think of the good these people do, of their self-sacrifices, and the beauty of character which they often display. They may contrast these with certain petty, disagreeable, embittered personalities among their married friends and remark, "How absurdly untrue is all this theory of the necessity of a normal sexuality!" One may be indulgent with such critics, but skeptical of their deductions, for any psychiatrist—or, for that matter, almost any family physician or minister—could tell how deceiving are these appearances. The pettiness, selfishness, and unhappiness of many married people exist because in spite of their opportunity, they often do not have a normal sexual life. And as for those persons who have adjusted themselves to continence (I dislike the pious hypocrisy of the word "chastity"), I venture to say that not even their most intimate counselors, but only they themselves know the price they pay in silent suffering and unseen penalties.

Some objectors will ask: Even granting the importance of a normal sexual life, is it not against public policy to remove the restraints that exist to curb its promiscuous expression? Are we not in danger of sexual license and the widespread dissemination of illegitimacy and venereal disease if we abandon completely the taboos that have attached for so many centuries to sexual manifestations? Does not the experience of the Romans during the decline of the Empire indicate that sexual freedom does not further the happiness of the human race? And is it not true that the Union of Soviet Socialist Republics found that the removal of barriers to divorce led to an unhealthy situation which had to be corrected by revision of the laws?

These are weighty questions, but in part they misconstrue the meaning of what I have said. I have nowhere suggested that the unregulated, uncontrolled expression of the sexual instinct is desirable or practicable. Sexual freedom is *not* promiscuity, as I have already made clear in dealing with such phenomena as the Don Juan type. As for the ancient Romans, I think we know too little about the actual life of the average Roman citizen to draw any fundamental conclusions, for the life led by rich aristocrats is not the life of the people of a country. And in Russia there are still too many conflicting elements for us to draw conclusions. For although both Marx and Lenin inveighed against profligacy and so-called freedom, no less than against puritanism, in the rush of the Revolution the pendulum swung from the one extreme to the other, and may now be swinging back. "When Lenin had criticized the 'hypocrisy of bourgeois morality,' he did not mean to attack such an institution as monogamy, but only the use and pious misuse of it under capitalism. 'Healthy bodies, healthy minds!' he had exclaimed. 'Neither monk nor Don Juan!' " [14]

In refuting these objections, the important point is that the exaltation of the sexual life does not and *should* not imply debauchery and promiscuity, for the reason is that these things are not love, even though they may use some of the physical techniques of love. Judas used the same technique to betray Jesus that a lover uses to reassure his sweetheart. The same act is performed by the reverent visitor to the Pope when the latter extends his hand and ring. And just as a kiss may have various connotations, so other forms of physical contact may vary in implication, taste, and wholesomeness.

Prostitution is promoted and supported by the taboo on sexuality, combined with the social ideal of compulsory monogamy and the lack of contraceptive information among married and unmarried women. It becomes a technique of experiencing physical pleasure without psychological obligation, and this encourages a split in the emotional life, with the result that the tender elements are bestowed upon one person and the physical elements upon another. This is just as illogical and just as unhealthful as it would be if only carbohydrates were served in legitimate restaurants and proteins and fats had to be obtained surreptitiously and illicitly from restaurateurs who had no social or business standing. Occasionally a man resynthesizes these elements, falls in love with the prostitute, and marries her. This is both because of her bad reputation and in spite of it. I say *because of it* in the sense that men are relieved to be able to discard the prudery with which sex is so frequently invested and to feel comfortable in the presence of one who is honest enough to make no pretense about her sexual wishes, even though it is surely not these that force her into prostitution as a means of livelihood. In addition to this, some men, for unconscious reasons, actually prefer women who have been sought after and possessed by other men. And I say *in spite of* her reputation because the selection of a prostitute ordinarily implies that the sexual relation is one from which the romantic elements have been stricken. In the conscious mind, the love object is looked

upon as a degraded one, but the natural tendency to identify the
tender and physical elements in sexual intimacy often overcomes
this social taboo.

These aspects of prostitution have been portrayed by poets and
playwrights for centuries. They have been repeatedly submitted
to the contemplation of readers and playgoers of the world, who
nod assent but show thereafter not the slightest evidence of any
change in their preconceptions. Let one try the experiment, in the
course of a discussion of social life, of suggesting the possibility
of improving prostitution—and observe the adverse emotional reactions that spring up like geysers.

And this is, of course, understandable. More and better prostitution is *not* the answer. If an honest, intelligent conception of
the significance of the sexual life can be brought to prevail in
place of the present hypocrisy and repression, if the importance of
the psychological content and the natural importance of the function of love can be established, if the cleavage between the tender
and the physical elements of sexual relations can be annulled (as
would be the case if the primary error were corrected), prostitution
would vanish like frost in the sunshine.

I am not such a dreamer as to suppose that any words of mine—
or, for that matter, anything that a thousand psychiatrists or ten
thousand philosophers might say—could revolutionize or even
considerably alter the prevalent social attitudes. Yet we know
that they do change, that they are changing, and this gives us some
hope for the future and some encouragement to speak out our
thoughts, however feeble their effect may seem to be. That the
world does change in its attitudes is hard for us to realize: it
seems incredible that less than sixty years ago a book of poems
by that most conventional, trite, Victorian poet, Ella Wheeler
Wilcox, should have been assailed with fury as "immoral"—a fact
as incredible as is the fact that the man to whom Miss Wheeler
had just become engaged wistfully pleaded with her to withdraw
the book from publication.[15]

Not only in regard to sex, but in regard to all human rights there has been a vast change in social attitudes. In spite of human frailties and errors, we may ultimately achieve a less artificial, more psychologically sound civilization. It is not impossible to conceive of a time when the expression of love—in all the forms in which it manifests itself—will be as natural, as spontaneous, and as magnificently organized as is the expression of rage and hate at the present moment.

Of that time I cannot predict the outward forms of life; but I know of no better expression of the spirit in which our lives could be lived than has been set down by Rebecca West in her contribution to *Living Philosophies:* [16]

"I have no faith in the sense of comforting beliefs which persuade me that all my troubles are blessings in disguise. . . . But I have faith in a process, in a particular process that is part of the general process of life, though it is sometimes annulled by it. I find an ultimate value in the efforts of human beings to do more than merely exist, to choose and analyze their experiences and by the findings of that analysis help themselves to further experiences which are of a more pleasurable kind. I use the word pleasurable in its widest sense; to describe such experiences as come from good food and wine, exercise, the physical act of lovemaking, the practice of a beloved craft or art or science, a happy marriage, the care of children or the sick or the old by those who enjoy it, the service of valid ideas, or the administration of worthy institutions, or the pursuit of agreeable sensations. *Trahit sua quemque voluptas.* By indulgence in these experiences life is made more pleasant from day to day. That is in itself of the first importance. That end would be worthwhile pursuing if no other benefit were obtained. But it also serves the purpose of furnishing each human soul with access to the avenue along which it can advance farthest toward the comprehension and mastery of life. Pleasure is not arbitrary; it is the sign by which the human organization shows that it is performing a function which it finds appropriate to its means and ends.

I take it as a prime cause of the present confusion of society that it is too sickly and too doubtful to use pleasure frankly as a test of value.

"But indeed we need no further argument in favor of taking pleasure as a standard when we consider the only alternative that faces us. If we do not live for pleasure we shall soon find ourselves living for pain. If we do not regard as sacred our own joys and the joys of others, we open the door and let into life the ugliest attribute of the human race, which is cruelty . . . the root of all other vices."

But before that day comes we shall have learned more about ourselves. We shall have conceded the existence of evil within us, of aggressive tendencies that cannot be permitted to find their expression spontaneously, following a course of least resistance. We shall have revised our ways of living to include more play, and our ways of working to insure more joy in work. The study of the child and the threats to his development will have been recognized not as a pretty little hobby for a few earnest missionaries and pedants but as a task equal in importance to the study of the stock-market and the compounding of poisonous gases.

We shall have put a higher estimate upon the beautiful as a criterion of creativeness. "When we discern the influence of creation predominating we are moved by something we call beauty, when we see destruction we recoil at the ugly. Our need for beauty springs from the gloom and pain which we experience from our destructive impulses to our good and loved objects; our wish is to find in art evidence of the triumph of life over death; we recognize the power of death when we say a thing is ugly." [17] We shall have gained the courage in that day to hate what is ugly.

We shall have accorded to love the pre-eminence which it deserves in our scale of values; we shall seek it and proclaim it as the highest virtue and the greatest boon. We shall not be ashamed to have "suffered much extremity for love," in the full realization that love is the medicine for the sickness of the world, a prescription often given, too rarely taken. We shall have realigned our faith in God to include more faith in human beings, and extended our identifications to include more brothers, more sisters, more sons and daughters in a vastly wider family concept. "For love is the desire of the whole, and the pursuit of the whole is called love." Plato said this, even before Jesus taught that "God is love," which means the same thing.

This goal is not unattainable in spite of past errors and present vicissitudes. For we have the courage to hope and the power to love. And for all the evil within us, we cannot escape the will to live. From that springs our determination to better our lot. By the use of our intelligence and our knowledge we can use the slave of science for the promotion of human happiness. Speed the day!

Source Notes

Chapter 1

1. Sigmund Freud, *New Introductory Lectures on Psychoanalysis*, Norton, 1933, p. 144.

Each new pronouncement of Freud was met by storms of opposition, refutation, ridicule and skepticism; time after time, following the initial storm, the reaction against his quiet proposals died down and his authority became established. I would not give the impression that every postulation of Freud has been substantiated because this is far from being the case. Freud altered and revised many of his original propositions and conclusions, some of them many times, and although he had the courage to venture into unknown territories armed only with the knowledge acquired in investigation of the human mind, he always recorded his ideas with a diffidence and tenuousness in sharp contrast to the eloquent positivism of some of his critics. Even at the present time his concept of the aggressive instinct, the self-destructive trend which he related to death just as he related the sexual instinct to life, is not universally accepted. In the interests of scientific honesty, I think I should state some of the objections that have been made to it and indicate why I feel these objections are unsound.

In the first place, there is what might be called a common sense objection. This objection is based on the following line of reasoning: If a person fights, he does so because he is threatened; therefore, his fighting is in self-defense and it is dictated by his instinct of self-preservation. This argument is the weakest one of all, although it is the most plausible. It ignores a part of the instinct theory, which is that successful living consists of being able to direct the destructive energy into just such useful channels of self-protection and it is just this which neurotic people, for example, are characteristically unable to do.

A variation of this objection is one made by some sociologists, anthropologists and others whose psychological ground work is relatively deficient. They admit that aggressiveness is frequently wantonly dispensed and even self-destructive, but they regard all this as being the result of "the culture" in which the individual lives. They make such nonsensical propositions as that all aggression is the result of frustration. Anyone who has had his toe stepped on, which is certainly not a frustration, knows how inadequate such a formula is. Furthermore, it completely ignores the question of where the aggressive energy comes from which is provoked by the frustration, and this is what the instinct theory attempts to answer.

Then there is the objection of the psychologists which is the most intelligent and rational objection although, in my opinion, not a sound one. Psychologists have used the word instinct rather narrowly to describe certain isolated patterns of behavior, such as nest-building in birds, for example, which they now interpret or explain quite differently. Many of them are ready to concede that there are fundamental drives, among which may be a drive in the direction of destructiveness in general and self-destructiveness in particular, but they (correctly) hold that it is impossible to demonstrate these experimentally and prefer to base their formulations upon concepts capable of laboratory reproduction. They object to the word instinct and they are skeptical about hypothetical constructions based on teleological interpretations, believing that instincts are best understood not if directed purposively, but in terms of their genetic antecedents and not as purposes. (See Teleology and the Emotions by Alden O. Weber and David Rapaport. *Philosophy of Science*, 8:69-82, Jan. 1941, and the references therein quoted.) It would probably be more accurate, in line with their criticisms, if instead of speaking of the "instincts" of hate or love, or of construction and destruction, we said, "the tendency to react to stimulation in constructive or destructive ways." But to substitute words like *tendency, trend, reaction capacity* and words of that sort for *instinct* does not seem to me to help matters very much. They are still indefinite and obscure.

Finally there is a philosophical objection to the instinct theory which is based in substance on the old quarrel between monism and dualism. Monistic philosophy would insist that to account for the energy is one thing but to consider it earmarked as destructive and constructive from the start is fallacious. Heat or cold are not two different things but only a relative presence and absence of heat; east and west are not two different directions but only different aspects of direction along the same line. I cannot answer these philosophical objections; we know empirically that anabolism and katabolism are apparently two different processes, even though they are combined to make up what we call metabolism. Life and death, so far as human judgment can perceive, are two different things. Dialecticism is a philosophical mode which attempts to solve the problem of duality by pointing out that the one is made up of an interaction of the two, for which reason some dialectically minded philosophers find nothing to criticize in our theory. This, however, is far beyond my scope. (For a didactic summary of the history and present status of this theory, see Bibring, Edward: The Development and Purpose of the Theory of the Instincts. *Int. J. Psa.*, 22:93-131, 1941.)

Chapter 2

1. Margaret Gray Blanton, "The Behavior of the Human Infant During the First Thirty Days of Life," *Psychological Rev.*, 24:456-483, Nov. 1917. See also Margarethe A. Ribble, "The Significance of Infantile Sucking for the Psychic Development of the Individual," *J. Nerv. & Ment. Dis.*, 90:455-463, October 1939; Phyllis Greenacre, "The Predisposition to Anxiety," *Psychoanalytic Quarterly*, 10:66-94, January 1941; and Wayne Dennis, "A Description and Classification of the Newborn Infant," *Psychological Bulletin*, 31:5-22, January 1934. (Dennis and others hold that the infant's anger appears only after it experiences frustration; however, frustration inevitably occurs almost from the beginning of life.)

2. Anna Freud and Dorothy T. Burlingham, "Report on Hampstead Nurseries," issued April 1942 by the British Foster Parents' Plan for War children, New York Headquarters, 55 W. 42d St.

3. Lawrence K. Frank, "Cultural Coercion and Individual Distortion," *Psychiatry*, 2:21-22, February 1939.

4. G. F. Weinfeld, "Pediatric Approaches in Infancy," *Am. J. Orthopsychiat.*, July 1941.

5. Erik Homburger Erikson, "Observations on Sioux Education," *J. Psych.*, 7:101-156, 1939, p. 138.

6. George Devereux, "L'Envoûtement chez les indiens mohaves," *Journal de la Société des Américanistes de Paris*, 2 (29), 1937, pp. 405-412.

7. Havelock Ellis, *On Life and Sex: Essays of Love and Virtue,* Garden City Pub. Co., 1937, 2:28-29.

8. Margarethe A. Ribble, "Disorganizing Factors of Infant Personality," *Am. J. Psychiat.* 98:459-463, November 1941.
There are numerous competent books of counsel to parents which respect these principles; e.g., C. A. and M. M. Aldrich, *Babies Are Human Beings,* Macmillan, 1938; Anna W. M. Wolf, *The Parents' Manual: A Guide to the Emotional Development of Young Children,* Simon & Schuster, 1941; Winifred DeKok, *Guiding Your Child Through the Formative Years,* Emerson Books, 1935; *Parents' Questions,* Child Study Association of America, Harper and Brothers, 1936; and Caroline Zachry, *Emotion and Conduct in Adolescence,* D. Appleton-Century, 1940.

Chapter 3

1. Virginia Woolf, *Three Guineas,* Harcourt, Brace, 1938, pp. 63ff.
2. Lillian E. Smith and Paula Snelling, "Man Born of Woman," *North Georgia Review,* 6:14, Winter 1941.
3. For an analysis of war in terms of the destructive impulses of the individual, see particularly: E. F. M. Durbin and John Bowlby, *Personal Aggressiveness and War,* Columbia University Press, 1939, and Edward Glover, *The Psychology of Fear and Courage,* Penguin Books, 1940, and *War, Sadism, and Pacifism,* George Allen & Unwin, 1933.
4. See, for example: Lewis M. Terman, *Psychological Factors in Marital Happiness,* McGraw-Hill Book Co., 1938; G. V. Hamilton and Kenneth Mac-Gowan, *What Is Wrong With Marriage,* Albert & Charles Boni, 1929; G. V. Hamilton, *A Research in Marriage,* Albert & Charles Boni, 1929; Katharine Bement Davis, *Factors in the Sex Life of Twenty-Two Hundred Women,* Harper & Bros., 1929; Laura Hutton, *The Single Woman and Her Emotional Problems,* William Wood & Co., 1935; Willard Waller, *The Family, a Dynamic Interpretation,* The Cordon Co., 1938; Carney Landis et al., *Sex in Development,* Paul B. Hoeber, 1940; Robert Latou Dickinson and Lura Beam, *The Single Woman,* Reynal & Hitchcock, 1934; H. Van de Velde, *Sex Hostility in Marriage,* Covici, Friede, 1931.
5. Ruth Mack Brunswick, "The Preoedipal Phase of the Libido Development," *Psychoanalytic Quarterly,* 9:293-319, 1940.
6. *Op. cit.,* 1:75.
7. Smith and Snelling, *op. cit.*

Chapter 4

1. George W. Henry and Hugh M. Galbraith, "Constitutional Factors in Homosexuality," *Am. J. Psychiat.,* 13:1249-1267, May 1934.
2. John Rickman, "On the Nature of Ugliness and the Creative Impulse," *Int. J. Psa.,* 21:294-313, July 1940, p. 309.
3. David Rapaport, "The Szondi Test," *Bull. Menninger Clinic,* 5:33-40, 1941.
4. Douglass W. Orr, "Pregnancy Following the Decision to Adopt," *Psychosomatic Medicine,* 3:441-446, October 1941. See references to H. Sellheim, A. Mayer, O. Schwarz, F. Kehrer and others in H. Flanders Dunbar's *Emotions and Bodily Changes; A Survey of Literature on Psychosomatic Interrelationships,* Second Edition, Columbia Press, 1938.
5. G. A. Studdert-Kennedy, *The Warrior, the Woman, and the Christ,* Doubleday, 1929, p. 40.

6. Smith and Snelling, *op. cit.*
7. Sylvia M. Payne, "A Conception of Femininity," *Brit. J. Med. Psychol.,* 15:18-33, 1935.
8. Thomas Mann, *Freud, Goethe, and Wagner,* Knopf, 1937, p. 112.
9. Joan Riviere, *Love, Hate, and Reparation,* Psycho-Analytic Epitomes, No. 2, London, Hogarth Press, 1937, p. 44. See Ch. 6, ref. 4, and Ch. 8, ref. 3.
10. J. F. Brown, *Psychology and the Social Order,* McGraw-Hill, 1936.

Chapter 5

1. Bertrand Russell, "What I Believe," *The Nation,* March 30, 1942, p. 414.
2. For a review of the evolution of the concept of sublimation, containing references to over 100 technical contributions, see Harry B. Levey, "A Critique of the Theory of Sublimation," *Psychiatry,* 2:239-270, May 1939.
3. W. C. Menninger, "Psychoanalytic Principles Applied to the Treatment of Hospitalized Patients," *Bull. Menninger Clinic,* 1:35-43, November 1936; and "Psychiatric Hospital Therapy Designed to Meet Unconscious Needs," *Am. J. Psychiat.* 93:347-360, September 1936.
4. This was pointed out by Freud, but elaborated and extended in a scholarly study by Franz Alexander (*Psychoanalysis of the Total Personality,* Nervous and Mental Disease Publishing Co., 1930), and applied by him to the study of criminals in particular in a book with Hugo Staub (*The Criminal, The Judge, and The Public,* Macmillan, 1931) and in a later book with William Healy (*Roots of Crime,* Knopf, 1935).

Chapter 6

1. Ives Hendrick, "Work and the Pleasure Principle," read before the 44th meeting of the American Psychoanalytic Association, May 18, 1942; and Siegfried Bernfeld, *The Psychology of the Infant.* Brentano's, 1929.
2. For a discussion of factors improving and impairing productivity in work, see A. C. Ivy, "The Physiology of Work," *Journal of the A.M.A.,* 118: 569-573, February 21, 1942.
3. Thorstein Veblen, the chapter on "The Instinct of Workmanship" in his *Essays in Our Changing Order,* Viking, 1934, pp. 78-96; and his book *The Instinct of Workmanship,* Viking, 1918.
4. Melanie Klein, *Love, Hate, and Reparation,* Psycho-Analytic Epitomes, No. 2, London, Hogarth Press, 1937, p. 67. Joint author: Joan Riviere.
5. T. N. Whitehead, *The Industrial Worker,* Harvard, 1938, Vols. 1:265 and 2:1-81; F. J. Roethlisberger and Wm. J. Dickson, *Management and the Worker,* Harvard, 1940.
6. See the following books: Arthur J. Jones, *Principles of Guidance,* McGraw-Hill, 1934; Donald G. Paterson, *Men, Women and Jobs: A Study in Human Engineering,* Univ. of Minnesota, 1936; Donald G. Paterson, *Student Guidance Techniques,* McGraw-Hill, 1938; Edmund G. Williamson, *Student Personnel Work, an Outline of Clinical Procedure,* McGraw-Hill, 1937; Harry W. Hepner, *Finding Yourself in Your Work,* D. Appleton-Century, 1939.
7. Voltaire in *Candide.*
8. Gabriele d'Annunzio, *Constitution of the Free State of Fiume,* Aug. 27, 1920.
9. Julia Menninger, "A Critical Investigation of Theories of Work and Play; Including a Preliminary Field Theoretical Approach." Thesis for Master's Degree, University of Kansas, June 1943.

Chapter 7

1. F. Schiller, *Essays, Aesthetical and Philosophical*, London, George Bell & Sons, 1875, p. 112.
2. Harry Emerson Fosdick, "Living for the Fun of It," *American Magazine*, April 1930.
3. John Eisele Davis, *Recreational Therapy*, Play and Mental Health, Barnes, 1938, p. 165.
4. Elmer D. Mitchell and Bernard S. Mason, *The Theory of Play*, Barnes, 1935, p. 52.
5. Moritz Lazarus, *Ueber die Reize des Spiels*, Berlin, F. Dummler, 1883.
6. Mitchell and Mason, *op. cit.*
7. Sigmund Freud, *Beyond the Pleasure Principle*, London and Vienna, Int. Psa. Press, 1922, pp. 11-17.
8. Ernest Jones, "The Problem of Paul Morphy; a Contribution to the Psycho-Analysis of Chess," *Int. J. Psa.*, 12:1-23, January 1931.
   See also:
   Isador Coriat, "The Unconscious Motives of Interest in Chess," *Psa. Rev.*, 28:30-36, January 1941.
   Ben Karpman, "The Psychology of Chess," *Psa. Rev.*, 24:54-69, January 1937.
   Karl Menninger, "Chess," *Bull. Menninger Clinic*, 6:80-83, May 1942.
9. Melanie Klein, *Psychoanalysis of Children*, Norton, 1932.
10. Erik Homburger Erikson, "Dramatic Productions Test," p. 552ff in Henry A. Murray's *Explorations in Personality*, Oxford, 1938.
11. Erikson, "Observations on Sioux Education," *J. Psychol.*, 7:101-156, 1939.
12. Ernst Simmel, "The 'Doctor Game': Illness and the Profession of Medicine," *Int. J. Psa.*, 7:470-483, July-October 1926.
13. Adrien Turel, *Bachofen—Freud, zur Emanzipation des Mannes vom Reich der Mutter*, Berne, Hans Huber, 1939, Ch. 5.
14. J. L. Moreno, "Psychodramatic Shock Therapy: a Sociometric Approach to the Problem of Mental Disorders," *Sociometry*, 2:1-29, January 1939.
15. N. Reider, Davida Olinger, and Jeanetta Lyle, "Amateur Dramatics as a Therapeutic Agent in the Psychiatric Hospital," *Bull. Menninger Clinic*, 3:20-26, January 1939. Mrs. Bernice Engle, who read this bulletin, comments: "Every high school teacher of expression should read this clear, simple, stimulating exposition of the inner values in dramatic work."
   See also:
   Myrl Anderson, "The Role of Prescribed Social Gatherings in the Treatment of the Mentally Ill," *Bull. Menninger Clinic*, 5:56-60, 1941.
   R. E. Hemphill, "The Aims and Practice of Recreational Therapy," *Bull. Menninger Clinic*, 1:117-122, March 1937.
   W. C. Menninger, "Bibliotherapy," *Bull. Menninger Clinic*, 1:263-273, November 1937.
   W. C. Menninger, "Psychoanalytic Interpretations of Patients' Reactions in Occupational Therapy, Recreational Therapy, and Physiotherapy," *Bull. Menninger Clinic*, 1:148-157, May 1937.
   W. C. Menninger, "Psychoanalytic Principles Applied to Treatment of Hospitalized Patients," *Bull. Menninger Clinic*, 1:35-43, 1936.
   W. C. Menninger and I. McColl, "Recreational Therapy as Applied in a Modern Psychiatric Hospital," *Occup. Therapy*, 16:15-23, 1937.
16. James W. Mower, "Comparative Study of Hobby Activities," *Bull. Menninger Clinic*, 4:82-87, May 1940.

17. Thorstein Veblen, *The Instinct of Workmanship*, Viking, 1918.
18. "Recreation for Morale; A Subjective Symposium," *Bull. Menninger Clinic,* 6:65-102, May 1942; see also W. C. Menninger, "Psychological Aspects of Hobbies: A Contribution to Civilian Morale," *Am. J. Psychiat.,* 99:122-129, July 1942.

Chapter 8

1. Sigmund Freud, *The Future of an Illusion*, London, Liveright, 1928, pp. 56-57.
2. Morris R. Cohen, *Reason and Nature*, Harcourt, Brace, 1931.
3. Joan Riviere (with Melanie Klein), *Love, Hate, and Reparation*, Psycho-Analytic Epitomes, No. 2, London, Hogarth Press, 1937, pp. 46-48.
4. Elmer Ernest Southard, *The Kingdom of Evils*, Macmillan, 1919.
5. *Works of Martin Luther*, translated with introductions and notes, Vol. IV, Philadelphia, A. J. Holman Company and the Castle Press, 1931.
6. Anton T. Boisen, *The Exploration of the Inner World*, Willett, Clark & Co., 1936; "The Problem of Sin and Salvation in the Light of Psychopathology," *Journal of Religion*, 22:288-301, July 1942; and "Religion and Personality Adjustments," *Psychiatry*, 5:209-218, May 1942.
   Carroll A. Wise, *Religion in Illness and Health*, Harper's, 1942.
   Seward Hiltner (Secretary of the Committee on Religion and Health of the Federal Council of Churches of Christ in America)—Various short articles, e.g., "Contributions of Religion to Mental Health," *Mental Hygiene*, 24:366-377, 1940.
7. Gregory Vlastos, *Christian Faith and Democracy*, New York, Hazen Foundation Series, Assn. Press, 1939.

Chapter 9

1. Ernest Jones, "The Concept of the Normal Mind" in *Our Neurotic Age*, ed. by Samuel Schmalhausen, Farrar & Rinehart, 1932.
2. J. F. Brown, *Psychology and the Social Order*, McGraw-Hill, 1936.
3. Franklin C. McLean, "The Happy Accident," *Scientific Monthly*, 53:61-70, July 1941.
4. E. B. Holt, *The Freudian Wish*, Holt, 1915.
5. Kurt Lewin, *A Dynamic Theory of Personality*, McGraw-Hill, 1935.
6. Holt, *op. cit.*
7. George Drysdale, *Elements of Social Science*, London, E. Truelove, 1882, pp. 332-333, 39. This extraordinary book, which I ran across in the stock of an old-book dealer, is a famous document. No copy of the first edition is known to be extant, but thirty-five subsequent editions were published and the book was translated into at least ten European languages.
8. *Education and American Life*, Report of Regents' Inquiry, McGraw-Hill, 1938.
9. Charles Beard, *The Unique Function of Education in American Democracy*, Educ. Policies Comm. of the N.E.A., Washington, D. C., 1937.
10. William G. Carr, *The Purpose of Education in American Democracy*, Educ. Policies Comm. of the N.E.A., 1938.
11. William G. Carr, *op. cit.*, p. 35.
12. K. S. Lashley, *Nervous Mechanisms in Learning*, Handbook of General Experimental Psychology, Clark Univ. Press, Worcester, Mass., 1934, p. 457.
13. Daniel A. Prescott, *Emotion and the Educative Process*, American Council on Education, 1938, p. 160.

14. R. Simmons, *The Relative Effectiveness of Certain Incentives in Animal Learning*, Comparative Psychology Monographs, Williams & Wilkins, 1923, p. 79.

15. Percival M. Symonds, *Personality Adjustment of Women Teachers*, paper read at the Amer. Orthopsychiatric Assn., Boston, February 1940.

16. John Dewey, *Education Today*, Putnam, 1940.

17. Karl A. Menninger, *Man Against Himself*, Harcourt, Brace, p. 420.

Chapter 10

1. Robert Burton in *The Anatomy of Melancholy*.

2. Sigmund Freud, *New Introductory Lectures in Psychoanalysis*, Norton, 1933, p. 144.

3. The affection of many people for animal pets and the faculty that some people have of dealing with them successfully is common knowledge. Precisely how the interchange of feeling takes place is not very well understood. Certainly love can be expressed by gentleness and in other subtle ways which defy description but which permit it to be perceived and reacted to even by wild animals. This has been reported in some scientific articles as well as in many legends such as that of Androcles and the Lion and such novels as White's *Andivius Hedulio*. I know of nothing more impressive, however, than the work of Grace Wiley of Minnesota and California who, originally terrified by all kinds of snakes, so completely overcame this fear and so skillfully mastered the technique of gentleness that she feeds and handles hundreds of the most dangerously poisonous and notoriously unpredictable snakes, including mambas and cobras. (Grace O. Wiley, "Taming King Cobras," *Natural History Magazine*, 39:60-63, January 1937, and "With Fangs Withheld," *Nature Magazine*, 34:429-432, October 1941.)

4. Flo V. Menninger, *Days of My Life*, Richard R. Smith, 1939, pp. 81 and 34.

5. W. Trotter, *Instincts of the Herd in Peace and War*, London, Benn, 1916.

6. Sigmund Freud, *Group Psychology and the Analysis of the Ego*, London, Int. Psa. Press, 1922.

7. S. I. Hayakawa, *Language in Action*, Harcourt, Brace, 1941.

8. Antoine de Saint-Exupéry, *Flight to Arras*, Reynal & Hitchcock, 1942.

9. Havelock Ellis, *On Life and Sex: Essays of Love and Virtue*, Garden City Pub. Co., 1937, I:64-66.

10. Francis H. Bartlett, *Sigmund Freud*, London, Gollancz, 1938, p. 103.

11. Lauretta Bender and Abram Blau, "The Reaction of Children to Sexual Relations with Adults," *Am. J. Orthopsychiatry*, 8:500-518.

12. Rebecca West, *Living Philosophies*, Simon & Schuster, 1940.

13. Havelock Ellis, *On Life and Sex*, I:61.

14. Arthur Behrstock, "Love Is Sweeping the Soviets," *Esquire*, October 1939, p. 49.

15. Katherine Woods, in a review in the New York *Times* "Books," Feb. 4, 1940, of *Period Piece: The Life and Times of Ella Wheeler Wilcox* by Jenny Ballou.

16. Rebecca West, *op. cit.*

17. John Rickman, "The Nature of Ugliness and the Creative Impulse," *Int. J. Psa.*, 21:294-313, July 1930, p. 313.

Index

Carr, William G., 236, 241, 300
Cassandra, 123
Castration, 93, 282
Catholic Encyclopedia, The, 200
Character formation, 15-23
Chaucer, 164
Chess, 175
Child, birth theories of, 207, 208
  frustrations of, 24-40, 296
  psychological and physiological interactions, 15-18
  repression of emotions in, 20, 204
  sexual curiosity of, 207, 208
Childbearing, avoidance of, 51, 222, 225, 228, 229, 232
  importance of, 52, 104, 223, 232, 233
  pain in, 97, 98
  see also Parenthood
Children, education of, 233-259
  effect of war on, 12
  encouragement of aggressions in, 258
  psychiatric treatment of, 38
  psychology of, 224, 231
  rearing, books on, 297
  unwanted, 223, 226
Child Study Association of America, 297
China, 125
Christianity, 192, 193, 195, 267, 279, 281, 282
  rite of communion, 273
Circe, 101, 113
Civilization, and child rearing, 23
  and sexual inhibition, 281-285
  defective, 3, 4, 227, 228
  effects upon women, 32, 105
  hostility toward children, 230, 232
  poverty in, 227, 228
  restrictions in, 22, 23
Civilization and Its Discontents, 281
Cohen, Morris R., 191
Collected Papers (Freud), 262
Collier, John, 22
Comenius, 237
Conscience, and aggressive instinct, 132
  and play, 187
  and religion, 203, 204
Coriat, Isador, 299
Cowley, Abraham, 214
Crawford, N. A., vii
Criminality, 128

Crouse, Russel, 53
Curiosity, 253
  as motive in religion and science, 206-208
Curriculum, 251-252
Czechs, 44

Dancing, as a form of play, 183
Dangerfield, Alice, viii
David, 265
Davis, John Eisele, 168, 299
Davis, Katharine B., 297
Day, Clarence, 53
Days of My Life, 227, 264, 301
Death, as loss of love, 198, 199
  as reality, 218
Death instinct, 5, 129
  objections to, 295
  see also Aggressive instinct
De Kok, Winifred, 297
Delilah, 101
Delusions, schizophrenic, 218
Dennis, Wayne, 296
Descartes, 246
Devereux, George, 22, 296
Devil, The, 282
Dewey, John, 235, 237, 301
Dickens, Charles, 227
Dickinson, R. L., 297
Dickson, William J., 298
Diseases of the Nervous System, 60
Dix, Dorothea, 100
Dolls, play with, 176
Don Juan, 289
Don Juanism, 59
Donne, John, 5
Dou, 260
Dreams, as hopes, 217
Drysdale, George, 227, 228, 300
Dunbar, H. F., 297
Durbin, E. F. M., 297
Dutch people, 44

Eating habits, 15-18, 21, 23, 39
Education, 233-259
  and teachers, 245, 253-257
  books on, 300, 301
  definitions, 234-235
  denial of emotions in, 239
  hypocrisy in, 243-245
  for change, 258
  for warfare, 242-245